FINLAND AND RUSSIA 1808–1920

STUDIES IN RUSSIAN AND EAST EUROPEAN HISTORY

Phyllis Auty and Richard Clogg *(editors)*

British Policy towards Wartime Resistance in Yugoslavia and Greece

Elisabeth Barker

British Policy in South-East Europe in the Second World War

D. G. Kirby *(editor)*

Finland and Russia 1808–1920: From Autonomy to Independence: A Selection of Documents

Martin McCauley *(editor)*

The Russian Revolution and the Soviet State 1917–1921: Documents

Further titles in preparation

FINLAND AND RUSSIA
1808–1920
From Autonomy to Independence

A Selection of Documents

Edited and translated by
D. G. KIRBY

in association with the
School of Slavonic and East European Studies
University of London

First published 1975 by
THE MACMILLAN PRESS LTD
London and Basingstoke
Associated companies in New York
Dublin Melbourne Johannesburg and Madras

SBN 333 16905 0

Printed in Great Britain by
THE BOWERING PRESS LTD
Plymouth

Contents

PART III REVOLUTION, CIVIL WAR AND
INDEPENDENCE

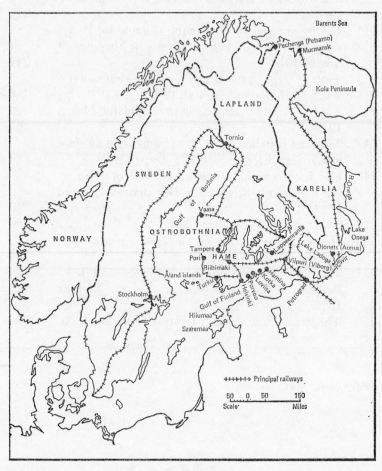

Finland in 1920

Introduction

In 1809 the Grand Duchy of Finland ended a connection of over six hundred years when it passed from the kingdom of Sweden to the Russian Empire. In uniting Finland to the Empire, Alexander I, anxious to secure a strategically vulnerable frontier area, chose to adopt a policy of consultation and conciliation. Whilst the war against Sweden still continued, representatives of the four Finnish Estates were summoned to a Diet in the small town of Porvoo. Here the Emperor promised to maintain and uphold the rights and privileges of each Estate in accordance with the 'constitutions' of the land. In return he expressed the hope that his new subjects, elevated to the rank of nationhood, would respond in a loyal and obedient manner to their new sovereign ruler.

Alexander's use of such politically loaded terms as 'constitution' and 'nation' was to provide posterity with ample material for debate. Finnish jurists and historians saw the Emperor as clearly having recognised the existence of a body of fundamental laws, which became the Finnish constitution. Russian nationalists countered this by arguing that the Autocrat would have been denying the very basis of his autocracy by turning himself into a constitutional, limited ruler in one part of the indivisible Russian Empire. In their eyes Alexander I had merely sworn to observe the existing rights and privileges of the Finnish Estates : he had not agreed to a wholesale adoption of the Swedish constitution. Both sides examined the semantics of the 1809 settlement in lengthy polemics, tinged with the nationalist and constitutionalist views of an age long exposed to these twins of the French revolution. But it is highly doubtful whether these ideas had begun to settle in the Finland of 1809. In essence the relationship sealed between Finland and Russia by the oath of loyalty of the Estates and the Imperial charter or *gramota*, was one of absolutist paternalism recognising the corporate rights of the Finnish Estates. The representatives of these Estates met as members of the community, anxious to preserve their own corporate interests. Raised in the traditions of Swedish aristocratic constitutionalism, their world view was monarchic-patriotic, and the suggestion that they were gathered as representatives of the sovereign Finnish nation would have been utterly alien to them.

This is not to say that the men assembled at Porvoo lacked all awareness of a fatherland. Patriotic sentiment ran very high amongst men such as the former army officer Major Aminoff : but loyalty was owed, in the end, to one's own estate and to the ruler rather than to the vague concept of the nation. Nevertheless, the implications of separation from Sweden were clear. No longer Swedes in any political sense, unwilling to become Russians, the natives of Finland would have to become Finns. Given a political existence by the Russian Emperor, they would have to find a national identity to match.

The search for a national identity was to cause a great deal of pain and bitterness. Finnish nationalists found in language the binding element of the nation. In Finland there could be no place for Swedish. The Swedish-speaking upper class would have to abandon its language, culture and traditions in favour of those of the great majority of Finnish speakers who lived in the country. As many Swedish speakers who did not support this course saw it, this involved the surrender of cultured values in return for an impoverished and debased peasant culture, isolated from the civilised western world. They were not only being urged to commit cultural and national suicide, but were also accused of disloyal hankerings after a return to Swedish rule. As the pace of political life quickened in Finland with the accession of Alexander II, the language conflict reached a new degree of intensity, and when the autocracy began to take active measures to diminish Finland's special status within the Empire at the end of the century, this conflict still bitterly divided Finns. Conservative Finnish nationalists argued that since Russia was undeniably the more powerful, Finland should try to comply with Russian desires and interests wherever possible in order to preserve the essential features of the nation. At the end of his life the leading exponent of Finnish nationalism, J. V. Snellman, gloomily predicted that the historical process seemed to be working in favour of the big nations of the world. These nations cared little for liberal principles when it was in their interest to suppress a subject nation. Twenty years later, his disciple Yrjö-Koskinen was faced with the *dies irae* foreseen by Snellman. He urged all Finnish nationalists to reject the divisive and disloyal passive resistance inspired by Swedish separatist elements, and seek to preserve the essential national identity of the country through loyal compliance with Russian demands. But many of the younger generation of Finnish nationalists disregarded this appeal. The conservative rigidity of the older generation and the excessive emphasis placed on language as the only pillar of nationhood seemed irrelevant and even dangerous when the nation as a political entity was faced with destruction. The passive resistance took its stand on the defence of constitutional liberties in face of oppression. The essential conservatism of the leaders of this resistance further alienated a number of young men, mostly Swedish-speaking members of the intelligentsia, who sought to combat the violence of oppression with the violence of the terrorist and direct action. These activists saw that only through the overthrowal of the autocracy itself could Finland regain her freedom, and to this end they were prepared to work with the Russian revolutionary movement.

The 1905 revolution proved to be a disappointment for the activists. The autocracy was shaken into granting reforms and rescinding much of the iniquitous legislation of the previous five years, but it still remained in control. The revolutionary movement had had its chance, but had not taken it. The Finnish socialists, whom the activists had regarded as their closest allies, were more interested in pursuing an uncompromising class conflict against the Finnish bourgeoisie than in leading national resistance against renewed Russian oppression. The democratically elected Diet failed to provide effective leadership for the nation, since it was either divided along ideological lines or forced to dissolve prematurely by the Emperor taking exception to words of protest uttered by the Speaker. Disillusioned, the activist movement lapsed into silence after 1907, leaving the task of propagating the ideal of Finnish independence as the only true end of the struggle against Russian oppression to the young men of the world war years.

During the first period of oppression (1899–1905) the struggle was waged primarily between the Imperial bureaucracy and military on the one hand and conservative defenders of Finnish rights on the other. During the second period of oppression which set in after 1907, other more vital elements were involved. In his speech to the Third Duma in 1908, Stolypin warned of the powerful new force of Russian nationalism which had been called into play by the attempts to create a new Russia. In Finland too, the political awakening of the masses during the revolutionary period of 1905–6 thrust the Finnish Social Democratic Party into the leading position in the reformed Diet. Prior to 1905 the 'national' line of co-operation with other groups in national resistance had won considerable support in party ranks. This was discredited during the strike week in 1905 when the constitutionalists failed to give the socialist strike leaders the consideration they felt they were entitled to, and later replaced by a rigid orthodoxist line of non-co-operation with the bourgeoisie forcefully argued by new, academically-trained recruits to the party such as O. W. Kuusinen. The principal task of the Finnish labour movement was seen to be the waging of a relentless class struggle against the Finnish bourgeoisie, whom the socialists accused of conniving with the forces of reaction in Russia to prevent the passage of reforms vital to the interests of the workers. The socialists constituted the largest single party in the Diets elected between 1907 and 1916, yet they refused to countenance any participation in the running of affairs of the bourgeois state. Thus, when 1917 burst upon them, they were forced into a hasty revision of ideology which did not sit easily upon the shoulders of the party. The party which had recoiled in horror at the idea of participation in government in the bourgeois state found itself holding half the seats in the Senate : and the party which had placed social reforms before national unity now found itself leading the fight to wrest a degree of national sovereignty from the inheritors of Imperial authority. In a sense, the Finnish Social Democratic Party forgot what it had always preached, that the struggle to live a decent life was more directly relevant to the majority of Finns than the preservation and expansion of autonomous rights. Social tensions in Finland were gravely exacerbated by the war. Finland's trade to the west was virtually cut off : foodstuffs were in short supply, prices rose rapidly and the value of the mark fell. The 1917 revolution worsened the situation. War contracts, which at the beginning of the year had provided employment for some 42,000 workers, gradually dwindled away. Thousands of men employed on construction of fortifications were laid off. Vital grain supplies from Russia trickled to a halt, and inflation threatened to become uncontrollable. In the heady atmosphere of revolution, many workers sought to alleviate their condition by direct action. A wave of farmworkers' strikes across southern Finland in the spring and summer left a trail of bitter and sometimes bloody clashes in its wake. Farmers in southern Finland soon began to form armed bands to defend themselves and their property : the workers responded by setting up workers' or red guards. Both sides continued to arm, although the red guards were probably less well equipped. It was for this reason that their leaders turned for help to the Bolshevik government in January 1918. Arms trains from Russia were attacked by the white guards before they could reach their destination. By mid-January 1918 armed conflict in Finland was a reality. The radicals in the Social Democratic Party, which had shirked from seizing power in November 1917, now saw the choice before them as one of either leading the insurgent workers or being swept aside by them. The Svinhufvud bourgeois government, voted into office by the Diet on 26 November, was committed to a restoration of law and order, and its first priority was the ejection of dissolute Russian troops from the newly independent country. The only force capable of performing this task, in the eyes of the government, was the white guards, composed of the armed groups established by farmers and units set up originally to fight for Finnish independence. The civil war which broke out in January 1918 became a struggle for power on a national scale when the Svinhufvud government declared the white guards to be the basis for the future Finnish army and entrusted their commander, General Mannerheim, with the task of disarming Russian troops in Finland and the Social Democratic Party executive committed the labour movement to a seizure of power. By choosing to identify with the warring white and red guards, government and party condemned Finland to a bitter national and class struggle, the effects of which were to remain for years.

Finnish independence was the final solution to the problem of the relationship between Finland and Russia, which had grown more acute with the revolution of 1917. Loyalty towards the ruler had been eroded during the years of oppression, and with his demise even that personal link was broken. The Provisional Gov-

ernment's appeals for loyal support of the revolution and the war
effort made little impact in a country whose political leaders were
seeking to make it virtually independent of the new Russia. As the
authority of the Provisional Government in Finland waned and
finally was extinguished, sovereign independence emerged as the
only replacement in the political vacuum. Nevertheless, the proclamation of the sovereign independent state of Finland in December 1917 was, in a sense, a political luxury. National liberation
was a fine thing, but at the end of 1917 freedom from hunger, unemployment, insecurity and want was of far more immediate
relevance to many thousands of Finns.

The traditional 'white' interpretation of the Finnish civil war
has tended to underplay the importance of social tension in the
country : the civil war is seen as one of liberation, the final elimination of the Russian presence from Finnish soil and the suppression of Bolshevik-inspired unpatriotic red elements. In the sense
that Finnish independence was forcibly *asserted* in war by the
victorious whites the term 'war of liberation' has some validity.
National identity in the form of a cleansing of the land of what
was seen as alien and hostile elements was achieved : but at the
cost of national division and social tragedy. The 'red menace'
was driven into Russia, and underground at home. It became what
the old Social Democratic Party had never been : communist-
revolutionary, vengeful, and in the course of time, utterly sub-
servient to Moscow. And throughout the interwar years the threat
of a 'red' Finland, whose embryonic form could be observed for
a time in the Karelian Autonomous Socialist Republic, continued
to haunt 'white' Finland.

Finland's union with Russia ended formally with the Soviet
government's acceptance of the *fait accompli* of the Finnish proclamation of independence. In the civil war which followed, the
Soviet government backed the red side, although severely
restrained by German pressure and domestic difficulties, thus en-
suring that the war would become elevated to the level of ideological struggle. This struggle continued during the period of
Allied intervention in Russia. In white Finnish eyes, their country
stood at the frontiers of western Christian civilisation, fighting off
the demonic Russian Bolshevik hordes and aiding oppressed kins-
men in Estonia and Karelia. The collapse of intervention and the
necessity of reaching some sort of agreement with the Soviet

Union at the peace conference in Tartu (1920) did not dim this vision. Geography compels Finland and Russia to be neighbours : but it took two bitter and costly wars between 1939 and 1944 to teach the Finns the political expediency of living on good terms with a neighbour more powerful than themselves.

* * *

I should like to express my gratitude to the directors of the Finnish National Archives and the Finnish Labour Archives for granting permission to publish in translation hitherto unpublished documents deposited in their collections; to Tiden Folkrörelseförlaget for permission to publish extracts from Eric Palmstierna's diary; and to A. & C. Black Ltd for permission to use the sketch map from *Finland Today* by Frank Fox. The publishers have made every effort to trace the copyright-holders but if they have inadvertently overlooked any, they will be pleased to make the necessary arrangement at the first opportunity.

The responsibility for errors of translation must rest with me, but I have greatly benefited from the advice of Dr Martin McCauley, Dr Will Ryan and Dr Isobella de Madariaga on the 'Russian' side of the fence, and Dr Michael Branch for his criticisms and ideas on the Finnish side. Especial thanks are also due to Professor Juhani Paasivirta, Dr Hannu Soikkanen, Dr Eino Lyytinen and Dr Jukka Nevakivi, whilst I am particularly indebted to Dr George Maude and Dr Bill Copeland for their special expertise which has provided me with much food for thought over the years. Finally, I owe an immense personal debt to my family and relatives for their kindness and unstinting support.

Part I

THE PERIOD OF AUTONOMY

The Union of Finland
with the Russian Empire

On 20 February 1808, Russian troops invaded Finland. By mid-summer much of the country, including the strategically vital fortresses of Svartholm and Sveaborg, was in their hands. These initial easy successes may have prompted Emperor Alexander I to abandon the policy of conciliation and consultation which he had outlined in his proclamation to the inhabitants of Finland on 18 February, in favour of a policy of simple annexation without conferment of special status, as advocated by the former Anjala conspirator Major K. H. Klick (7). The manifesto issued on 17 June spoke simply of union with Russia, although it did promise the preservation of ancient laws and privileges (1).

By the end of 1808 the situation had somewhat changed. In St Petersburg, the advocates of the idea convening the Finnish Estates, led by another former Finnish army officer G. M. Sprengtporten, received additional support from an elected Finnish delegation to the capital. The stiffening of resistance in Finland and the uncertain European political situation caused Alexander I to revert to the idea of a Diet as a means of settlement in Finland (2). It is clear that the Emperor wished to win over the loyalty of the Finnish people in order to obtain military security on the north-western frontier of the Empire (4, 10). In order to do this he was prepared not only to confirm ancient privileges and laws, but to extend the degree of control exercised by the Finns over their own affairs. The obvious parallel for this was Peter the Great's treatment of the conquered Baltic lands a century earlier. It is unlikely that Alexander I or even his mentor Speransky, who played a vital role behind the scenes in 1809, ever considered using Finland for constitutionalist experimentation. No further Diet was summoned until the reign of Alexander II: government remained for the most part in Finnish hands, but it was bureaucratic in character and in no way representative or responsible to anyone but the Emperor/Grand Duke.

The method and manner of Finland's union with Russia were to prove the source of endless debate in future decades. In 1838–40, A. I. Arwidsson, an early Finnish nationalist forced to leave his native land because of his views in 1822, contested the views of the Swede Israel Hwasser that Finland had acquired some sort of separate identity before the final peace with Sweden, although he went on to say that under Russian rule a growing sense of national identity had emerged (12, 13). Fifty years later, Count Rumyantsov's letter to his Emperor was to be cited by the Finnish nationalist Danielson-Kalmari as evidence of Finland's acquisition of statehood at the Diet of Porvoo (9). The Russian nationalists for their part claimed that the assumption that Alexander had ever intended to take into his Empire an alien constitution was contrary to the spirit of legitimacy (zakonnost') on which the entire autocracy was founded. Alexander had merely confirmed the privileges and certain basic laws of the Swedish era but did not, because as Autocrat he could not, embrace any fixed body of fundamental laws (14, 16). The Finns countered by quoting Alexander's references to the elevation of Finland to nationhood and by stout defence of the inheritance of Swedish constitutional laws (15). Nevertheless, in spite of the efforts of Finnish jurists to construct a theory of statehood on the basis of these laws, the Finnish case could not in the end rest on crystal-clear clauses but had to rely on the spirit of the law, as Danielson-Kalmari himself admitted.

1   HIS IMPERIAL MAJESTY'S GRACIOUS MANIFESTO CONCERNING THE UNION OF FINLAND WITH THE RUSSIAN EMPIRE, 17 JUNE 1808

In accordance with the will of the Almighty, who has blessed Our arms, We have united the province of Finland to the Russian Empire for all time. We have been pleased to observe that the inhabitants of this province have sworn a solemn oath as a pledge of their loyalty and eternal affection for the Russian crown. For Our part We have solemnly undertaken to retain this province which the will of the Almighty has ordained unto Us, unchanged and intact, in an eternal union with the Russian Empire.

The inhabitants of conquered Finland are to be numbered from this time forth amongst the peoples under the sceptre of Russia and with them shall make up the Empire; only the will and resolve of the Almighty can separate them from this great whole. We trust that God in His wisdom, having afforded protection and aid to Our brave warriors in the conquest of this province, will also help Us in the future to preserve it intact.

Inhabitants of Finland! Let this principle be graven in your hearts. Many peoples live in peace and happiness under the protection of Our sceptre. The happiness and welfare of everyone, including you who are now part of Our Empire, is dear to Our heart. In becoming part of Our Empire you have acquired the same rights as other peoples to Our solicitude and benevolence. The ancient laws and privileges of your country shall be solemnly maintained. Furthermore, new opportunities for your diligence and industry lie before you. Under the mighty protection of Russia your agriculture, commerce and other sources of wealth and prosperity will be further stimulated and developed. We shall soon know of your requirements and We shall not refuse you aid and support. Our arms shall defend your frontiers and protect you should an enemy dare to disturb your peace. In return We demand and confidently expect unity, loyalty and absolute obedience.

Inhabitants of Finland! Do not trust the rumours and hearsay which Our and your enemy may seek to spread amongst you; the fate of your country is irrevocably determined. Any futile notion of the possible reinstatement of the former Swedish dominion would therefore not only be a delusion but also a cruelly calculated means of preparing your destruction. Those who allow themselves to be drawn into the spreading of such rumours do so at their own peril.

We are aware that some of your fellow-countrymen are still serving with the Swedish forces and are therefore turning their weapons against you yourselves. Our patience would by now have been exhausted by their procrastination if, moved by sympathy for their helpless families who remain, We had not still shown willingness to accept them as loyal subjects and to erase for ever from Our memory their folly, provided that they hasten home within a period of six weeks from the day of publication of this

manifesto. Let them cease to obey and serve an alien power : let
them return to the fold of the fatherland : but let them hasten
home within the time prescribed, for all repentance thereafter
will serve to no avail.

Loyal inhabitants of Finland ! Continue in your firm and steadfast devotion to Russia ! We have promised to maintain you in
an undivided union. Our promise is immutable and assures you
for all time of Our Imperial benevolence and good will.

*(Samling af Placater, Förordningar, Manifester och Påbud ...
Första delen 1808–1812, (Åbo 1821) pp. 9–11.)*

2   THE ORDER FOR THE CONVOCATION OF THE DIET OF PORVOO, 20 JANUARY/1 FEBRUARY 1809

We Alexander the First, by the grace of God Emperor and Autocrat of All the Russias ... Grand Duke of Finland ...

The Grand Duchy of Finland having been united for ever to
Our Empire by the decree of Providence and the success of Our
arms, the wellbeing of its inhabitants is one of the first claims to
Our attention. In the conviction that all the estates in Finland
will be desirous to support Us in Our efforts to attain this beneficial goal, We have resolved, in conformity with the constitutions
of the country, to convene a Diet; We have therefore ordained
and do hereby ordain that a general Diet be summoned for the
tenth of March of this year in the town of Porvoo.

*(French original in Akty dlya vyyasneniya politicheskago polo-
zheniya Velikago Knyazhestva Finlyandskago, ed. G. Borenius,
(Helsingfors 1890) pp. 1–2.)*

3   ALEXANDER THE FIRST'S CHARTER, GIVEN AT THE DIET OF PORVOO, 27 MARCH 1809.

1. TRANSLATION OF THE RUSSIAN TEXT

We Alexander the First, by God's grace Emperor and Autocrat
of All the Russias ...

Let it be known : Having by the will of the Almighty entered
into possession of the Grand Duchy of Finland, We have hereby
seen fit once more to confirm and ratify the religion, basic laws,[1]
rights and privileges which each estate of the said Duchy in par-

---

[1] 'korennye zakony'.

ticular and all subjects therein resident, both low and high, have hitherto enjoyed according to its constitutions, promising to maintain them inviolably in full force and effect : in confirmation of which We have graciously signed this Charter[2] with Our own hand.

Given this day, the fifteenth of March 1809, in Porvoo.

2. TRANSLATION OF THE SWEDISH TEXT

We Alexander the First, by God's grace Emperor and Autocrat of All the Russias . . . Grand Duke of Finland . . .

Let it be known : That whereas We by the will of the Almighty have entered into possession of the Grand Duchy of Finland, We have hereby wished to confirm and ratify the religion and fundamental laws[1] of the country as well as the rights and privileges which each estate of the said Duchy in particular and all the inhabitants in general, both low and high, have hitherto enjoyed according to the constitution : Promising to maintain all these privileges and laws inviolably in full force. In confirmation of which We have signed this act of assurance[2] with Our own hand.

Given this day, the fifteenth/twenty-seventh of March 1809, in Porvoo.

(The Russian text, with detailed comment, is printed in K. Ordin, *Pokorenie Finlyandii*, vol. 2 (St Petersburg 1889) p. 335 ff. The Swedish text is in J. Danielson, *Finlands förening med ryska riket*, (Borgå 1890) p. 113.)

4 ALEXANDER THE FIRST'S SPEECH AT THE CONCLUSION OF THE DIET OF PORVOO, 19 JULY 1809

In convening the Estates of Finland to a general Diet, I sought to ascertain the desires and feelings of the people in regard to their own true interests.

I have drawn your attention to the matters most important to your wellbeing. Confident in your loyalty and steadfast, moreover, in the purity of my intentions, I have allowed you full freedom in your deliberations. No outside influence or authority has dared cross the threshold of these portals. I have watched over

---

[1] 'grundlagar'.
[2] 'gramota', 'försäkringsakt'. For the debate on these terms, see pp. 28–31.

the independence of your views. Even when absent, I have sought to be with you by vowing that I would not cease to work for the success of your labours.

The pronouncements you have just made bear the stamp of wisdom and patriotism. I shall take them into consideration in the vital work I am contemplating for your wellbeing.

Your labours are now at an end. But in going your separate ways, you have essential duties to fulfil. Carry into the distant parts of your provinces, impress upon your compatriots the same confidence which has presided over your deliberations here. Inspire in them the same conviction, the same assurance of the most important features of your political existence; the maintenance of your laws, personal security and the inviolability of your property.

This courageous and loyal people will bless Providence, which has determined the present course of events. Placed from this time on amongst the rank of nations, under the governance of its own laws, it will remember nothing of past domination except in order to foster friendly relations when these are re-established by peace.

And I, for my part, shall have gathered the full harvest of my labours when I see this nation, outwardly at peace, enjoying internal freedom, devoting itself to agriculture and industry under the protection of its own laws and good customs, by the very fact of its prosperity doing justice to my intentions and blessing its lot.

(Printed in the original French, with footnotes on the draft text of the speech, by K. Ordin, *Pokorenie Finlyandii*, vol. 2 (St Petersburg 1889) pp. 407–8.)

5 HIS IMPERIAL MAJESTY'S INSTRUCTIONS FOR THE ESTABLISHMENT OF A GOVERNMENT COUNCIL IN THE GRAND DUCHY OF FINLAND, 18 AUGUST 1809

Amongst the means of strengthening the happiness of Finland, the establishment of a national government has seemed to Us to be of the utmost importance. For the common good of the state, government officials in the provinces ought to have a central point or government to give them a lead, to maintain conformity in basic principles, to give the laws strength and force, to watch over the administration of justice and to provide a useful motive force for the advancement of public enlightenment and industry.

A special committee of Finnish citizens, noted for their knowledge and devotion to their fatherland, has been entrusted with the task of drawing up the first proposals for the establishment of such an institution, in accordance with the principles which We have laid down. After considering these proposals in the light of the common interest, We have graciously directed them to the further deliberations of the Estates of the country now assembled.

Having received their comments on the proposals, and convinced that a national government, armed with sufficient powers for the protection of the laws and founded upon noble principles, would actively contribute to the good of the country, We have decreed the following to be universally observed and obeyed :

Section One

Concerning the composition of the Government Council.

General regulations

1. The general administration of Finland shall be entrusted to a Government Council, consisting of two departments, of which one shall be for the administration proper of the law, and the other shall be for the direction of the national economy.

2. The president of the Council shall be the Governor-General of Finland.

3. In his absence, the chair shall be taken by the most senior official of either department.

4. The Council shall consist of fourteen members. The number of other officials and servants shall be determined in the supplementary statutes.

Paragraph II

Concerning the length of service of members

11. The list of members of the Council shall be determined by His Majesty the Emperor once every three years. His Majesty shall also appoint in the event of a seat on the Council falling vacant.

12. The Council shall inform His Majesty the Emperor of the need to appoint a new Council six months before the termination of their period of office.

13. It shall be a matter for His Imperial Majesty's pleasure whether a new group of members shall be named or the former Council, either wholly or in part, shall be retained . . .

Paragraph III

Concerning the general functions and rights of the Council

15. All matters connected with the administration of justice and the public economy shall be the concern of the Council; with the exception of certain matters which in law appertain to the powers of decision of the supreme power. Such matters are : appointments to all higher offices, the dispensation of pensions, gifts and certain ecclesiastical offices, the enfeoffment of crown estates and rents, permission to exchange a house belonging to the crown, and in general anything which according to the laws depends upon the especial and direct commands of the ruler.

16. The Council cannot on its own initiative levy new impositions or taxes, neither can it provide for any expenditure which has not been already appropriated for that year, since no extraordinary expenditure can be incurred without the express command of His Imperial Majesty.

17. As a general rule, no legislative measures can be made by the Council. Its activities are circumscribed by laws already passed, and it has no right to alter, interpret and even less to repeal them.

18. The Council shall however possess the right to inform His Majesty of the clarifications which are considered necessary in regard to the decrees of a statute or the laws. Any such proposals shall receive careful consideration and shall be invalid without the consent of His Imperial Majesty.

(Samling af Placater, Förordningar, Manifester och Påbud . . . Första delen 1808–1812, (Åbo 1812) pp. 23–6.)

6   EXTRACTS FROM MAJOR BERNDT AMINOFF'S NOTES, MADE DURING THE YEAR 1808–10.

[February 1808]

I shall never forget that day when, together with my son-in-law, I was awoken early in the morning with the news that 15,000

Russians had crossed the frontier and were rapidly approaching the town [of Loviisa, where Aminoff was staying]. We hastened out into the town. Oh merciful God, what sights met our eyes: everything in motion, weeping and lamentation everywhere, the roads into town choked with those who were fleeing from their peaceful abodes with their infants in their arms, without even a piece of bread to see them through the day, their homes perhaps already ablaze. Before my departure I was able to read in the town the Emperor's manifesto to the inhabitants of Finland. It promises us that persons and property will be fully respected: the slightest act of violence will be punished most severely, there will be no need for any conscription of troops, everything down to the smallest item will be paid for in cash. But how can one rely on the good faith of an enemy . . .

[After the fall of Sveaborg, May 1808]
Almighty God, I take up my pen with a feeling of deepest affliction. Oh my dear fatherland, weep over thy fate, thy only hope has gone . . . I can see no further hope for thy salvation after the surrender of Sveaborg, with the entire land and sea defences of Finland, by such unspeakable treachery. Such godless treason is without equal since the creation of the world. Where now is that Swedish fortitude, virtue and honour, so famed and reputed? Ah, my unhappy fatherland, in nearly all thy wars thy country has been divided by the treachery of thy own compatriots, and this last act will see the end of the entire Swedish monarchy . . .

[April 1809]
The Diet has been opened and we have already been in session for several days, employing the procedural forms consonant with the established fundamental laws of Sweden. No alteration of our privileges has occurred. The Emperor has handed over his proposals to the Estates for their deliberation. Not one of them goes against our liberties or our laws, on the contrary, they are for the good and welfare of the country. The Emperor himself opened the Diet with a speech from the throne, in which he guaranteed our former laws, liberties and privileges with the most solemn assurances and high-minded phrases, and this assurance he has confirmed before the altar and presented in writ-

B

ten form to the Estates. In magnanimous terms he expressed the desire that the Almighty might grant him the strength and ability fitly to govern this noble Finnish nation, and he has left it to the Estates to work now for their own future happiness and felicity, which was his dearest wish . . . Our Emperor captivates all who see him, he appears noble and good, and his clear countenance affords me the conviction that he will truly provide for our contentment, if he has his own way. God, hear our prayer, since our present status as Russian subjects cannot now be altered.

[Later reflections, probably in 1810]
Which is now my fatherland, Sweden or Finland? According to my way of thinking, my fatherland is the place where I was born, where I imbibed patriotic sentiments with my mother's milk, where I was raised and brought up. This must of necessity be my true fatherland, whoever rules over it. Since the peace gave Finland to Russia, and Sweden has publicly withdrawn our bond of allegiance to her, what duties do we Finns have left to fulfil? Well, it now behoves every honourable Finn to seek in all ways imaginable to make his own contribution to our Emperor's noble vision of making our native land happy . . . What do we Finns now have to complain of? We are a free people as we were before, governed according to our time-honoured laws; native-born men administer the course of justice and we have been allowed to choose them from those amongst us in whom we have most confidence; our expenses are reduced and we are protected by a great and powerful monarch. I say that, if we may enjoy all these advantages we now possess, Finland is the most fortunate country in Europe in regard to its situation . . .

('Annotationer gjorda under 1808 och följande år', *Svenska Litteratursällskapet i Finland, Förh. och Uppsatser 2*, (Helsingfors 1887) pp. 76-88.)

7 MAJOR KARL HENRIK KLICK'S VIEW OF THE SITUATION IN FINLAND IN 1808

What ought to be the object of the ruler of Russia in entering upon this war? Undoubtedly nothing less than the destruction of Sweden by the conquest of Swedish Finland; the advantages which will accrue thereby to Russia are even greater than is commonly thought, although it is not the purpose of these reflections to enter into details.

To conquer Finland is a simple enough matter at the present moment, and to retain it safely is hardly more difficult, if the confidence and affections of the nation are won; how this may be done merits closer consideration.

The nobility, which is sufficiently enlightened as to its interests, will soon be warmly disposed towards Russia, especially as it has shown its hatred of Sweden on several occasions in the past. If assured of the maintenance of its privileges and the reduction of taxes, it can be counted upon.

The military is for the most part composed of nobles and shares their sentiments, having been put to the test in 1788.[3] If they are assured that they may keep their estates which they hold in consequence of their military service, Russia can count on the loyalty of the officers.

The clergy, one of the estates of the realm, plays a role which cannot and must not be preserved under Russian rule, and undoubtedly it wishes Finland to remain a Swedish province; but the priests must be won over because of the influence they have over the peasants. They can be made to act in the interests of Russia by threats and cajolery.

The bourgeoisie ought to be soon won over; it will be plain to them that the union of Finland and Russia will both extend and enrich their trade; for the rest, their influence in general is very insignificant.

The peasants bear a marked hostility towards Russia, which stems from their ignorance and the false rumours put about by the deceased King of Sweden during the last war. But if they are assured in a most solemn manner that they will never be serfs, that they will have the same rights of possession to their lands as before, if His Majesty the Emperor lessens the taxes or abrogates them for a year or two, these peasants will soon become the most faithful subjects of Russia.

---

[3] Klick is referring here to the League of Anjala conspiracy of 1788, in which a number of Finnish officers were involved in an attempt to reduce the powers of the Swedish king. Klick himself was one of the officers involved, and was condemned to death in his absence: he fled and took service in the Russian army.

To reiterate : the effort must be made to win over Finland, but this does not mean that one should enter into some sort of negotiations with the Finns. Conquest having been achieved by force of arms, any advantages one has resolved to give them should be made as an act of grace. Any sort of negotiation supposes a certain equality between the contracting parties and could lead to misunderstanding and dangerous differences. The conqueror, on the other hand, dispenses acts of grace which are received as such, with no reason to pretend otherwise, no other stipulations having been made.

(French original, probably written in the spring of 1808, published in 'K. H. Klickin valtiollisia kirjoituksia vuonna 1808', *Historiallinen Arkisto* 10 (1889), pp. 268–70.)

8   THE TREATY OF HAMINA, 17 SEPTEMBER 1809

Article IV

His Majesty the King of Sweden irrevocably and for all time, on his own behalf and that of his successors to the throne and Kingdom of Sweden, relinquishes in favour of His Majesty the Emperor of Russia and his successors to the throne and Empire of Russia all privileges and titles pertaining to the provinces hereafter enumerated, which have been conquered from the crown of Sweden in the late war by the arms of His Imperial Majesty, namely : the provinces of Kymenkartano, Uusimaa and Häme, Turku and Pori with the Åland islands, Savo and Karelia, Vaasa and Oulu, together with a part of Västerbotten as far as the river Tornio, as shall be defined in the next article on the drawing up of frontiers.

These provinces, together with their inhabitants, towns, harbours, fortified places, villages and islands, with their possessions, privileges, rights and receipts, shall henceforth belong, with full rights of ownership and lordship, to the Russian Empire, and remain therein incorporated.

In consequence hereof, His Majesty the King of Sweden promises and most solemnly swears on his own behalf and that of his successors and of the whole Kingdom of Sweden never to make any direct or indirect claim to the above-mentioned provinces, islands and districts, whose inhabitants, on the basis of the above-mentioned renunciation, are to be freed of their oath of loyalty to the crown of Sweden . . .

Article VI

Since His Majesty the Emperor of Russia has already given the most incontestible proofs of the mildness and justice with which His Majesty is determined to rule over the inhabitants of his newly acquired country, and has already generously and of his own accord assured them of the free exercise of their religion, rights to property and privileges, His Swedish Majesty considers himself discharged from the otherwise sacred duty of making stipulations to the advantage of his former subjects . . .

> (Swedish text printed as an appendix in T. Torvinen, *J. R. Danielson-Kalmari Suomen autonomian puolustajana*, (Porvoo 1965) p. 448.)

9 COUNT RUMYANTSOV TO ALEXANDER THE FIRST, 9 SEPTEMBER 1809

[Rumyantsov and Alopeus were the Russian negotiators of the peace treaty at Hamina: their Swedish counterparts were Stedingk and Skjöldebrand.]

. . . In concluding this despatch I must inform Your Majesty that when M. Stedingk frequently and repeatedly talked of the necessity of drafting an article which would guarantee the liberty of the religion, laws, privileges and inviolability of property in Finland, I was unwilling, Sire, to admit discussion of such an article, holding that all this was a matter of internal administration and should not be treated as the subject of a diplomatic agreement. M. Stedingk cited in support of his view several treaties in which the power ceding provinces always made stipulations in favour of the subjects over which it renounced its rights. I did not dispute the justness of this, but found no difficulty in showing him how little analogy there was between earlier acquisitions and those lately made by Your Majesty. Your Majesty had won the love of the Finnish people, had appeared amongst them as their Sovereign before the treaty, had personally received their oath of allegiance, and had, as their Sovereign, opened the Estates of their Grand Duchy. This argument served me well. M. Skjöldebrand alone has since drafted a project for an article, which he has given to M. Alopeus, in the belief, he said, that it was so constructed as to agree with my principle and their demands.

. . . I have made no reply as yet, but I may inform Your Majesty that with a slight amendment the article will be acceptable. It does not in any way weaken, but rather strengthens the dignity of my principle, which was to show that Your Majesty was Sovereign ruler of Finland before the treaty.

(Original French text, with English translation, in J. R. Daniel-son, *Finland's union with the Russian Empire*, (Helsingfors 1891) pp. 160–2)

10 ALEXANDER THE FIRST'S SECRET INSTRUCTIONS TO GOVERNOR-GENERAL STEINHEIL, 26 SEPTEMBER 1810

The present state of affairs in Sweden give no cause for alarm in political terms,[4] but in view of local conditions in Finland, the newness of its government and the many ties which still exist with Sweden, steps must be taken to ensure that the new order in Sweden does not have an adverse effect upon Finland.

I have therefore considered it necessary *firstly* to inform you of our present political relations with Sweden and *secondly* to outline the policy which you are to pursue.

I. Relations with Sweden

With the union of Finland to Russia, We have achieved the main object of our endeavours concerning this country. Two principles follow from this.

1. Absolute non-interference in Sweden's internal affairs.
2. Finland's internal structure is to be arranged in such a way that the people of that country, united to Russia, have incomparably more privileges than they enjoyed during the period of Swedish rule . . .

The following conclusions can be deduced from these two principles :

1. That Russia has never sought nor even wished to exert influence in the election of a successor to the Swedish throne.

[4] The instructions were written as a consequence of the election of Bernardotte to the succession to the throne in Sweden.

2. That it has no reason to believe the recent election danger-ous or a menace to its interests.

3. That therefore those who may try to see in this election a reason or a guarantee of war to regain Finland, do so without foundation. It is natural that Sweden should wish to reconquer Finland; but that would demand forces which the election of a successor to the throne has in no way brought into existence. Every time war has broken out against Russia, it has had to be prepared to repel Swedish designs; the real difference is not to be found in the ruler, but in the theatre of war.

4. In determining conditions in Finland, my intention has been to give the people of that country a political existence, so that they would not consider themselves conquered by Russia, but joined to it by their own self-evident interests; therefore

(a) Not only the civil but also the constitutional laws[5] of that country have been preserved.

(b) The administration itself has been entrusted to a Finnish council under your control.

(c) Many taxes have been abolished.

(d) The country's army has been dissolved.

(e) The nobility and army officers have been given privileges which Sweden could never have given them.

(f) The merchant class has been freed from the monopolies and the obligation to trade principally with Sweden.

These are the main outlines of the present situation of Finland in relation to Sweden.

(Printed in J. R. Danielson, *Suomen sisällinen itsenäisyys*, (Helsinki 1892) Finnish text pp. 72–5, Russian text pp. 75–8.)

11 ALEXANDER THE FIRST'S MANIFESTO ON THE FINNISH SENATE, 21 FEBRUARY 1816

We Alexander the First, by the grace of God Emperor and Auto-crat of All the Russias and Grand Duke of Finland . . . declare to all people :

From the moment of union of the Grand Duchy of Finland to Our Empire, the happiness of this country has always been a

---

[5] The Russian original reads: 'ne tol'ko grazhdanskie, no politicheskie ego zakony'.

treasured object of Our desires and attentions. In consequence, We have turned all Our endeavours to that end at every opportunity so that Our Finnish subjects, by Our actions solely directed to the common good, might be disposed to the allegiance and devotion which We, invested by Providence with supreme power over them, have the right to expect, and of which We have been especially pleased to see many infallible proofs. Assured that the constitution and laws which, adapted to the customs, culture and spirit of the Finnish people, formed from ancient times the basis of their civic liberty and institutions, could not without damage be limited or altered, We on assuming the governance of this country have not only most solemnly confirmed the constitution and the laws as well as the special rights and privileges of every Finnish citizen which are founded upon these, but, having first consulted the assembled Estates of the country, We have set up a special government, which under the name of the Government Council, consisting of native Finlanders, has until now administered the civil government of the country and has resolved judicial matters as a supreme court, independent of any other authority save that of the laws and Our sovereign will. Having in this manner shown the good will which We have and will continue to bear towards Our loyal Finnish subjects, We hope that We have sufficiently confirmed for all time the promise given by Us concerning the sacred preservation of a separate constitution for this country under Our sceptre and that of Our heirs.

Having now successfully concluded, with the aid of Our allies and through God's help, the affairs relating to the safety of Our Empire and the peace of Europe, and having found the long-awaited opportunity to devote Our attention to the internal affairs of Our Empire, in particular to the matters concerning Finland, unhindered by foreign worries, We find it convenient to show more clearly Our intention for the local government of this country and to show its direct relation to Our person by giving to the supreme government of Finland, in conformity with the nomenclature of the supreme government of Our Empire and of the recently annexed Kingdom of Poland, the name of Our Senate for Finland, without however changing its actual composition or even less the constitution and laws which We have confirmed for Finland and herewith do further confirm in all respects. We hereby solemnly promise that the members of Our Finnish Senate shall in future, as hitherto, be chosen only from native Finlanders, or those domiciled in Finland and having Finnish citizenship, and We order all Our loyal Finnish subjects as well as others whom this may concern to carry out all those ordinances which the Imperial Finnish Senate, hitherto known as the Government Council, shall promulgate in Our name and on Our behalf, and to carefully observe this Our decree. In confirmation of which We have signed this with Our own hand.

(Swedish text in J. R. Danielson, *Finlands förening med ryska riket*, (Borgå 1890) pp. 182–5.)

12 ISRAEL HWASSER ON THE SEPARATION OF FINLAND AND SWEDEN IN 1809

Before Sweden ceded all its claims to Finland in favour of Russia at the peace of Hamina, Finland had in fact already freed itself of its former relationship and had concluded a separate peace with the Emperor of Russia through the agency of its Estates assembled at the Diet of Porvoo. By this peace, Finland not only ceased to be a Swedish province, a part of Sweden, but became a state in itself, with a fine constitution, its own form of government and its own laws, entitled to employ its public resources for its own advancement. By virtue of the fact that this new state had acknowledged the Autocrat of Russia as the reigning Grand Duke, its independence in regard to foreign relations was circumscribed; it was unable to become a free member of the European league of states and to defend its own existence, but in regard to internal administration its independence was fully acknowledged by the conqueror and solemnly confirmed; he further strengthened its national vigour by ceding to Finland territory which had previously been conquered and incorporated into the Russian Empire.[6] This recognition of Finland as an independently existing community, or of its national independence, was also acknowledged and confirmed by Sweden at Hamina.

(I. Hwasser, *Om allianstractaten emellan Sverige och Ryssland år 1812*, (Stockholm 1838) pp. 15–16.)

[6] This refers to the return of 'Old Finland', the area ceded to Russia in 1721 and 1743.

13   A. I. ARWIDSSON'S VIEW OF THE SEPARATION OF FINLAND AND SWEDEN IN 1809

With regard to Finland's position in Russian eyes, we see . . . that
the Russian armies, in accordance with the statement made by
the supreme commander, attacked the province in order to sub-
due the King of Sweden's blind hatred of Napoleon. There was
no indication whatsoever of an 'emancipation' of Finland; the
country was to be taken *under his* [the Emperor's] *protection
and occupation*, to *provide him* with *rightful satisfaction*.[7] During the course of the war, when the Finnish army victoriously
drove back the encroaching enemy, the inhabitants of Finland
were urged to swear an oath of loyalty to the Russian monarch,
not under expressed threats of punishment, but under the threat
of losing *'the protection of life and property'*.[8] About the same
time, the whole country was disarmed and shortly afterwards was
declared *'united* to the Russian Empire *for all time'*, the inhabitants of Finland being 'numbered from this time forth amongst
the peoples *under the Sceptre of Russia and with them making
an Empire'*.[9]

Thus far have matters developed, and now the 'separate peace'
is about to be concluded at Porvoo. The contracting parties are,
on the one side, the mighty victor, and on the other, the conquered province whose inhabitants have sworn loyalty to the new
ruler and already have become his subjects, with whom there is
no need to discuss any sort of special conclusion of peace. And
indeed, there was never any question of such a settlement . . .

> ('Pekka Kuoharinen' (A. I. Arwidsson), *Finland och dess fram-
> tid jemte eringrar vid en sednare skrift; Om Borgå landtdag
> och Finlands ställning 1812*, (Stockholm 1840) pp. 17–18.)

14   K.   ORDIN   ON   ALEXANDER   THE   FIRST'S CHARTER OF 27 MARCH 1809

From the original text it is clearly apparent that with this new
charter the Russian Empire *once more*, that is, not for the first

---

[7] Proclamation of the Russian commander-in-chief Buxhövden, February 1808.
[8] Circular issued by the Turku High Court, 27 May 1808.
[9] Imperial manifesto of 17 June 1808.

time declared to the country in general and to the Diet in particular the privileges he wished to grant for the governance of the country. One can furthermore note that he had *already entered into possession* of the Grand Duchy, not on the strength of some sort of agreement or even less by a treaty, but exclusively *by the will of the Almighty*, as manifested by the victories granted by Providence. These words embody the principle, not of a constitutional, but of an autocratic monarch who derives his authority from God.

Furthermore, *he recognises the common good* – that is, he acted of his own accord in issuing this charter for the preservation of the privileges of Finland. Finally there is the statement that religion would be protected for each and every one as well as the *basic* laws and the privileges of each estate according to the *constitution*, that is, according to the statutes. Here it is necessary to distinguish the above-mentioned *basic* laws from those which in the Russian state code are termed 'fundamental' laws,[10] which define the foundations of the order of government and administration. These last-named may be very recent in origin and therefore may not be basic, that is, determining elements of general, deep-rooted and ancient origin. In the present instance, such basic laws are, for example, the personal liberty of the peasant in contradistinction to the serfdom of former times in Russia, the right of all to own land, and the rights of exemption from military service. The peculiarly 'fundamental laws' of the Swedish constitution, on the other hand, did not have the significance of basic laws. They were only comprehensible to a limited number of educated people and their very origin, despite their revolutionary character, can be traced to the years 1772 and 1789, not so very long ago. The more important of these laws conflicted with the existence in Russia of a form of government which has already been outlined.

Moreover, the form in which these fundamental Swedish laws was established raised the question of the feasibility of their transplantation to Russian soil. In this respect, there might well be very

---

[10] The whole of this passage, and indeed the debate between Russian and Finnish commentators on the words and intentions of Alexander I is concerned with semantics which cannot be adequately conveyed to the English language. Basic laws *(korennye zakony)* were ancient and immutable principles, often unwritten, whereas fundamental laws *(osnovnye zakony)* covered a much more limited field, as Ordin attempts to show.

grave doubts as to which Swedish constitution is regarded as valid. The constitutions in Sweden were changed according to circumstances. The fundamental Swedish laws of 1720 were recognised as valid by Russia in the Peace of Nystad [Uusikaupunki] of 1721. This constitution was even guaranteed by Russia as a form of government which, stimulating internal party conflict and weakening the power of the crown, made Sweden impotent. Could Alexander have desired the transfer of this sort of constitution to a Russian province, even if it were to be tacitly ignored? Of course not. Later, Gustav III, encumbered by his lack of authority, engineered a revolution in 1771, after which an agreement was made with the officers of state which became the 'Form of Government' of 21 August 1772. Seventeen years later however, after the League of Anjala,[11] i.e. yet again after an attempted revolution, the same officials consented to the Union and Security Act of 3 April 1789; this, together with the law of 1772, is the basis of the Swedish constitution . . .

Hence it can be seen that by the charter of 27 March 1809 the Emperor Alexander only guaranteed to each and every one his religion, rights and privileges, but in no way obliged himself to adopt on his own behalf or that of the government of Russia the entire Swedish constitution, as this was logically and practically incapable of realisation. It might be assumed that he somehow wished to preserve certain legal statutes, which would invariably have accompanied the charter in the form of a list, but this was not done either at the time or at a later date, and everything remained subject to the will of the Russian Emperor. An expression of that will was the convening of the Diet of Porvoo, the appointment of a minister of justice and other officials 'for the time being': a further expression of that will was the confirmation of the ceremonial, which followed the manner and form observed in Finland during the period of Swedish constitutional rule: but this was as far as it went. The confirmation of the Swedish constitution as the fundamental law of the land by the Emperor Alexander would not only have been directly contrary to his sacred duty towards Russia, a duty solemnly acknowledged before the face of God at his coronation, but would have also

[11] The League of Anjala was a conspiracy of army officers during the early months of the Russo-Swedish war of 1788, in which a number of Finnish officers were deeply implicated.

placed him in a completely inimical position with regard to the Empire.

(K. Ordin, *Pokorenie Finlyandii*, vol. 2 (St Petersburg 1889) pp. 335–7.)

15 EXTRACT FROM J. R. DANELSON'S CRITIQUE OF K. ORDIN'S WORK, 'THE SUBJUGATION OF FINLAND'

The more carefully we read the Emperor Alexander's utterances during the Diet, the more fully we understand his real intentions for the future of Finland. At the opening of the Diet, besides having promised to maintain the Constitution and the fundamental laws, he declared: 'Cette réunion fera époque dans votre existence politique'. In the speech which we have just quoted,[12] he exhorted the members of the Estates to diffuse, among their countrymen all over Finland, the same confidence with which they themselves were inspired 'sur les objets les plus importans à votre existence politique'. Referring to the Finnish people, he continued 'placé désormais au rang des nations, sous l'empire de ses loix'. It lay neither in Alexander's, nor in any human power to give the Finnish people a place among the nations from an ethnographical point of view, for they had been in possession of such a place since the earliest dawn of the Middle Ages – but it did lie in his power to give it a political existence of its own. This and nothing else was his intention. He declared that the Finnish people should be, under the protection of their laws, 'libre dans l'intérieur,' independent in their interior government of all laws and authorities, except their own. Mark well however: independent only in this respect. The Emperor does not promise Finland any independence with reference to Foreign Powers. All his promises are based on the theory, that Finland stands, not in a personal, but in an indissoluble union with Russia, that it forms a part, a subdivision of the Empire with reference to Foreign Powers, though not with reference to legislation and administrative government. In accordance with this theory, the Estates declared their allegiance to Alexander, not only as Grand Duke of Finland, but also as Sovereign of the Empire.

[12] 19 July 1809. See pp. 15–16.

(J. R. Danielson, *Finland's Union with the Russian Empire.
With reference to M. K. Ordin's 'Finland's Subjugation',*
(Borgå 1891) pp. 149–50)

16   W. F. DEUTRICH ON THE 'FUNDAMENTAL LAWS', 1909

. . . In confirming the Swedish 'fundamental laws' for Finland, the
Emperor Alexander I never, in any single act, indicated what
Swedish laws he was pleased to extend to the Grand Duchy. This
much, at any rate, is indisputable, that he could not confirm all
Swedish 'fundamental laws'. In the following Swedish acts, viz.,
the Form of Government of 1772, and the Act of Union and
Security of 1789, which the Finnish politicians and jurists regard
as forming the basis of the Finnish Constitution, and as partaking
of the nature of Finnish Fundamental Laws, provisions are to be
found which are in conflict with the Russian mode of government.
Thus, the King of Sweden, or his present substitute, the Emperor
of Russia, must profess the Confession of Augsburg, adjure autocracy, not leave the country without the consent of the Diet, and
forego the right to appoint Governors-General. The Russian Autocrat obviously never undertook any such obligations, nor could he
do so. In regard to the 'fundamental laws' and the 'constitution'
of the country, the conqueror could have confirmed so much only
as was not in conflict with the mode of government of his own
Empire, and so much only as was granted to Finland under the
Swedish laws. According to the Swedish Constitutional Acts, viz.,
the Form of Government of 1772 and the Act of Union and
Security of 1789, Finland was not regarded as a separate state,
united to Sweden in the person of a common Sovereign only, but
as an ordinary province, which was governed from Stockholm
and shared the state institutions of the Swedish Kingdom. In the
Acts just quoted Finland is not mentioned once. The Russian
Emperor thus, in confirming the 'root laws' of the Grand Duchy,
or, according to the terminology of the Finlanders, its 'fundamental laws', has confirmed to it its organisation as a province, but
not as a state. In order to create a new Finnish state in lieu of the
Finnish province conquered from Sweden, it was not sufficient to
confirm the Swedish 'root laws' only, or even the 'fundamental
laws'. For this purpose it would have been necessary to draw up

and issue an act creating a new Finnish state. Such an act has never been issued. The Emperor restricted himself to notifying the maintenance for the population of Finland of its 'fundamental laws' and privileges, and nothing more.

(Extract from a speech by W. F. Deutrich, given at the session of the Russo-Finnish committee in 1909, printed in *The Russo-Finnish conflict. The Russian case, as stated by representatives of the Russian government*, (London 1910) pp. 13–14.)

The Growth of Nationalism

Towards the end of the eighteenth century there had developed a growing interest in academic circles in Finland in the origins of the Finnish nation and its culture. Under the inspiration of teachers such as H. G. Porthan (1739–1804) and of the German Romantic movement, numbers of young academics were to carry out much of the research necessary for the establishment of a Finnish cultural identity. Union with the Russian Empire in 1809 gave an additional impetus to the search for an identity, though it also posed numerous difficulties. Separated from the country with which the Swedish-speaking ruling class of Finland felt a common cultural and political affinity, Finland was now united to an autocratic empire on terms which seemed on the one hand to preserve and even enrich the essential features of the community, and yet failed to provide an adequate basis for the development of a national identity. Many of the Finnish ruling class chose to join the ranks of the bureaucracy which administered the country, or even to seek service in Russia: and they all tended to adopt the attitudes which were the hallmark of those who served the Emperor. Integration and assimilation for the sake of better centralised government: indifference to national aspirations: suppression of political dissent: such was the tone of bureaucratic government in Finland for much of the early nineteenth century (18, 21).

The great mass of the population, the peasantry, remained isolated and ignored behind the barriers of class, language and cultural tradition. Only by breaching that barrier could any real national idenity be established: this was the basic tenet of that section of the ruling class, the intelligentsia, which sought to realise some sort of historical and cultural heritage for their country (17, 19, 20). This they did by diligent research, publication and propagation, all intended to create a store-house for future generations. The political implications of this work were scrutinised in detail by the Hegelian philosopher and journalist J. V. Snellman. Snellman saw that these diligent labours could not be regarded as an end in themselves. They would serve no purpose without a concomitant effort to establish a political consciousness: and this could only be done if the ruling classes abandoned their Swedish language and cultural traditions in favour of a Finnish identity (19, 25).

Snellman's uncompromising position on the question of national identity not surprisingly provoked a reaction (24). He himself was compelled to take stock of Finland's political position when the Scandinavists and sections of the Swedish and European press started talking about the possibility of detaching Finland from the Russian Empire (26). During the Crimean war, a Finnish poet who moved in Scandinavist circles had pointed out, as had Arwidsson before him, that the awakening of national consciousness in Finland would preclude reunion with Sweden as a mere province (22). Nevertheless, the possibility of a return to Sweden continued to crop up in times of crisis, and increasingly came to haunt the minds of the Russian bureaucracy, which identified the Swedish element in Finland as obdurate separatists (30).

The accession of Alexander II seemed to promise an end to the period of 'frozen constitutionalism'. Preparations for a Diet were in the air from 1856. The growing unrest in Finland, which came to a head during the time of the Polish revolt, probably persuaded the Emperor to ease the situation by calling a Diet for September 1863. In his opening speech to the Estates, Alexander II conceded the need for reform and development in the Grand Duchy (28). In 1869 it was decreed that the Diet should henceforth meet every five years. In 1882, this period was shortened to three years, and four years later the Diet was given the right to initiate a limited degree of legislation. Both Alexander II and his successor thereby conceded to the Estates a share in the governance of Finland, a concession which was taken up in a spate of legislation which, if not meeting the demands made by the liberals in 1863, considerably extended the scope of Finnish autonomy – and increasingly angered the Russian nationalists (27).

Official recognition of the status of the Finnish language brought increasing tension (29, 33). Finnish nationalists, intent on the finnicisation of the ruling class, were not entirely satisfied with the provisions of the edicts (38). Swedish nationalists feared the cultural chaos and isolation which would follow from the implementation of the edicts: and moderates came to view the internecine language conflict with disquiet as the threat of assimilation grew (34, 35, 37). The conservative Finnish nationalists, dominated by the figure of Y. S. Yrjö-Koskinen, stressed the necessity and value of good relations with Russia and the primacy of the struggle for the victory of the Finnish language, but a number of 'Young' Finns, increasingly disenchanted by the harsh and dogmatic ideology of the 'Old' Finns, began to pay more attention to social questions and in particular to the defence of the constitutional liberties of Finland, now threatened by Russia (37, 39).

17   J. G. LINSÉN ON THE FINNISH LANGUAGE, 1819

. . . The language is indeed undeveloped, but it is young and fresh and still retains its pristine qualities. The fact that its cultivation has been delayed and hindered must not lead one to suppose however that such cultivation is impossible, as long as the Finns remain the same vigorous and unspoilt people they have always been. But what are the major obstacles to cultivation? There are but two, and both so easy to remove that hardly anything more than *good will* is required. The first obstacle is *the exclusion of the Finnish language from the circles of the educated classes and its neglect as a written language.* Hitherto the Swedish language has prevented our tongue from enjoying its birthright. It is freely admitted that the former has gained nothing from this usurpation; that the Finnish language has suffered a grievous loss thereby is a truism which every sensible person understands. The language is not the only loser; the people as a whole have suffered a defeat. The language and the people are inseparably united. Since the Finnish language does not command the higher levels of culture, the people as a whole have been deprived of the benefits of culture. One seeks in vain to influence a people if the spirit of its language is not seriously and fully understood; and with very few exceptions the educated classes in Finland, even the teachers of religion, have failed to do this . . . It is moreover a great mistake to think that the educated classes themselves have not suffered from this neglect. They have had to pay for the contempt with which they have treated the language of the people. If the lower orders of society need the guiding influence of its more educated classes, the latter are equally dependent upon the influence of the former. Unless a culture is rooted in the people, it cannot properly exist : knowledge, genius, heroism, every civic virtue is inevitably to be found there, and everyone must obtain his first nourishment from it. If not, the flower will wither and the fruit shrivel up.

The other reason why the cultivation of the Finnish language has been hindered is that *the Swedish language has also replaced Finnish as the official language*, i.e. the latter is not used in the courts, public offices and official documents of the land. The consequences of this defect are, if anything, even more regrettable than those of the first-mentioned drawback. I appeal here to every citizen in whose breast there still survives a flicker of patriotic sentiment; can anything be more indecent than that matters of vital importance to the people are determined in a language which the people do not themselves understand? Is it not the same as binding the eyes of a person entrusted to one's care so that he, suffering from the torments of unease, may not know what is to happen to him? Is it not likely to create coldness and contempt amongst the officials towards those dumb citizens whom they should be treating with love, and to provoke a justifiable suspicion amongst the people? As long as this fearful barrier stands, there can be no drawing together . . .

(From J. G. Linsén's article in *Mnemosyne*, nos. 60–1 (1819), translated and printed in T. Hultin, *Suomalaisuuden herätys*, (Helsinki 1892) pp. 16–18.)

18 THE STATUS OF THE RUSSIAN AND FINNISH
    LANGUAGES – AN OFFICIAL VIEW, circa 1835

. . . The study of the Russian language in Finland has markedly failed to make the progress which might justifiably have been expected by the government as a result of its decrees and measures.

As long ago as 1812 His Majesty the Emperor Alexander was graciously pleased to ordain, in accordance with a proposal made by the chairman of the Committee for Finnish Affairs in St Petersburg [Count Gustaf Mauritz Armfelt], that after a period of five years had elapsed no-one should be appointed to public office in Finland without a knowledge of Russian.

... [In 1824] this decree was once more enforced and it was again prescribed that anyone who wished to hold public office in Finland had first to pass an examination in the Russian language, as well as other examinations, at the university. In spite of this, these examinations have up to now been mere formalities and have not produced the anticipated beneficial results.

The same applies to the Finnish language, which is moreover the language of the country, in other words, of the people, but which is so little used in the university and schools that there is a large number of civil servants who cannot even understand a word of the language, let alone speak it.

If it is the intention of the government gradually to make Russian, as well as the Finnish language more generally used in the country, it is absolutely essential that more appropriate measures to this end be taken now, and a more consistent and durable system worked out.

[A number of proposals follow, such as the establishment of a Chair of Finnish Language at the university, and the elimination of Swedish as a language of instruction in schools in favour of Russian and/or Finnish.]

The aim of the government must be to bring the two countries closer together, and to fuse the two nations together as far as is possible, something which could have been done a long time ago if the least sort of principle had been adhered to.

The most certain method of attaining this objective is to attract as many Finns as possible into Russian service, and above all, to allow them to advance in that service, if they are able and intelligent, and then to return them to their native land after completion of their political education, after they have been as it were assimilated into the great Russian Empire.

(Swedish translation of the original French-language memorandum, written by the Governor-General's aide, Alexander Armfelt, printed in H. Hirn, *Alexander Armfelt. Början av en statsmannabana 1832–41, Skrifter utgivna av Svenska Litteratursällskapet i Finland* no. 315, Helsingfors 1948) pp. 175–9.)

19 LANGUAGE AND THE NATIONAL CONSCIOUS-NESS – THE SNELLMAN-CASTRÉN CORRESPONDENCE, 1844

SNELLMAN TO CASTRÉN, KUOPIO, 1 OCTOBER 1844

. . . I would begin by claiming that he who seeks to persuade himself that the nationality of an oppressed people can ever be aroused to consciousness without entering into *ipso facto* opposition is a coward and would conceal the truth from himself. This consciousness is after all no more than the return of a people to its own self, a process in which opposition is an essential element.

One may well argue that this opposition must be purely theoretical . . . The people experience life in a more concrete form. They do not devote their attention to the whole world but only to those matters with which they have dealings, and the shortest and most natural course for an oppressed nation to achieve an awakened national consciousness is to adopt an attitude of resistance to those who oppress its nationality.

It is perhaps sufficient for the literary men of the nation to adopt this [theoretical] attitude of resistance – very quietly, of course. Their work would otherwise lack passion and usefulness, one has to admit. But this cover of silence does mean that they must labour in such a way and in such a spirit which must not be revealed. You will no doubt say : grammars, dictionaries etc. can be composed on the language of the nation and the theory of language be developed without this spirit of resistance revealing itself. But for what purpose are grammars and dictionaries needed? Surely not so that an unending stream of similar works can be turned out? No, they are needed for a national literature. Well then, how can there be a national literature without a clear-cut national spirit; and where does the consciousness for this come from, if it is not to be found in the nation? Turn whichever way you wish. There is no national literature without a conscious national spirit, for the former is nothing more than the expression of the latter, and that in its turn only exists as the antithesis of other nationalities, principally of that which threatens its existence. Without this, even your work is a futile exercise. It is our misfortune at present that the national consciousness of the Finnish people is primarily subjected to the pressure of a different force from that which controls our political independence. If these two were one, then there would be no other choice but defeat or victory, that is, to risk all . . . But there will come a time when both powers are one, and resistance to the one will mean open rebellion against the other one as well. In other words, how many dictionaries or works will have to be bound in calfskin before the nation can know that it is or will be a nation? The most marvellous volumes of all will indeed be produced in one day, if on the morning of that day the nation is aroused to consciousness; but the Finnish Literary Society may fill whole depositories with world-famous books in vain, as long as this consciousness does not exist . . .

CASTRÉN TO SNELLMAN, HELSINKI, 18 OCTOBER 1844

. . . In order that resistance be soundly based and achieve the results for which we strive, it must have a political direction – it must be a resistance of the sword. If this sort of resistance were now to be employed, it would inevitably lead to the destruction of Finland, i.e. the opposite of what resistance is intended to achieve. You appear to be thinking of a different means for our salvation – opposition to Germanic culture, liberation from its chains. Great events must take place in Finland before this great hope can be fulfilled. How can the generation which now abases itself and meekly bends its back before the blows of the Russian whip ever dare to think so boldly? History also demonstrates that spiritual liberty has advanced nowhere where political liberty is oppressed. And the subtly cunning Russian policy must surely invent ways of destroying any advancement of spiritual liberty. This is why I regard all our efforts now merely as preparation for revolt, not in the sense that we would be able to bring this about by our own efforts, but in that we might take advantage of any opportunity. The Russian will sooner or later come to blows with the Turks, who will receive support from the Kirghiz, the Tatars and the whole of the Caucasus. Poland only awaits such an opportunity to take up arms. At that moment we too will cry destruction to the Muscovite from the Finnish morasses. But until that time I believe that we must refrain from all forms of uproar, particularly as resistance cannot be kept up or even carried out . . . I regard all resistance as inappropriate, even against Germanic culture, because we cannot hope to achieve anything better in its place. The best thing in our present situation is to inspire and sustain the newly awakened love for our bog-country.[1] . . .

Above all else we must save our language, the cornerstone of our nationality . . . Because it is the policy of the Russians to seek openly and surreptitiously to hammer their language into our heads, I see no sense in aiding the Russians by forcibly banishing the Swedish language at a time when Finnish is by no means sufficiently developed to be adopted as an official language. But we must work for the advancement of the language so that it might eventually become the noble language of the realm.

(Finnish translation in J. V. Snellman, *Kootut teokset*, vol. 12, (Porvoo 1931) pp. 116–21.)

20 A STUDENT ASSOCIATION FOR THE ADVANCEMENT OF THE FINNISH LANGUAGE, 1847

Sorrowfully and with bitter feelings we have observed how slowly and painfully the Finnish language and the Finnish cause is advancing both amongst the educated classes in general and amongst our educated Finnish youth in particular. We know that the sacred cause of our fatherland and mother tongue will never emerge from this deplorable state unless it first fires the as yet still undefiled hearts of the young.

With steadfast hope and firm devotion we, young people of the Finnish University, have therefore decided to save ourselves first from the dominance of an alien nationality and then to show others the way. To this end, we consider our first need to be:

The teaching of the Finnish language to those who have the misfortune to be strangers to their true mother tongue by those who have already acquired a knowledge of it.

This shall be our first duty which must be immediately undertaken. From this will follow:

The use of Finnish and the avoidance of Swedish within our

[1] Castrén had earlier defined his task to be 'to show the Finnish people that we are not a solitary people of a bog-country, isolated from the world and world history, but related to at least one-sixth of humanity'. The term 'bog-country' is probably a play on words with the Finnish word 'suomaa', an already discredited interpretation of the meaning of 'Suomi'.

own circle and with others whom we think comprehend what we say and write.

Those of us who know our mother tongue wish to carry out all our promises immediately, those of us who do not yet have that knowledge as soon as our first promise is in some way completed.

We seek the victory of enlightenment in our country.

It is therefore our duty to carry enlightenment to the common people and to further love of the fatherland and national culture by all means available and on all occasions.

This is our firm and united resolve, this we promise by the sacred name of that end dear to us, and from this no hindrances shall swerve us in our course.

Helsinki, 28 March 1847

AUG. AHLQVIST	KARL COLLAN	ANDREAS WARELIUS
AKSEL ASPELUND	FREDR. POLÉN	D. E. D. EUROPAEUS
P. TIKKANEN	OSCAR TOPPELIUS	AUG. SCHAUMAN
C. F. FORSIUS	NESTOR TALLGREN	

(Original Finnish and Swedish text in the Ahlqvist papers preserved in Suomen Kirjallisuuden Seuran arkisto. Printed in *Suomen historian dokumentteja*, vol. 2 (Helsinki 1970) p. 62.)

21 EXTRACTS FROM S. G. ELMGREN'S DIARY ON UNIVERSITY LIFE, 1853–5

[1 January 1853]

Finland has gone through hard times of late, and one cannot look back without feeling sad. Hence I prefer to turn my gaze to the future in the hopes of better times to come . . .

How hard the blows were which our fatherland has recently had to endure can be seen from the following: the printing of works in Finnish was forbidden in 1850, with the exception of spiritual and economic literature; proctors were introduced into the University, on the Russian model, uniforms were made compulsory in order to crush any feeling of common human dignity; the new statutes[2] abolish the chair of philosophy altogether as harmful and the assistant posts as unnecessary, whilst the very name of philosophy is not permitted: the student nations are

[2] These statutes for the University were introduced in 1852, and bear the stamp of post-1848 reaction.

abolished as they are regarded as breeding-grounds for liberty and republican institutions, the students are declared to be minors in the eyes of the law and under the authority of non-elected deans and non-elected counsellors. A new and strict customs duty has been introduced, even for all books which must undergo the most stringent censorship and are frequently confiscated . . .

[13 February 1855]

Last Thursday a number of speeches were made at the meeting of the Philology Faculty which have aroused much unease amongst the authorities. One student declared that those who travelled to Russia on Russian scholarships were unworthy of the respect of their comrades and traitors to their fatherland. Another student declared that the severity of having to wear uniforms was unlawful, unreasonable and absurd. A third student satirised the present Vice-Chancellor in a dramatic poem entitled Genghis Khan . . .

Last Sunday a large number of students had assembled to draw up a note to the Vice-Chancellor and to elect a delegation to go to see Nordenstam [the Vice-Chancellor]. The delegation complained about the insolence of the proctors, who behaved rudely and arrogantly towards the students, thereby provoking disturbances and regrettable incidents; they therefore asked that the proctors be kept in better order by the Vice-Chancellor . . . Nordenstam seems to have met them with courtesy on the whole, without however making any firm promises . . .

(Printed in *S. G. Elmgrenin muistiinpanot, julkaissut A. Maliniemi*, (Helsinki 1939) pp. 37–8, 141–2.)

22 EXTRACTS FROM PEDER SÄRKILAX'S BOOK, *FENNOMANI OCH SKANDINAVISM* (1855)

And Finland, whose culture is European, which formerly possessed a freer social order, which during the period of union with Russia has perpetually held in its heart a secret fear and resentment against its ruler, on whose final defeat and withdrawal it has counted upon as a liberation for itself – would not Finland, now the hour seems at hand, prove true to its innermost instinct, and at least hasten towards that moment in hope, if nothing else? And the spirit of nationality, by which we mean not only that of the Finnish-minded,[3] but also that prevalent amongst the Swedish-Finnish population, which has been awakened in Finland in recent times, would this not, since the feeling of nationality is the very foundation upon which the search for independence and liberty of all peoples is based, would this not, we say, of necessity become an ally of all those who in the general interest wish to liberate Finland?

. . . Although this national spirit is still quite young and, as we have seen, dates only from the time of Finland's separation from Sweden, when it developed spontaneously as a consequence of Finland's isolated position and as the only sure foundation for a natural force of resistance to the Russian lust for assimilation – although it can therefore perhaps be said that it was brought into being and shaped by Finland's union with Russia, it would be a great mistake to suppose that, as soon as the menacing threat of oppression from Russia has vanished, this spirit of nationality would also vanish and Finland would show itself willing to become united with just any other liberal, civilised European community, Sweden of course springing first to mind, as a province. . . . For nearly fifty years, Finland, both internally and externally, has had a separate identity, with its own government – the Senate – its own administration and legislation, and it has already grown accustomed to the shadow, if not of freedom, then of a kind of independence and unity. The question of a provincial reunion with Sweden would thus meet with the most determined resistance from officials of all classes, from the lowest to the highest . . .

(Peder Särkilax, (Emil von Qvanten) *Fennomani och Skandinavism. Sednare Haftet: Kunna Sverige och Finnland åter förenas?* (Stockholm 1855) pp. 30–3.)

23   A HOSTILE VIEW OF FINNISH AS A BASIS FOR A NATIONAL CULTURE (1855)

. . . However much the Finnish language may possess qualities of inflection and euphony, it is still highly doubtful whether it can ever develop into a cultural language in any real meaning of the word. Any word which bears the slightest degree of reference to the circumstances of life beyond the lowest level of barbarism is

[3] This is the best term for the Swedish 'Fennomani'.

borrowed from Swedish, in the same way as all the rudiments of education are Swedish as well. Not one of the great family of peoples in Europe has played such an insignificant role and displayed such a poor aptitude and ability to take an independent place amongst the nations as the Finnish, or the Tschudic race.[4] Ingrians, Ostyaks, Permyaks, Mordvins, Cheremiss, Voguls and Lapps are all dying tribes, lacking an inner life-force, lacking any conspicious urge towards civilisation. The fact that the tribes who came under Swedish rule and whose descendants live within the frontiers of the area now known as Finland do not present a similar sorry spectacle does not in any way mean that their nationality contained a more intense internal force and was independently developed, but on the contrary, it is because they were adopted by a free and noble civilised people and to a degree participated in the spirit, culture and institutions of that people. Without the implant of these outside elements they would stand at quite the same level as the other Finnic tribes; and if these outside elements should be eliminated and the Finnish national element in Finland begin to make their own foundations in isolation from the contacts and influences of Swedish culture, then the way to barbarism and annihilation will be covered in as many decades as it took centuries for Swedish culture to lead the Finnish people, whom it had taken under its care and protection, to civilisation, self-esteem and independence.

To seek to build hopes of a genuine Finnish culture on the basis of the *Kalevala* and the other Finnish folksongs . . . is a poetical heresy into which no-one should allow himself to be enticed if he has any sort of knowledge of cultural history and is able to appraise the situation with any sort of dispassion. That the *Kalevala* is quite noteworthy as a piece of poetry, and it was quite natural that it should attract much attention on its appearance, we have already hinted; but the Finns, in a transport of delight over this attention and fame have completely overstated the real importance of this cycle of poems by seeking to read into them evidence of an ancient high degree of culture amongst the

[4] The term *tsud'* presented something of a problem to the early nineteenth century ethnographers: Sjögren identified the language as Vepsian, but the term came to be used in a pejorative sense by the Swedes in Finland and Sweden to describe the Finnish language and race.

Finns as well as a definite basis for the development of their own Finnish nationality.

(A. Sohlman, *Den unga Finland. En kulturhistorisk betraktelse,* revised edn. (Helsingfors 1880) p. 12)

24 THE NATIONALITY QUESTION – A SVECOMAN VIEW (1860)

If, as Prof. Snellman argues, language is taken to be the expression of nationality and as the only or the principal means of defining the nationality of a people or an individual, it therefore clearly follows (as has already been stated in *Litteraturbladet*) that we Swedish-speaking Finlanders can in no way be called Finns in any national sense but 'Swedes from the former province of Finland', who together with the Finns themselves make up the Finnish, or more properly, the Finlander people . . .

If, as I sought to demonstrate in my first article, the word people (populus) is taken to mean those who obey the same laws and the same higher authority, and the word nation (natio) is taken to mean individuals who speak the same common tongue, one cannot therefore speak of a Finnish nation inhabiting Finland. In the case of most nations, they do not form separate peoples; most peoples are composed of different national elements. Thus the Swiss people consist of Germans, Frenchmen and Italians, the Austrian people of Slavs, Magyars, Germans and Italians, and so on. The same applies to the Finnish people, composed of Swedes and Finns plus a small number of Lapps, Germans and Russians. As a reaction to this long-standing political division of the nations of Europe has arisen the so-called national movement of the present time, whereby each nation is seeking to become a people, a political whole. This is the aim of Scandinavism, Germanism and Panslavism; it is also the principal objective of the Italians. We Finns have something similar, the so-called Fennoman movement, which is nevertheless a quite exceptional phenomenon in the history of the nationality question. Everywhere else we see nationalities in conflict with each other, but here a nationality is fighting against itself: elsewhere, one nationality is striving to crush the other or defend itself whilst here, one nationality is seeking to defend another and defeat itself. In Hungary for example, the Magyar seeks to establish his language at the expense of the German, whilst the German attempts to defend his privileged position against the Magyar : here, the Finn corresponds to the Magyar and the Swede to the German, but the Swede is not only playing the role which the Finn should by rights by playing, but he is also fulfilling his own role in a manner completely contrary to that which is expected of him . . .

One who fights for the advancement of the education of the Finnish people and the development of the Finnish language is to be wished all success, providing his participation in this work does not come before a more national-minded form of activity. But this sort of work should not be aimed at depriving Swedish of its present rights at some future date, or robbing the Swedish speaker of his nationality, for such activity by Swedish men is of an unnatural character, one might even say that it is a form of national suicide.

(A. Freudenthal, *'Några ord om nationalitetsfrågan'* (part 2), printed in a hand-written student newspaper, *Nylands Dragon*, 8 February 1860, and published in A. Mörne, *Axel Olof Freudenthal och den finlandssvenska nationalitetstanken*, (Helsingfors 1927) pp. 68–71.)

25   J. V. SNELLMAN ON THE FINNISH NATION

'NEW YEAR'S GREETING, 1861 – A YEAR LATE'

. . . Let us admit that we Finns, more than most other European peoples, have ourselves experienced the recognition of the justification of nationalities. Before 1809 the world had not even heard of the Finnish nation. Even when the Swedish government bought peace with the surrender of Finland, there was no mention of it in the peace treaty, as we know. But even before the conclusion of peace, the Emperor Alexander had acknowledged the nationhood of the Finnish people and had declared that Finland would be included in the ranks of nations. This good fortune that has befallen Finland is without comparison in the history of peoples . . .

Over the course of half a century the people have of course come to know the fluctuations of fate. Not every day has been so promising for Finland. But what of that. A nation is not created in a matter of decades, or just for a decade or two. A freer social order is without doubt a blessing if the cultural level of the nation can accommodate it. Civil liberties, the security of the law and equality before the law are our most precious inheritances from our union with Sweden, much more precious than those of many a great and powerful nation. Our political rights on the other hand are just as insignificant as they were at the end of that union. History has placed us in a position in which their further development cannot rest with us alone. Sooner or later a parliamentary constitution will be an essential for the preservation of every European state and the material and intellectual advancement of all peoples. When this happens, Finland may also hope for a parliamentary system, when it will no longer be a matter of chance whether or not the Diet slumbers for half a century at a stretch. At the present moment the most important thing for the Finnish people is probably not this or that particular political institution, but the knowledge that can maintain and preserve them as a nation.

The self-awareness of the individual is strengthened the more he sees the results of his own intellectual endeavours, and the same is true of national awareness. A people must have some object which it can *recognise* as its work, so that it possesses this awareness of its own existence . . .

A people can cultivate its land, build its canals, railways, dwellings and workplaces, more or less in the same way as any other. But no nation can borrow knowledge and customs from another. A national language is the basis and foundation of national consciousness in the same way as one's native country is the basis and foundation of national wealth and the people's awareness of this. The unity which custom provides is the unity of action and deed. Custom is often understood in such a narrow sense that it ostensibly covers only the forms of domestic and social life . . . But in fact all the deeds and action of the individual are based on custom. The quality of upbringing within the family, civic and patriotic life, these all stem from national custom and usage; and where there are no customs common to the people, when the core of national consciousness is missing, there is no strong sense of patriotism. It is quite certain that a unity of custom implies a common sense of awareness, a unity of intellectual culture, and only the most thoughtless ignorance could lead one to suppose that there can be no common awareness amongst a people without unity of language. The Finnish people are in this respect in a worse position than any other, because the difference of language still separates the educated social classes from the great mass of the people. Language, as the basis of an intellectual national consciousness, differs from that which we have called the basis of national consciousness in the material sense in that it is in itself a product of the intellect. People win for themselves a fatherland, but their language makes it ...

(First published in *Litteraturbladet* no. 12, 1861 : the article's publication was delayed for nearly a year by the censor – hence the title, and the circumspect style of writing. Finnish translation in J. V. Snellman, *Kootut teokset*, vol. 6 (Porvoo 1929) pp. 491–6.)

26 'WAR OR PEACE FOR FINLAND' (1863)

... The present position of our country is briefly as follows :

It is not certain whether there will be war or peace; if war should break out, the coasts of Finland would certainly be put under blockade, though it is not certain whether or not the enemy would attack our country.

In these circumstances the Finnish people are being talked of in the newspapers of Europe as a people who not only hope for and expect success in war, but are also prepared to rise up in revolt and join the enemy.

These statements about the Finnish people first reached the public through letters sent from Finland to the Swedish press and through the speeches and writings of former Finns now living in Sweden. These have been seized upon and embroidered as usual by some European newspapers. Events in our country, such as the national addresses and the attitude of our own newspapers,[5] have hardened opinion, but as every patriot knows, this is more apparent than real. It has however left the impression outside Finland that it is real.

In these circumstances it is not surprising if the belief that the Finnish people, in the event of war and an invasion, wish to rise

---

[5] The Polish revolt prompted numbers of Finns to send addresses of loyalty to the Tsar, but it also prompted the liberal newspaper *Helsingfors Dagblad* to raise the question of Finland remaining neutral in the event of a war developing.

up in revolt and go over to the side of Russia's enemies has gained
ground in Russia too and if the Russian troops now pouring into
our country come here in the belief that they are surrounded by
a potentially rebellious population . . .

I do not need to say how disastrous war would be for our
country. War is always destructive, but does afford the compensation of an elevated national spirit, independence and power to
the nation which wins. But for such an insignificant and politically non-independent nation as the Finns, which does not in-
augurate war but is on the receiving end, which has therefore no
national interests to protect and which is in no way able to determine the final outcome – for such a nation war can bring only
disaster. I do not say that the Finnish people, having enjoyed the
blessings of half a century of peace without having had any say
in the matter, should not be responsible for bearing some of the
burdens of war. But this does not alter the fact that war for Finland is and will be nothing but a disaster.

(Article first published in *Litteraturbladet* no. 5 1863, Finnish
translation in J. V. Snellman, *Kootut teokset* vol. 7, (Porvoo
1930) pp. 239–51.)

27   A POLITICAL PROGRAMME FOR FINLAND, JULY 1863

. . . The very manner of Finland's existence has hitherto suffered
and continues to suffer from the rather glaring discrepancy between the development of its people in a national and cultural
sense and the external conditions and institutions to which they
are bound . . . The entry of the Finnish people in the league of independent nations is indeed well known, but our relationship to
our present associate state, Russia, has not fully lived up to expectations, and our interests have had to suffer in a war which
was not fought for our benefit and which has left us with a financial crisis for which we are not responsible.

. . . The most noticeable defect in our political system is the
undetermined period of time which elapses between the occasions
when the monarch and Estates gather together to deliberate upon
the affairs of the country. We must therefore hope that *a fixed
period – three to five years – may be legally decreed for the convening of Diets.* A similar drawback, which, although we have not

had occasion to experience in practice, will never permit the full development of trustful co-operation between government and people until eliminated, is caused by the fact that the Diet may only deliberate upon the matters brought before it by the government, and may not itself make proposals for the sanction of the monarch. We must therefore also hope that *the right to initiate proposals is granted to the representatives of the country at the Diet* . . . We must also hope that *this right, by the joint decision of the government and Diet, will be clad in the same sanctity as other constitutional regulations.* Furthermore, to quote the words of our own fundamental laws, 'true freedom is the giving of what is deemed necessary for the preservation of the state'; it is thus necessary for the promotion of our freedom that the practice of imposing duties and other indirect taxes without consent of the Estates be abolished *and that it be legally ordained that all state revenue of whatever kind be dependent upon the consent of the Estates* . . . We must also hope *that the Estates be granted full rights of control over finances and the voting of taxes* . . . It is also essential that high officials of state be made more responsible than hitherto to the high courts or the Estates for the measures taken within their departments which might come into conflict with existing fundamental laws. We must finally hope, therefore, *that the heads of departments within the Economic Section of the Senate be made answerable to the government and the Estates in this manner* . . .

In regard to our relations with Russia, we must hope above all for *the total separation of the Russian military forces from the Finnish and the withdrawal of the former from the country, and the freeing of the Finnish mint from the Russian,* or what amounts to the same thing, a decree that only hard currency will be accepted as legal tender in our country.

('Hvad Finland har att önska?', *Helsingfors Dagblad*, 1 July 1863.)

28 ALEXANDER THE SECOND'S SPEECH TO THE DIET, 18 SEPTEMBER 1863

. . . My attention has long been directed to a certain number of questions which have arisen concerning the most serious interests of the country. These questions have remained in suspense because their solution required the co-operation of the Estates. Certain major considerations which are reserved for My judgement, have prevented Me from convening the representatives of the four Estates of the Grand Duchy during the first years of My reign. I have nevertheless already taken some preparatory steps to the attainment of this end, and now that circumstances are no longer such as to cause a further postponement, I have convoked you in order to lay before you, after having previously heard the report of My Senate for Finland, the projected measures and administrative business which will require your attention in the course of the present session. In consideration of their importance, I have had them examined first by a committee composed of persons enjoying the confidence of the nation. The publicity given to the debates of this committee has acquainted you beforehand with the object of your deliberations and you have also had the opportunity of studying these projected measures by consulting the opinions and needs of the country. Consequently, in spite of their number and importance, it will be possible for you to complete a thorough investigation of them in the period fixed by law . . .

Many of the provisions of the fundamental laws of the Grand Duchy are no longer applicable to the state of affairs existing since its union with the Empire; others lack clarity and precision. Desirous of remedying these imperfections it is My intention to have a draft law carefully prepared which will contain explanations and supplements to these provisions, and which will be submitted to the scrutiny of the Estates at the next Diet, which I contemplate convening in three years' time. Whilst maintaining the principle of constitutional monarchy inherent to the customs of the Finnish people, and of which principle all their laws and institutions bear the impress, I wish to include in this projected measure a more extended right than that which the Estates now possess in regard to the regulation of taxation and the right of initiating motions, which they formerly possessed; reserving for Myself however the initiative in all matters concerning the alterations of the fundamental laws.

You know My sentiments and My wishes for the happiness and wellbeing of the people entrusted to My care. None of My acts has been such as to interfere with the good understanding that ought to prevail between the sovereign and the nation. I desire that this understanding may continue, as in the past, to be the guarantee of the good relations which unite Me to the brave and loyal people of Finland. It will greatly contribute to the prosperity of a country very dear to My heart and will provide Me with a new incentive to assemble you periodically.

It is for you, representatives of the Grand Duchy, to prove by the dignity, moderation and calmness of your discussions that in the hands of a wise people, determined to work in agreement with the sovereign in a practical spirit for the promotion of their well-being, liberal institutions, far from being a danger, become a guarantee of order and prosperity.

I declare the present Diet open.

(French, with English translation, in J. Danielson, *Finland's union with the Russian Empire*, (Borgå 1891) pp. 176–80.)

29   THE LANGUAGE EDICT OF 1 AUGUST 1863

We, Alexander the Second, by the grace of God, Emperor and Autocrat of All the Russias, Tsar of Poland and Grand Duke of Finland, etc., etc., let it be known : In consequence of the applications and addresses which the Finnish population of the Grand Duchy have from time to time presented to Us, and as We are always desirous to promote all which may be to the advantage and benefit of Our Finnish subjects, We, as a permanent memory of Our visit to the Grand Duchy, have graciously decreed the following :

1. Although the Swedish language will still remain the official language of the country, the Finnish language is hereby proclaimed of equal status with the former in all such matters which directly concern the Finnish population of the country; in consequence whereof, papers and documents in the Finnish language shall henceforth be admitted without hindrance in all courts and offices in Finland.

2. The status of the Finnish language, hereinbefore affirmed and decreed, shall be enforced by the end of 1883 at the latest in regard to those documents which are drawn up by the courts and officials; however, those magistrates and officials who now have a sufficient knowledge of the Finnish language and sufficient experience in writing in it to be able to draw up minutes and docu-

ments in that language may undertake to do so as soon as they are asked to, and

3. It shall be left to Our Finnish Senate to deliver their humble proposals to Us on how and in what sort of order the Finnish language shall hereafter be introduced into the usage of the judiciary and bureaucracy of the country, in addition to the other undertakings and actions consequent upon this Our gracious statute. Which let all concerned humbly obey.

Helsinki, 1 August 1863
(*Suomen Suuriruhtinaanmaan Asetus-Kokous*, no. 26 (Helsinki 1863).)

30   GOVERNOR-GENERAL ROKASSOVSKY'S REPORT TO ALEXANDER II, MAY 1865

. . . Finally, I consider it my duty to say that the frequent demands for new privileges inevitably provoke thoughts about the secret activity of the radical party. Recently much has changed amongst the Finnish public, new ideas about the country's independence have sprung up, with a separatist aspiration and a persistent tendency towards securing the future. This activity came to light rather clearly in the reform of the currency. Little by little special concessions, in themselves unimportant, but which have in the end accomplished the separation of the Grand Duchy from the Empire, have been systematically procured.

Behind the present projected measure [concerning the reorganisation of the Senate] . . . one cannot but detect the same radical party, which has ceaselessly propagated its views and has even designated the person who would merit the leadership of the government. In this connection I ought not to hide the fact that the radicals' programme has long been known to me, and that only a part of it has been designated at present for consideration in committees.

But despite all this, I would think it best to allow the existing institutions to continue in their present form. However much the interests of the Finns in their regular advancement and the happiness of their country is dear to me, I cannot however desire this to the detriment of the interests of the Empire, presupposing that

new concessions do not satisfy the radical party, but merely lead
to new desiderata impossible to fulfil.

(Printed in E. Berendts, *Till den finska frågan*, (Stockholm
1912) pp. 22–3.)

31 'THE NATIONAL DEBT OF GRATITUDE' (1876)

. . . It has become the custom with regard to the Finnish people
to attach a quite singular importance to the particular gratitude
which as a consequence of our past history we feel towards
Sweden. For party political purposes, in fact, attempts have been
made to stress and stress again that the Finnish people have always been, are still and will forever be themselves incapable of
achieving anything good, and that all good things come to them,
not from the supreme mover of the fate of peoples on high, but
from Sweden and the Swedes. That truly noble work and influence of the Swedish people in regard to Finland, and that amity
which for that reason resides in the heart of every Finn, is in this
way misused for purposes which are too well known to be mentioned here. The main purpose is of course to show the Finnish
people the sheer impossibility of their task, to crush their self-
esteem, to kill their national spirit. 'Even the ability of self-
advancement' has supposedly come to us from Sweden. And it is
presumably for this very reason that we owe an eternal debt of
gratitude to Sweden, a debt which binds us in all matters concerned with our domestic affairs.

. . . Used thus for party political purposes, 'the debt of gratitude
to Sweden' has become a magic word, which the reactionaries in
the nationality question presumably hope will provide an effective
form of salvation against the demands of the Finnish language.
The 'Fennomen' are therefore branded as the principal ingrates
towards Sweden, even as instigators of hatred against the Swedish
people and the Swedish tongue.

. . . We also owe a not insignificant debt of gratitude to Russia.
Nearly seventy years of amicable coexistence and the establishment of our independent status during that time has completely
changed the ancient prejudices of the Finnish people towards
Russia. As a *debt* of gratitude this changed sentiment naturally
means no more that other national debts of gratitude; but it does
have a greater significance in that we are in true union with

Russia, a union which contains mutual obligations and mutual
interests. Russia protects us and knows it has a loyal companion-
at-arms here; we for our part are ready to defend to the best of
our ability this corner of the Russian Empire, and in doing so we
know that we are defending the national and political position we
have achieved ...

('Kansallisista kiitollisuusveloista', (Y. S. Yrjö-Koskinen) *Kir-
jallinen Kuukauslehti*, January 1876) pp. 3–10.)

32   FINNISH NEUTRALITY – 'THE AFGHAN QUES-
TION AND FINLAND' (1885)

... We in Finland cannot want a war in which we have nothing
to gain and much to lose. Any war waged by Russia against a
European power is a great misfortune for Finland, and especially
a war waged against the world's leading seapower. We cannot
blame Britain if, in accordance with the traditional laws of warfare, it intercepts our merchant fleet, sailing under the Russian
flag, or if it treats our timber products as contraband: in any
war between Britain and Russia, fate has made us an enemy of
Britain. In the event of a war we would have to bear all these
misfortunes. Furthermore, the lack of a complete defence system,
which we have demanded for our country, will mean the influx
of masses of Russian troops into Finland. What would be the
compensation for us if Russia emerged victorious from the struggle? Nothing.

If Finland were to possess the advantage of a guaranteed
neutrality, however, things would be very different. We would of
course have to be prepared for defence in the event of a threat
to neutrality in the form of operations directed against Petersburg, but even so, our country would be free from the ravages of
war, our trade commodities would be treated in the same way as
those of any other neutral state, and our merchantmen, under the
protection of the flag of their own country, would avoid the risk
of capture.

A neutral area may have the same ruler as a belligerent area.
There are even precedents for this: at the Congress of Vienna,
the provinces of Chablais and Faucigny in northern Savoy, which
bordered the Lake of Geneva, were declared to be covered by the

same neutrality guaranteed to Switzerland in the declaration of 20 March 1815 . . .

The belligerent powers would only benefit from Finland's neutrality, both Russia and her opponents. The Russian fleet would not have to protect and patrol a long and dangerous coastline. Petersburg would be better protected from attacks from the north than it would be by fortifications and armies and Finland by virtue of the peaceful development of its industry and maritime trade, would be in a position to supply its eastern neighbour with quantities of necessary articles, which would otherwise become very expensive or even run out of stock during wartime.

('Afganska frågan och Finland', *Helsingfors Dagblad*, 20 March 1885.)

33   THE LANGUAGE EDICT OF 18 MARCH 1886

The gracious Edict of His Majesty the Emperor and Grand Duke on the use of the Swedish and Finnish languages in official business and correspondence.

Given at Gatchina, 6/18 March 1886.

To Our Governor-General of Finland.

In order finally to obtain equal status of the Finnish and Swedish languages in Finland, We graciously command you to announce that all administrators and officials in the country shall be allowed in official business and correspondence to use both the Swedish and the Finnish language.

A proposal regulating these matters, which should be adequate to cover the use of one or the other language, must be presented to Us without delay, after you have consulted with Our Finnish Senate.

(*Suomen Suuriruhtinaanmaan Asetus-Kokous*, no. 11. (Helsinki 1886.)

34   A LIBERAL VIEW OF THE LANGUAGE CONFLICT
(1886)

. . . It is of course a well-known fact that the Finnish party places the nationality principle high up on its programme. The aim of

the party is indeed not only to work for the advancement of the
Finnish language and the acquisition of the rights which it should
rightfully possess, but also to arouse and inspire the national consciousness of the Finnish people through the creation of a *Finnish
national* culture. What the party, especially the more advanced
groups of the party, understands by Finnish and national is something of a mystery. The programme in its crude form has been
published in the Finnish press, in particular in a number of provincial papers. Finns are those who have the Finnish language as
their mother tongue, national is that which is clad in the garb of
the Finnish tongue, The other section of our people is Swedish
and alien, all other endeavours not specifically Finnish in aim are
alien, not national, and there is little room for doubt as to how
anything not national is regarded. Finland for the Finns! is the
battle cry. This other section of our people must either change
their language and become completely assimilated into the pure
Finnish element, or they must seek out another fatherland : 'Ôtez-
vous en que je m'y mette'. It is humiliating, so the line goes, for
the Finnish national consciouness that another language possesses
the same rights as Finnish, and that Finnish is not the sole mother
tongue of the country's educated class; this consciousness can
only be satisfied when 'the poet's dictum on one language and one
people, which shall unite the Finnish people in harmony' has become a reality.

The party on the opposite extreme, the Swedish party, is also
built around a nationality programme. 'We are not Finns and
will not be Finns!' – this well-known slogan flung out in Tammi-
saari had been officially denied, to be sure, by the leading organ
of the Swedish party, but nevertheless it offers an insight into
feelings within the party. The recent talk about the Tschudic
race, even within the circles which now lay claim to be moderate
and reasonable, is also nothing more than an expression of the
same sentiment. The Swedish party has been careful to preserve a
sharp distinction between the two 'nationalities' in our country; it
has branded as a crime against the Swedish nationality, its inheri-
ted rights and its cultural-historical mission, any concession which
might afford the Finnish language any advance at the expense of
the role which the Swedish language has hitherto played. And
even if all these ideas of nationality, as a result of circumstances
and the numerical inferiority of the Swedish party, have not taken

on the same crude, pronounced forms associated with the utterances of the Finnish national extremists, it does not require much perspicacity to see, behind the more reserved pronouncements, the lurking feeling that blood other than that of the 'Tschudic' race flows in Swedish veins, and that great importance is laid upon the wish not to see Swedish extraction mistaken for that of the vulgar Finnish masses.

In this way, by a sort of mutual friction, by the advocacy of exaggerated and rigid national consciousness by both sides, a consciousness of what 'dignity' demands, a nationality movement has managed to emerge in our country. It is not a national struggle which will lead to the creation of *one* strong and united nation by all the inhabitants of our fatherland, strong and able to wrest for itself a firm and sure position 'amongst the ranks of nations', to secure its own independent place in the cultural work of humanity; it is not this sort of national movement that has been produced here, but a movement which sets brother against brother, which divides where it should unite, which permits numerical superiority on the one side and ancient tradition on the other to count for more than respect for the natural rights of others; which will divide our strength in internecine struggle, further weakening our powers to fulfil the aims laid before us by history.

(*Tankar i politiska frågar af Nemo* (L. Gripenberg), (Helsingfors 1886) pp. 3–5.)

35   *NYA PRESSEN* ON THE CONSEQUENCES OF FINNISH BECOMING AN OFFICIAL LANGUAGE (1886)

. . . With the establishment of Finnish-language grammar schools, a new avenue of social change was opened up in that large numbers of the population were thereby afforded the opportunity of acquiring a good education. In the meantime, however, the language of the civil service was Swedish, and anyone wishing for advancement in the service was compelled to acquire sufficient command of that language so as to be able to write and speak it without difficulty. But now that both languages have been placed on an equal footing as official languages, this state of affairs in some way must alter. More and more people having Finnish as their mother tongue will compete for entry into the service of the state. The passing of a written examination in Swedish will not be sufficient preparation to deal with major problems. Once in the civil service, they will take the opportunity as often as possible to employ their mother tongue, Finnish, in correspondence . . . It will become a competition to see if Finnish will outdistance Swedish . . . In this respect we do not entertain any worries, as long as our Swedish-speaking inhabitants are fully aware of their duty towards their country, themselves and their mother tongue. But if the so-called equality of the languages is to be based on grounds which make it compulsory for civil servants to employ the language which is in use in the minutes of the local authority, and to deal with every matter in the language of the original application, then this will mean a radical alteration of circumstances[6] . . .

The necessity of using, in the main, the Finnish language will cause an influx of Finnish-language speakers into the civil service. We can therefore expect an ever stronger recruitment of elements straight from the masses into the educated class, together with a continuous remoulding of our educated class with regard to language. The consequence of this must be the speedy supersession of the Swedish language by Finnish within the ranks of the educated; the general lowering of the standard of education with the mass entry of this new element, and a heightening of the already existing unease and discontent amongst the Swedish population, which will deprive our country of indispensable strength.

As Swedish ceases to be the language of the educated class and our country becomes an isolated Finnish cultural area of less than two million people, so must it become even more difficult for our people to keep up with developments in the field of culture. As our political existence so closely depends upon this, we can only expect a debilitated spirit of resistance against external influences, in a word, a weakened political position in face of a future which is impossible to predict . . .

('Språkfrågan och senatens minoritet', *Nya Pressen*, 18 May 1886.)

[6] This refers to the attempt by the Fennoman minority in the Senate to make the language used in the minutes of local administrative areas the official language of correspondence for local civil servants.

36 AN APPEAL TO STAND FIRM AGAINST ASSIMILATION (1890)

In a number of Russian and even foreign newspapers there have recently appeared several articles describing our present circumstances in the most gloomy terms as greatly out-of-date, and seeking to convince the world that the true people of Finland welcome those measures which have been undertaken to bring Finland into closer union with the Empire, in other words to russify Finland. Official circles – so we are told – and titled landowners, for whom all the Finnish press acts as spokesmen, are supposedly oppressing the peasantry and are now opposing those measures which are intended to liberate the people from their yoke. Our circumstances are indeed better known in Russian government circles, but nevertheless it would appear that even there they are unaware of the views of our people on these attempts at change. We Finns well know that the Finnish people are of one mind in these matters, but this knowledge is not enough: we must also let our sovereign and the world know that the entire Finnish people, i.e. all social classes without exception stands as one man against these moves. This is the duty of the Finnish people to itself and to the future, its task to silence all detractors. *We propose that every Finnish parish elect, at specially convened meetings, representatives to present our sovereign with their humble feelings of sorrow that have been aroused by the changes which have partly taken place, and are still being planned concerning the Finnish postal, monetary and customs systems, and to express the humble desire of the parishes of Finland that these measures be repealed.* The present moment demands this sort of spontaneous popular demonstration, whether it is productive or not. The fact that the Diet will soon convene does not render it unnecessary for many reasons. Let us therefore act resolutely and with enthusiasm!

We hope that other newspapers will carry this exhortation in their columns.

A GROUP OF COUNTRYMEN

('Kehoitus', *Uusi Suometar*, 18 September 1890.)

37 'WHAT THE PRESENT SITUATION DEMANDS': THE FINNISH VIEW (1893)

What the present situation is should be clear to everyone. The legally confirmed national existence of the Finnish people has been questioned in the Russian press by an inflammatory campaign inspired by a large and powerful party in the Empire. This campaign has already caused us one or two distinct setbacks, which have encouraged the victors to renew their efforts with even more violence ...

Frankly, the nationalists must bear in mind that they alone form the only party at the present moment which can be said to represent the general opinion of the Finnish people in political matters. Constitutionally, no doubt, all the members of the Diet in every Estate and party represent the Finnish people, and all have the same right with regard to the drafting of laws. But in those delicate matters which may be brought up at this Diet, only the pronouncements of the national party have any significance ...

Nowadays there is a lot of talk of the necessity of unanimity. Unanimity is a good thing, and may even be necessary, but the word has a double meaning. From the point of view of the Swedish nationalists it is most often understood to mean that the Finns must follow the lead of the Swedish party in political matters, and should in no way be offended if in practical matters the things they stand for are belittled and their leaders deliberately insulted and abused. This sort of unanimity is therefore nothing more than the continuation of control exercised by the Vikings.[7] For political reasons it is now essential that a final end be made to that control, since it is already becoming very dangerous for the security of the country for a sect to continue to exist in certain circles, which so deceives the eye with its anti-national programme that it is for instance allowed to hatch plans for foisting upon the Finnish people a language wholly alien to it through the medium of the elementary school.[8]

[7] Perjorative term for the Swedish party, originating from the title of the Svecoman mouthpiece of the 1870s.

[8] This is a reference to a suggestion by certain members of the Swedish party for Swedish to be used as the language of tuition in Finnish-language schools.

Unanimity should indeed be brought about, but on quite different terms, that is by the fulfilment of the justified demands of the Finns. And as for the present sensitive state of affairs, unanimity is only to be achieved by the national party taking over the leadership and the Swedish party willingly following it . . . Only the Finnish party at the present moment speaks for the Finnish people.

('Mitä nykyinen asema vaatii', (Y. S. Yrjö-Koskinen) *Uusi Suometar*, 21 September 1893.)

. . . When matters concerning the happiness and interest of the *whole country*, every Finnish citizen, are brought up, matters whose political significance is just as important and just as dear to every inhabitant of Finland irrespective of language, party political attitudes must give way, and the Diet is, and must be, as one man. In such matters there can be no justification for making distinctions between different parties and individuals belonging to different parties . . . That point of view which refuses to recognise solidarity between the parties in matters most dear to the fatherland we cannot but regard as short-sighted and incomprehensible in view of the exigencies of the situation . . .

('Entinen asema ja mitä nykyinen vaatii', *Päivälehti*, 5 October 1893.)

38 J. R. DANIELSON-KALMARI ON THE LANGUAGE QUESTION (1897)

. . . The Finnish people cannot fulfil their historical mission and it is doubtful whether they will even preserve their present political position, if the language of the majority of the people does not become the main language used by the educated classes as well . . . There have already been a number of indications that our country will not escape the wrangles over social issues which have caused such deep and bitter conflict between the social classes in the Europe of our day. If these break out here at a time when the language conflict still causes bitterness and when the Finnish-speaking majority is faced with an educated class dominated by those who speak Swedish . . . can you guarantee that all the different social classes will stand as one man against threatening dangers from outside? It would be an unforgivable act of folly to ignore the possibility of a renewal of such outside threats. I repeat my question : if they are renewed at a time when not only the language conflict but also the social question divides the upper and lower classes in our country, can you guarantee that the masses will then, fired by passion, remember and understand that the destruction of the fatherland is also their own destruction? If they give up or remain indifferent, we, the so-called educated, will be unable to maintain the building . . . Therefore in order to bring about the necessary unity we must renew the demand, renew it until it is realised, that just as the great majority of our people are Finnish-speaking, so must our social and political life become Finnish . . .

(Speech by Danielson, reported in *Uusi Suometar*, 4 December 1897. Extract printed in T. Torvinen, *J. R. Danielson-Kalmari Suomen autonomian puolustajana*, (Helsinki 1965) pp. 208–9.)

39　A FOREIGN VIEW OF FINNISH POLITICS (1894)

. . . The Old Finn party is at present the government party in Finland. In one respect this is its strength and in another, its weakness.

At the Diet of 1882 the leader of the Finnish party, Y. S. Yrjö-Koskinen was appointed to the Senate. With the aid of a less than average amount of talent in general and a talent for intrigue in particular, this former party leader is now the undisputed leading figure in the government where his will is law. This triumph has been however brought at almost ruinous cost to the party whose power and influence Mr Koskinen represents.

The leader of the Finnish party has in fact achieved his influence in the Senate and in Petersburg by following a political programme of which the principal rule is; concession, concession without end, even beyond the limits of constitutional infringements. . . . At the commencement of the last Diet, Senator Koskinen made an energetic attempt to consolidate his position. He laid before the Finnish party a sensational party programme, which clearly spelt out the intention of pushing the troublesome Swedish party to one side and of proclaiming the duty and right of the Finnish party to 'speak alone for the Finnish people'. The aim was clear enough : the Finnish party was to be declared synonymous with the Finnish people, and in the position of absolute dictator within his party Senator Koskinen would be even more justified than ever in asserting his claim to represent both the people and government of Finland . . .

It has also been revealed that Mr Yrjö-Koskinen overestimated his authority within the party when he issued his party political piece 'What the present situation demands'. The rank and file of the party did not go along with him; the Young Finn group and its leader, Mr Jonas Castrén, began to separate from and revolt against the old party leadership more and more, and all the signs seem to indicate that the schism within the Finnish party is on the way to becoming even more pronounced in the forthcoming Diet . . .

The schism within the Finnish party is of course not new. From the beginning there have been differences of opinion on the language question itself. A section of the younger members put forward a very radical language programme, demanding that the Swedish party should be told straight out what their aims were and that there should be no involvement in compromises . . . Gradually the divergence of opinion in the language question was erased, but other divisions have taken its place. The deep-rooted conservatism of the Old Finns became more pronounced, whilst amongst the younger party members the ideas of a new era had made inroads. The old leaders' preference for clericalism, protectionism, anti-semitism and all other illiberal tendencies was an abomination for the young. This antagonism grew ever stronger with the emergence of major political questions when the defence of Finland's constitutional liberties pushed all other interests into the background. The tactic pursued by the old had no appeal to the young, who could have no confidence in a government which published the manifesto concerning the postal system and the suspension of the penal code without protest and which issued the decree on the State Secretariat and the Chancery of the Governor General . . .

The Swedish party in Finland commands . . . a decisive majority in both the Estates of Nobles and the Estates of Burghers, but it is rather poorly represented in the other two Estates. Its position in the Diet is thus considerably stronger than party numbers would warrant. The Swedish-speaking element in Finland in fact comprises no more than one-ninth of the entire population.
. . . Some twenty years ago, it was the 'liberals' – also called,

after the main party paper, the 'Dagblad party'[9] – which occupied
the leading position amongst the Swedish-speaking element, and
the Swedish party proper – the 'Vikings' – played an unenviable,
though noteworthy role. . . . The liberal party has since been
decimated . . . The liberals of today go to the meetings of the
Swedish party and may thus be reckoned amongst the number of
that party . . .

(O. von Zweigbergk, *Finska studier. Bref från Aftonbladets
specielle korrespondent*, (Helsingfors, januari-februari 1894,
(Stockholm 1894). Unpaginated offprint.)

[9] *Helsingfors Dagblad*, which ceased publication in 1889.

Part II

AUTONOMY THREATENED (1890-1917)

The First Period of Oppression (1899-1905)

Russian awareness of the existence of a politically sophisticated, autonomous nation on the doorstep of the capital, so graphically portrayed by a Finnish official in 1889, was to have ominous consequences for Finland (40). Alexander III's orders to the Governor-General in 1891, with his use of terms such as 'frontier region' and 'general state laws', were a clear indication of the new course of Russian policy towards a strategically vulnerable area (41). Governor-General Heiden's proposals for the administration of the provinces foreshadowed the measures outlined by Governor-General Bobrikov less than ten years later, and revealed to the Finnish people in the February manifesto of 1899 (42, 45, 47). The dies irae of pitiless assimilation feared by Snellman in 1880 seemed at hand. The Senate split over whether or not to promulgate the February manifesto, with the vice-chairman's casting vote determining the issue. In 1900, most of the Senators resigned rather than sign the order to promulgate the Language Edict, but those who stayed were joined by others who felt it their duty to remain at the helm to save what could be saved (49). Yrjö-Koskinen defended the actions of those who remained and urged the Finnish nationalists to rally in defence of the language and in support of the government (50). This so-called 'compliance line', which found a more flexible interpretation in the writings of Danielson-Kalmari, Yrjö-Koskinen's successor to the leadership of the Finnish party, sought to recognise the sad fact that Russia was all-powerful and likely to remain so for the foreseeable future, and to meet the demands of Russian national interest halfway in the hopes of preserving the essential features of Finnish national identity intact (51, 53).

The Young Finn and Swedish constitutionalists who formed the passive resistance took their stand on the defence of the law from unwarranted attack (52, 54). The fact that churchmen in Finland were required to proclaim all new laws from the pulpit

*involved the Lutheran church in the conflict; civil servants,
teachers and doctors, all in positions of authority became involved
(55). The most successful prolonged act of resistance was directed
against the enforcement of the military service law of 1901, which
replaced the Finnish army created in 1878 with selective conscription for Russian military units. It is however unlikely that passive
resistance would have saved Finland from thoroughgoing assimilation in the long run. Its effectiveness was indeed questioned at
the time by members of the younger generation, keenly aware of
the underlying conservatism of the constitutionalist leadership
(59).*

*A few Finns looked beyond their own country and sought to
establish closer links with oppositional groups within the Empire,
a move frowned upon by the leadership of the passive resistance
(57, 58). By 1904, an activist movement of a few determined
young intellectuals, mostly Swedish-speaking, had come into being,
with close links through the person of Konni Zilliacus with the
Russian revolutionary movement (61, 62). Active resistance as
such in Finland was minimal. The assassination of Bobrikov in
1904 was committed by an individual on the outer fringes of the
movement. The importance of the activist movement was its
ability to break with the idealistic conservatism of the constitutionalists and to consider a future Finland emerging from a
revolutionary situation. Unlike the author of 'Scandinavia and
Finland', who harked back to the liberal ideal of Finnish neutrality guaranteed by the major powers, the activists sought to ex-
ploit the internal situation in Russia to secure a new political deal
for their country (63, 64).*

40 THE RUSSIAN VIEW OF FINLAND – A FINNISH INTERPRETATION (1889)

. . . It would seem as if Russian statesmen have only just woken up
to the fact that they are now faced with a quite new and remark-
able phenomenon which has grown and matured silently whilst
their predecessors were either sleeping the sleep of indifference or
were looking the other way. They are surprised and annoyed to
see that small embryonic state which Alexander at the stormy
dawn of the century hastily created 'somewhere the other side of
Viipuri' now grown into an autonomous state within the course

of three-quarters of a century, and possessing all the attributes of such a state in more or less fully developed order. They see furthermore that those few hundred thousand Tschudi who were grubbing about in the bogs and forests of the conquered province, clad in rags, with birch-bark shoes on their feet and nourished on birch-bark bread, ruled by a handful of 'Swedish noblemen', now, at least in their eyes, form a nation of two and a quarter million people some twenty miles from the gates of the capital : a nation which claims a more ancient culture than their own and which on top of that speaks and demands to be addressed in a language which the Russians in their pride have been accustomed to compare with the bellowing of cattle and the howling of dogs. Before their astonished eyes appears a well organised, self-governing society with thousands of schools, where, *horribile dictu*, the language of the Empire is not taught, with its own industry which in part competes with their own markets, and with its own firmly secured finances and credit system in the world markets, which many richer countries might even envy ...

(Johannes Gripenberg to Y. Yrjö-Koskinen, 15 April 1889 : letter in the Yrjö-Koskinen archives, Finnish State Archives. Printed in P. Rommi, *Myöntyvyyssuuntauksen hahmottuminen Yrjö-Koskisen ja suomalaisen puolueen toimintalinjaksi*, (Helsinki 1964) p. 77.)

41 ALEXANDER THE THIRD'S RESCRIPT TO THE GOVERNOR-GENERAL OF FINLAND, 12 MARCH 1891

After you had opened the Diet of representatives of Finland on 8/20 January of this year in accordance with My instructions, the Marshal of the Nobility and the Speakers of the Estates, in expressing the humble sentiments of loyalty of My subjects, felt it their duty to inform Me of the mood of unrest prevalent in the country, brought about by certain of My plans to bring the Grand Duchy into closer union with the other parts of the Russian Empire.

My unfailing solicitude for the welfare and domestic progress of Finland and the many manifestations of My goodwill towards its people does not justify this sort of mood in a frontier region.

Only a false interpretation of the foundations on which the

relations of the Grand Duchy to the Empire and the supreme authority are based, and the dissemination of these misconceived notions amongst the people to the detriment of their true interests could have led to this unfortunate state of affairs.

Finland, which has belonged to the Russian Empire from the beginning of this century, and even earlier, as is the case with one of its constituent parts, received by the wish of the Emperor Alexander I of blessed memory its own special internal administration, as well as a most merciful assurance of the preservation of its rights, privileges, religion and fundamental laws. His Imperial successors have also confirmed this assurance.

These rights and privileges, the ecclesiastical structure and the laws of the land are not only still in force, but have also been further developed to meet the needs of the Finnish people. Thus, the lot of the Grand Duchy under the Sceptre of Russia has demonstrated that the union with Russia has not prevented the free development of its local institutions, and the prosperity attained by Finland irrefutably proves that this union meets Finland's own interests. However, the lack of uniformity between certain of Finland's statutes and the general state laws, as well as the lack of sufficient clarity in those decrees which relate to the Grand Duchy's position in regard to the Empire, regrettably give rise to misunderstandings of the real significance of the measures which are being taken to achieve the common aims of all parts of the Russian Empire. I trust however that the commonsense of the Finnish people will overcome this misunderstanding and that a proper understanding of their own interests will cause them to strive for a strengthening of the bonds which unite Finland to Russia.

It shall be your task to inform in My name all My loyal subjects in Finland that I wish to show the same goodwill, solicitude and trust towards the Finnish people as hitherto, maintaining unchanged the rights and privileges granted by the monarchs of Russia, and that I have no intention of altering the basis of the internal government of the country.

I believe the sentiments of loyalty of all the estates of the land, expressed by the Marshal of the Nobility and the Speakers of the Estates, and I am entitled to expect of the Finnish people an interests in the unanimous co-operation of My people for the realisation of that which I have outlined for the purpose of strengthening the political union of the Grand Duchy and the Empire.

(Printed in F. Yelenev, *Finlyandskiy sovremenny vopros*, (St Petersburg 1891) pp. 220–3.)

42 GOVERNOR-GENERAL HEIDEN'S PROPOSALS FOR THE ADMINISTRATION OF THE PROVINCES OF FINLAND (1891)

4. The provinces of the Grand Duchy of Finland have their own internal administration and local powers of legislation distinct from the other parts of the Empire.

Some sections of this internal administration are authorised by special statutory provisions, and are subject to the general laws of the Empire.

6. Laws which concern both the Grand Duchy of Finland and other parts of the Empire shall be issued in the manner prescribed by the laws of the realm and published in the country by the Imperial Senate for Finland.

In the event of measures concerning the general laws and ordinances of the Empire, which may also concern Finland, the appropriate ministers and chief civil servants shall confer with the Minister State-Secretary for the Grand Duchy.

7. ... In any such matters concerning the local government of Finland, which deal with questions relevant to the general administration of the realm, the Governor-General shall, if he finds it necessary, present a report to the committee of ministers, if no alteration in the existing statutes of the country is necessitated by these matters.

8. ... The Governor-General may be present at the State Council when measures concerning the issuing of such general laws of state which concern Finland and which require alteration in the existing statutes of the country are under consideration.

In such measures which concern local administration and which also affect other parts of the Empire, the Governor-General shall confer with the relevant ministers and civil servants in the Empire.

9. All subjects of the Russian Empire, who possess the right to enter into the civil service on the basis of the laws of the Empire, may also be appointed to the civil service in Finland.

10. The right to be represented in the Estates, as well as other rights and privileges provided for by the local laws of Finland, shall be enjoyed by all subjects of the Russian Empire who are of the Christian faith, enrolled in one of the Estates of the country ...

13. Bills concerning the amendment, supplementation or repeal of the laws of the land in the following categories shall be presented to the Estates for their consideration : (1) ecclesiastical, dealing with the Evangelical Lutheran faith (2) civil (3) concerning the privileges and rights of the estates (4) concerning the payment of taxes *in natura* (5) concerning the levying of direct taxes (6) concerning the rights of private ownership (7) paragraph 11 of the decree of 9 December 1867 concerning the Bank of Finland (8) the procedure of the Diet (9) paragraphs 1–6, 9, 13, 19, 20, 120–3 of the law on military service for the Grand Duchy of Finland and (10) the law on the right of non-Lutherans to hold office in the country. These laws shall be acknowledged as the fundamental laws of Finland.

The Estates shall give their opinion of other government bills in accordance with the decision of the supreme authority.

14. The Minister State-Secretary for the Grand Duchy shall, before submitting bills for new local laws, as well as the proposals made by the Diet, obtain the opinion of the relevant ministers on the matter, if it falls within their competence, and shall then add the views of His Imperial Majesty and of the Governor-General of the country, as well as the pronouncements of the ministers to the said bills and proposals.

15. All local laws for the country shall be drafted in the language of state, Russian, with official translations into the local Finnish and Swedish languages provided.

(Typewritten translation, entitled *Nedanstående reglemente, uppgjordt af generalguvernör, är afsedt att läggas till grund för förhandlingar inom den i Petersburg sammanträdande kommiteen för kodifikation af Finlands grundlagar*, Helsinki University Library)

43 A FINNISH INTERPRETATION OF THE CONSTITIONAL POSITION OF THE GRAND DUCHY (1892)

. . . As Finland makes up a part of the Russian Empire, its position within that Empire may be changed by a law issued by the Emperor in his capacity as supreme head of state, but before this can be done, it is necessary for a law *in conformity with the Finnish constitution* to have been made to permit such a state law to have legal validity in this country. Since the fundamental laws of Finland embodied the sanctity of the law for that part of the Empire which constitutes the Grand Duchy, it follows that laws cannot be made for the Grand Duchy other than in concordance with the said constitution. We have already demonstrated that this constitution does not recognise the validity of decrees made independently of its statutes : consequently, only decrees made in conformity with these statutes have the sanctity of law in Finland.

There can be no appeal to the power of autocracy against this principle, for the law in relation to this power, as we have shown, has no validity on Finnish soil. The Grand Duchy has a constitution which declares that laws cannot be made without the consent of the Estates and that the constitution itself cannot without violation of the rights of the people be altered other than with the consent and agreement of the representatives of the people, and this means that *on Finnish soil* the powers of the monarch are circumscribed by a law which acknowledges the people's right to consent to the making of law; the law which ascribes unlimited powers to the monarch is *not* valid on Finish soil, because limited and unlimited monarchical powers cannot simultaneously exist within the same area. We do not wish to reiterate here the many instances which show that this was indeed the opinion of the Emperor Alexander I, who laid the foundation of the present judicial system of Finland. But we cannot refrain from mentioning the speech from the throne which the Emperor Alexander II made in person at the opening of the 1863 Diet, in which the Emperor personally declared that the constitutional monarchic principle – *le principe monarchique constitutionel* – prevailed in Finland . . .

(R. Hermanson, *Finlands statsrättsliga ställning*, (Helsingfors 1892) p. 313.)

44 GOVERNOR-GENERAL BOBRIKOV'S SPEECH TO THE SENATE, 12 OCTOBER 1898

. . . Our monarch knows the devotion of the Finnish people, but His Imperial Majesty is also aware that a false interpretation of the basis of Finland's relationship with Russia has regrettably been disseminated in the country. Under the harmful influence of such interpretations, certain Finns have not shown sufficient sympathy towards the measures which have been taken to strengthen the bonds which link the country to the other parts of the Russian Empire. Russia is one and indivisible, one and indivisible is its Imperial throne, under whose protection the Grand Duchy has attained its present prosperity. It would therefore seem that every effort to bring about uniformity with Russia should be a natural sentiment in the breast of every Finn who holds the interest of his fatherland dear.

In the rescript entrusted to me by His Majesty, he has referred to the necessity of strengthening this sentiment by instilling in the minds of His Majesty's subjects in Finland the conviction of the importance of uniting Finland with the centre. Leaving intact the characteristics of Finland's ecclesiastical institutions, rights and privileges as well as her internal government, as defined in the rescript of 1891, insofar as these do not come into conflict with the interest and dignity of Russia, the power of the state cannot however permit a further extension of anything which might hinder the union of the whole Empire . . . I shall regard myself as fortunate if, under my governance, the Finnish people, who have repeatedly shown evidence of their loyalty to their monarchs, are filled with an awareness of the unavoidable necessity of good and cordial relations with Russia, since it is surely unthinkable to separate attachment to the monarch from attachment to the state as a whole. Within the boundless regions of Russia, there is only allegiance and a common love of the fatherland for all under the mighty sway of the Tsar. May God help us to fulfil the steadfast will of the monarch and to serve faithfully the wellbeing of our dear Russia. I sincerely hope for your firm co-operation in all things, and in particular I count upon the united support of my closest colleagues in the Imperial Finnish Senate. And so, with God's help, we may begin at a happy hour.

(Printed in Swedish translation in K. Zilliacus, *Ur Finlands nyaste historia*, vol. 2 (Stockholm 1901) pp. 102–3.)

45 GOVERNOR-GENERAL BOBRIKOV'S PROGRAMME FOR FINLAND

Finland, having been conquered by Russian arms, has come into Russian possession in accordance with the rights of conquest . . . as from 1809 the country has belonged to the Russian Empire and . . . is forever united with it. Its inhabitants are irrefutably Russian citizens and subjects of the Tsar of All the Russias.

The conquest of Finland was necessitated by the need to move our northern frontier further away from Petersburg. But despite an association of ninety years, the purpose of this conquest has to date not been achieved . . . In the place of a foreign state a frontier area has been created which has up to now remained alien to its benefactor, Russia, and openly seeks to establish its rights as a constitutional state, united to Russia simply by a common supreme authority.

The Finnish frontier country is today as foreign to us as it was during the time before its conquest.

Under such circumstances it is not easy for the representative of Russian authority in Finland, in addition to looking after the interests of the state, to find common ground with the present experts of the country in this field and to get to work on these matters. It will take not a little time to study the question on the spot and then to clarify and establish the system which best meets the main interests of the state.

In order to achieve the most thorough and comprehensive investigation of Finland's present position, it is essential that a revision similar to that carried out by Senator Manassein in the Baltic provinces[1] be performed by Russians. Finnish separatism could however be limited before the results of this revision are published by (1) carrying out an amalgamation of the army together with an adjustment of the burden and costs of maintenance of troops; a reformation of the Finnish Cadet Corps in a Russian manner; the establishment in Helsinki of an officers' club for Russian and Finnish officers (2) abolishing or limiting the im-

---

[1] Manassein was chairman of an investigating committee into the government of the Baltic provinces, 1882–4.

portance of the State-Secretariat, in addition to which the
Governor-General shall be accorded the right, albeit in matters of
particular importance, to be present at the submission of reports
by the Minister State-Secretary (3) carrying out a codification of
the laws of the land and establishing a special procedure for the
inspection of matters which are common to the Empire and Grand
Duchy (4) introducing the Russian language into the Senate,
schools and civil service (5) permitting Russians to enter into service in the institutions of the Grand Duchy without the qualifications imposed on them in this respect by the law of 1858[2] (6)
arranging for supervision of the university and inspection of all
textbooks used in Finnish schools (7) abolition of the separate
customs and coinage institutions (8) founding an official Russian
newspaper and permitting Russians to publish newspapers in
Russian or one of the local languages (9) simplifying the present
ceremonial followed at the opening of the Diet (10) modifying
the instructions provided in 1812 for the Governor-General . . .

(Extract from Bobrikov's diary, published in M. Borodkin,
Generalguvernör Bobrikovs minne, (Helsingfors 1905) pp. 11–
12.)

46 GENERAL BORODKIN ON THE FINNISH QUES-TION (1905)

. . . The only link between us is the person of the monarch. The
Finns do indeed recognise him, but it is impossible for us to be
satisfied with this meagre sort of link . . . Russia needs natural
frontiers and must protect its capital.

But if Russia has *need* of Finland then it is clear that we cannot be satisfied with its present relationship to the Empire; we cannot allow it to remain a country completely foreign to Russia. If
Russia needs Finland, then the political and vital interests of the
state demand that it must have *full powers* to carry out a policy
of unifying the Grand Duchy with the other parts of the Empire.
The interests of the Russian Empire demand that Finland be
closely welded to the centre. The needs and interests of a great
empire are the supreme judges of its own cause, and against this
judgement there is no appeal.

. . . Which general principle should become the linking bond

[2] These were mostly language qualifications.

between Finland and Russia as a united political unit? In our Russian view, it should be the principle of autocracy. In order to be strong, Russia must be united and indivisible, with an unlimited and all-compensating supreme authority at its head. These are the vital interests of our Empire; but Finland does not recognise the principle of autocracy.

(M. Borodkin, *Generalguvernör Bobrikovs minne*, (Helsingfors 1905) pp. 4–6.)

47 NICHOLAS THE SECOND'S SPEECH FROM THE THRONE AT THE OPENING OF THE DIET, JANUARY 1899

Representatives of the Finnish people!

You are convened in an extraordinary Diet as an indication of the particular importance of the matters which have been laid before you for your consideration.

Indissolubly united to the Empire and under the protection of the state of Russia, Finland has no need of an army separate from that of the Russian Army. The law on military service in this country must therefore be brought into line with the law which obtains in the Empire.

As We nevertheless desire that the new law which is to be introduced may be as far as possible in conformity with the local conditions peculiar to this country, We have thought it appropriate to deliver the bill and the basic rules for a 'decree concerning the organisation and administration of the Finnish troops' to the Diet for a preliminary consideration, in the firm conviction that the Estates will fulfil the task punctiliously and thereby justify Our gracious confidence in them.

The main principles which are the basis of this bill, which are directed to the protection of the frontiers and security of the whole Empire, were in principle approved by the Emperor Alexander III of blessed memory and by Us as fully in accordance with the precepts of justice.

May God help you to fulfil the work before you for the good of the loyal Finnish people, which is as near to Our heart as is the welfare of all Our faithful subjects ...

(Printed in *Värnepliktsfrågan i Finland. Handlingar tillkomna i ryska riksrådet vid den därstädes våren 1901 försiggångna behandlingen af den finska värnepliktsfrågan,* (Stockholm 1902) p. 9.)

48 THE 'FEBRUARY MANIFESTO', 15 FEBRUARY 1899

We, Nicholas the Second, by the grace of God Emperor and Autocrat of All the Russias, Tsar of Poland, Grand Duke of Finland . . .

Let it be known to all Our faithful subjects : the Grand Duchy of Finland, which has been part of the Russian Empire from the beginning of this century, has, in memory of the Blessed Emperor Alexander and with the gracious consent of His Noble Descendents, special institutions for its internal administration and legislation which are suited to the circumstances of the country.

But disregarding these local legislative matters which stem from the social institutions peculiar to Finland, there occur in the administration of the state other items of legislation concerning Finland, which, as they are intimately related to the good of the state as a whole, cannot solely be dealt with by the institutions of the Grand Duchy. The legislation at present in force contains no precise directions for the determining of these matters, and this has led to considerable inconveniences.

In order to do away with these inconveniences, We, forever solicitious of the welfare of all Our faithful subjects without distinction, have seen fit, in order to supplement the statutes at present in force and to comply with the appropriate institutions of the Empire and the Grand Duchy, to ordain a firm and inviolable decree for the preparation and issuing of general laws concerning the state.

In retaining the regulations governing the promulgation of local statutes solely concerned with the need of Finland, We have also deemed it necessary to reserve for Ourself the right to define more closely those matters of general Imperial legislation.

For this purpose We have furthermore confirmed with Our own hand a series of basic regulations on the preparation, inspection and promulgation of those laws which are to be decreed for the Empire, the Grand Duchy of Finland therein included.

As did Our crowned forefathers, so do We consider the closest association of Finland with the Empire to be one of the conditions for its wellbeing. Protected and safeguarded by the Russian Empire, Finland has during the course of almost a century ceaselessly followed the path of peaceful development and We have been pleased to see from the recent assurances of the Estates of the Duchy that the feeling of affection towards Us and Russia is strong in the hearts of the Finnish people.

We trust that an integrated relationship between the institutions of the Empire and the Grand Duchy of Finland, based on a firm regulation of the codes of law in those legislative matters which concern both parties, will be an even greater guarantee of the real advantages and benefits of the state of Russia.

(*Suomen Suuriruhtinaanmaan Asetuskokoelma*, no. 3. (Helsinki 1899.)

49   THE LANGUAGE EDICT, 20 JUNE 1900

We Nicholas the Second, by the grace of God Emperor and Autocrat of All the Russias, Tsar of Poland, Grand Duke of Finland ... Let it be known : after the union of the Grand Duchy of Finland to the Russian Empire, it was decided at the wish of the Emperor Alexander I of blessed memory that the Russian language should be gradually introduced as a main language in the conduct of business relating to the government of the country. This gracious order, which resulted from a desire to strengthen the unity of the state, has not so far been enforced because the Russian language has not sufficiently permeated into Finland. In order to do away with this problem, certain steps have been taken, and recently a knowledge of the language of the Empire has been made compulsory for entry into all high office in the country. As We deem the time now right for the Russian language to assume its rightful place in the official correspondence and business of the offices of the Grand Duchy, We have set up a special conference to consider the matter. The opinion of this conference, which corresponds with Our intentions, is that the matter should be expedited in a consistent manner. Attention has also been given to the needs of the private individual, who in future is to be guaranteed the opportunity to use his mother tongue in dealings with government institutions as freely as he uses it socially or in private life. In approving the views of the special conference, We command that :

1. The office of the State-Secretary for the Grand Duchy of Finland, the chancery of the Governor-General of Finland and the Finnish passport office shall, from 18 September/1 October 1900, conduct business and correspondence solely in Russian.

2. The Imperial Finnish Senate (Economic Department) is, from 18 September/1 October 1900, to draft its humble submissions and pronouncements and all its correspondence with the Governor-General in Russian. Where necessary the above-mentioned department of the Senate is to append to documents a translation of submissions, statements and papers in the local language. From 18 September/1 October 1903, both written and oral business in the Senate and its departments (with the exception of the Department of Justice) shall be conducted in Russian, with the following reservations : (a) original documents relating to the matter in hand may be read aloud in the language in which they are written (b) when copies of the decisions of the Senate are published, a Swedish or Finnish translation may be appended at the request of an applicant, and (c) for a period of five years after the above-mentioned date, the chairman of the Senate sessions shall permit members of the Senate to make oral statements in Swedish or Finnish.

3. Administrative bodies under the Imperial Finnish Senate, provincial governors, their deputies and administrative offices shall, from 18 September/1 October 1905, conduct their correspondence with higher officials such as the Governor-General, Senate, etc. solely in Russian.

4. Administrative bodies in the Grand Duchy of Finland, in which Russian is the language of business, must accept and consider in the manner prescribed the applications of individuals which are written in one or other of the local languages.

5. Russian-language applications and documents are to be accepted in all government institutions in the Grand Duchy of Finland . . . These applications and documents are to be translated into the local language where necessary . . .

6. The officials concerned must, subject to the direction and control of the Governor-General of Finland, take steps in good time and in the manner prescribed to see that the composition of the departments and offices under their supervision is so

organised as to meet the requirements for the successful introduction of Russian into the conduct of business and correspondence within the civil service, during the periods outlined above.

(*Suomen Suuriruhtinaanmaan Asetuskokoelma*, no. 22. (Helsinki 1900.)

50 'AN OPEN LETTER TO MY FRIENDS' – YRJÖ-KOSKINEN ON THE SPLIT IN THE FINNISH PARTY, DECEMBER 1900

Today I celebrate my seventieth birthday, and my friends had intended to hold a celebration dinner in my honour. I am grateful to those many friends whose names are on the list of guests, but for reasons which I shall make clear I have refused to accept this honour . . .

The fact of the matter is that in regard to the position of the Finnish party in the present circumstances, I am at odds with a number of my esteemed friends. On the whole I have to express my doubts as to the existence of a Finnish party at this moment, at any rate in terms of what that party formerly stood for. It is difficult to detect any sort of programme followed by the party at present, for silence is no programme and inactivity is no standpoint. A party which shows no sign of life, and whose members follow all kinds of banners or follow none at all, truly seems to have ceased to exist.

My doubts in this respect would seem to be supported by the events of last summer and thereafter. It is no secret that a certain vociferous clique, apparently in the name of 'public opinion', proclaimed that the Senate should refuse to promulgate the edict issued by the sovereign, and that because of this selfsame edict every Senator was under obligation to resign. Many influential people on the Finnish nationalist side have either supported this view, or have silently agreed with it. In this manner, a flood of insults has been unleashed against those government figures here at home who interpreted their duty to the country and the people in a different light. Nor is this the only illustrative example of the way things are going at present. During the prevailing adverse conditions of censorship, attempts have been made both in public and in private to bring about a general state of terrorism, which in my view can do nothing but harm. Finnish nationalists have

D

helped create this wretched situation, at any rate by their timid silence.

My views in these matters have been and are still not those of many of my good friends. Speaking only of the Senate question, I wish to point out :

Firstly : the Senate had no legal right to refuse to promulgate the edict.

Secondly : in regard to the resignation of the Senators, there surely can be no question of right or obligation; it is a matter for each individual to decide. But in the case now under discussion those who have remained in the Senate to bear their heavy responsibilities have, in my opinion, rendered a better service to the Finnish people than those who have opted out by resignation . . .

Although it has to be admitted that the situation at present is difficult – especially as no-one can predict how far it is intended to go with the measures aimed against us – I believe that it is absolutely essential that the Finnish party, behind which stands the Finnish people, does not cease to exist. Existence implies the need for a programme and a standpoint, if only in the form of general outlines for a programme. These outlines I hereby make so bold as to present as representative of my own views.

The first stipulation is the breaking of all ties with that group which at present goes under the name of the Swedish party. In actual fact this so-called Swedish party is made up of the most intransigent Vikings, to whom the existence of the Finnish people is as nothing compared with the dominance of the Swedish language. The fact that they are followed by a certain wagging Finnish tail does not alter the state of affairs.

The second stipulation is that the Finnish party supports in principle the government at home by assuming that this government is doing what it can to clarify the situation and protect the rights of the people.

The third point of the programme, which I regard as the most important since it is aimed at the future, is that the Finnish language and nation be more vigorously strengthened, as events have in this respect run ahead of us and time no longer brooks delay . . .

('Avoin kirje ystävilleni' (Y. S. Yrjö-Koskinen) *Uusi Suometar*, 11 December 1900.)

51 J. R. DANIELSON-KALMARI'S PROGRAMME OF ACTION (1900)

There are two basic principles . . . which in my view we must follow in all our activities.

The first is that the Finnish people as a whole and as individuals must frankly and fearlessly express their concept of justice. This must be done in such a way as to leave not the slightest doubt of what the humblest as well as the highest in this land thinks of the legality of recent decrees. This must be done in the first place to preserve the honour of the present generation and to win a brighter future for the coming generation, but it is also our clear duty to the ruler, who may on any occasion demand from his subjects, especially servants of the state, loyal and absolute frankness.

The second principle is that whatever may happen, the Finnish people must never embark on a course of action which finally and irrevocably breaks the relationship between them and the ruler. Finland is an inseparable part of the Russian Empire and no-one, who remains within the realms of reality, can imagine a different political situation for our country even in the future. We must build up the fortunes of our people, protect their internal independence and national advancement in association with the Russian Empire. It is for this reason that concern for the welfare of our people urges us to avoid anything which might lend weight to the argument that the prestige of the ruler of a world power necessitates the elimination of opposition and the thorough destruction of that which the rulers of the Empire have created with their own generous consent for the happiness of the Finnish people over the past century . . .

('Aseman selvittämiseksi', MS. article in the Danielson-Kalmari papers, Finnish State Archives (probably for newspaper publication, 1900). Extract printed in T. Torvinen, *J. R. Danielson-Kalmari Suomen autonomian puolustajana*, (Helsinki 1965) p. 236.)

52   A PASSIVE RESISTANCE APPEAL FOR PATRIOTIC JOINT ACTION (1901)

The events of recent years, so significant for our country and people, have everywhere aroused patriotic sentiment. Nevertheless, not every citizen by any means has grasped the full significance or extent of what has happened or what is at present being planned for the destruction of the political independence of our country and of the national existence of our people. Many a citizen does not yet believe in the existence of such dangers, since misfortune has not yet crossed his own threshold.

But although the national awakening has begun to the extent that those unlawful attacks against all that the people hold sacred and dear – religion, the laws, language, customs, free institutions, national and local self-government – have provoked bitter feeling amongst more and more people in different parts of the country, there is still a lot to do before our people are sufficiently educated to recognise their duty to *translate those feelings into action*; to sacrifice their own interests and welfare and to place the happiness of the fatherland above all other things. A spirit must be created whereby everybody, wherever he may be, must contribute to the common cause. No-one should remain inactive in the belief that others will surely take care of what needs to be done. In particular, there is a danger that the countryside, relying on what is done in the capital, will let the opportunity for action pass by.

It is no longer simply a matter of officials fulfilling their patriotic duty; insofar as misfortune hits all citizens, so must everyone be prepared to act as duty dictates.

The inability to act independently and at the right time which has already been noted has often been the result of *insufficient awareness of the situation*. To correct this, everyone who wishes to act for the common cause must carefully follow the course of events and pay careful attention to when and how he himself should act. To achieve this end, arrangements must be made to disseminate quickly and safely all information on what is happening and what the situation demands.

A second factor which has clearly deterred independent action is the uncertainty prevalent in many places as to *what is permis-*

sible within the limits of the law. It is therefore extremely important that information is circulated on what we are *entitled* to do, and everyone must be convinced of the justice of a resistance, which is founded on the laws which constitute the social order guaranteed by our ruler, and which have not ceased to be the surest guiding principles for the citizen because of a few new, illegal decrees. It must be strongly stressed that what we are *entitled* to do in accordance with these laws, we are also *duty bound* as citizens to do. And far more emphasis than hitherto must be placed on the conviction implicit in our conception of the law and justice that the law stands above authority, *that the law is our supreme authority.*

A great deal will have been achieved if people are educated to feel the responsibility which rests upon everyone who shirks his civic duty. But it is not enough that everyone is aware that something *must* be done; people must also be convinced that there is much which *can* be done. We must prevent citizens with honourable intentions and good motives being overwhelmed by despair. Despair will vanish if everyone realises that he is not alone in his patriotic work and self-sacrifice, but that his endeavours are shared by hundreds and thousands more. Independent activity must therefore be completed and supported by united *joint action*. Those who work for the common goal must be brought into personal contact with each other.

('Fosterländsk samvärkan/Isänmaallista yhteistyötä' *Kagaalin arkistoa – Ur Kagalens arkiv*, ed. E. Estlander (Helsinki 1939) pp. 226-8.)

53 YRJÖ-KOSKINEN ON THE PASSIVE RESISTANCE AND THE NEW MILITARY CONSCRIPTION LAW, OCTOBER 1901

'Passive resistance' means that no citizen, public official or any other may observe or obey illegal orders.

The programme is admirably clear and logical.

The Senate may not publish illegal statutes. As this in all probability will lead to the suspension of the home government and its replacement by an alien administration, well, what of that! The better will the illegality appear before the world! Someone may indeed point out that there are a lot more affairs for the government to see to : justice, supervision of the economic affairs of the country and of all institutions of education, as well as management of public funds. How these would make out under an alien government is apparently unimportant. The main thing is to be able to show the world how much farther we have progressed along the path of illegality . . .

As regards the matter of the military call-up in particular, this is to be prevented apparently by all means available. Priests may not present the lists of those liable for military service, but must hide their church records if anyone else tries to use them. The census official must also act in the same way. The functions performed by doctors and other officials at the call-up shall be the affair of the Russians. Finally, not even the parishes may choose their representatives for the conscription office. If the call-up takes place without these representatives, no-one may recognise the legality of such a call-up, nor may those liable for military service allow themselves to be taken into the army except by force. Thus we have strayed beyond the perimeter of *passive* resistance, an *active* resistance has begun, which in the common tongue is called *rebellion* – no doubt for the benefit of legality, but hardly for the salvation of the fatherland. Let there be no doubt but that *some* government will take over if the normal institutions have ceased to function. This may well give rise to the destruction of our national institutions, perhaps even the ruin of the Finnish people itself. But what of that ! Let the Finnish people perish, but let them perish with honour ! Will not history make a fine commemorative speech at the graveside – unless posterity chooses to remark (as it has already judged the Polish people) that the Finnish people in their impatience committed a miserable suicide . . .

We must not forget that in this fight we, despite our rights, are inevitably the weaker party, and that we must strive for a tolerable compromise if we do not wish to imperil the position, even the very existence of the Finnish people . . .

It is no secret that the country and people are in an adverse frame of mind as a result of the new law, and the recent address has indeed brought this in a pertinent, if slightly unsuitable manner to the notice of His Majesty. But all the same, we must for the time being give way before it, until we are able to have it changed. There is no point in trying to prevent the carrying out of a law by tiny pinpricks since in any event we have no weapons but pins; even if we had, it is clear that the law in its present form or in an even more destructive form will now be put into force in spite of resistance here. The only sensible policy is therefore to be patient for the time being until the time for compromise comes and more favourable circumstances dawn . . .

('Passiivinen vastarinta ja Uusi velvollisuuslaki' (29 October 1901. *Kagaalin arkistoa – Ur Kagalens arkiv*, ed. E. Estlander (Helsinki 1939) pp. 588–91.)

54 THE REPLY OF TWO OLD FINNS[3] TO YRJÖ-KOSKINEN'S COMMENTS ON THE PASSIVE RESISTANCE (1901)

. . . It is your opinion that the Finnish people must give up all forms of passive resistance and thereby give an aura of respectability to those illegal laws which are crushing our constitution. Your view is based on the fear that any other course of action would deprive us of all the privileges yet remaining of our former internal independence. The fear of even greater destruction to come is therefore to be the guideline of present and future policy for the Finnish people, according to this view. But fear is a very uncertain adviser; it has a tendency to exaggerate danger and to see everything in a gloomy light. Perhaps you have forgotten that this was the case when the February manifesto was promulgated in 1899. At the time, it was said that the Senate would be destroyed if the manifesto were not immediately promulgated, so to save the Senate the majority decided to promulgate without first making any objection to the illegality of the manifesto. The following year, 1900, the edict on the enforcement of the use of Russian in our administration was promulgated. At the time, it was also said that the Senate would be abolished if it did not immediately promulgate the edict. This it did not do, however, but sent in its objections to the illegality of the edict. This action did not have the consequences which many had feared. It would seem clear from all this that the fear which motivated the action of the Senate in the previous year was not sufficiently justified. Are you certain that you are not now exaggerating the dangers

[3] K. F. Ignatius and Otto Donner, both members of the passive resistance.

which it is thought might ensue from a passive resistance which stays entirely within the bounds of legality ? ...

But is the passive resistance of any use at all to us? Is it not merely a sort of irritation of those concerned in the form of pin-pricks, and is it not 'clear that the law in its present form or in an even more destructive form will now be put into force in spite of resistance here'? Not at all. The group which is now in power in Russia and to which the present Governor-General and Minister State-Secretary for Finland belong has, as is well known, a powerful and influential party opposed to it. Circumstances have made the Finnish question a sort of watershed between the ruling party and its opponents. It is claimed that the former party has assured the Emperor that the Finnish people are content with the reforms : this is clearly apparent from the statements put out by the Governor-General and his newspapers. If we can use all the means at our disposal to bring out the opposite point of view, then the party of the liberals and those sympathetic to our cause in Russia will have a weapon which, if properly used, is far more effective than any amount of pins. Bobrikov knows this very well, and this is why he is so annoyed with the mass address, the refusal of the clergy [to read out the military service act from the pulpit], etc. The only hope of promoting the downfall of our present enemies thus lies in our passive resistance ...

('Kahden vanhan suomenmielisten vastaus senaattori, vapaa-herra Yrjö-Koskisen lausunnosta'. *Kagaalin arkistoa – Ur Kagalens arkiv*, ed. E. Estlander (Helsinki 1939) pp. 600–1.)

55 ARCHBISHOP JOHANSSON'S PASTORAL LETTER CONCERNING THE MILITARY SERVICE LAW OF 1901

Dear colleague,

In view of the letters urging the clergy to refuse to proclaim the new military service law from the pulpit which have been sent to members of the clergy, and even to me, I, having discussed the matter with representatives of the Estate of Clergy from different bishoprics, regard it as my duty to voice my disagreement ...

A heavy blow has befallen our people; their sense of justice has been deeply violated. Such a state of affairs could hardly have been anticipated. We have not offended against the ruler, even less against the Empire, but we are guilty in the eyes of God, and His chastisement weighs upon us. Only from God is help forthcoming, and for this reason, we must remain steadfastly faithful and obedient to His will.

It is the legal obligation of the priest to proclaim the laws of the government in church, and it is not incumbent upon him to prove their legality. If he fails to proclaim them, he is setting himself outside the law and in opposition to authority. To be able to involve himself in this manner, he must know with certainty that such an act of resistance is consonant with the Will of God. It is true that a variety of arguments have been advanced to show that it is the duty of a priest to refuse to announce the military service law : but it is clear to me that the Will of God does not support such an act of resistance. If this were a matter of faith or creed then the duty of the priest would be apparent, but this is a question of making an announcement, an obligation which the church has for many years sought to be completely freed of : this announcement relates to a military matter, which does not fall within the competence of the priest. The clergy cannot hope to effect a change in this sad business by refusing to make the announcement. Such a refusal, even if only a minority of the clergy is involved, is such a delicate matter that it would cause untold damage to our church and our people : and it has yet to be demonstrated that such a step would be justified as an act of political wisdom. It is maintained that a law only becomes definitely valid when it is proclaimed by the priest from the pulpit : but this is not proven, for it must lie within the powers of the government to determine in which way a law shall be promulgated, and failure to make the proclamation cannot invalidate a law. Furthermore, the consequences of a refusal would not be as insignificant for the priest himself as many suppose, for he would be risking his post and his stipend . . .

Karjaalohja, August 12, 1901
GUSTAF JOHANSSON

(Printed in : *Kagaalin arkistoa – Ur Kagalens arkiv*, ed. E. Estlander, (Helsingfors 1939) pp. 311–12.)

56   THE CALL-UP RIOTS IN HELSINKI, APRIL 1902

. . . The muster of those to be conscripted took place in Helsinki
on 17 April. Of the 870 called up, only 57 appeared. At the
inspection the following day, only 38 of these appeared, and 31
were unfit for military service. A number of spectators gathered
at the places where the call-up took place . . . and showed their
displeasure with those who turned up at the illegal call-up with
derisive shouts and whistles . . .

On the morning of 18 April there was a slight clash amongst
the crowd gathered outside the guards' barracks, when a Russian
gendarme started to lay about him with a drawn sabre, wounding a worker in the hand and by mistake, wounding the assistant
to the police chief, a certain Maximov, in the face.

In the meantime, the crowd learnt that the Senate, which had
hitherto declared its intention of remaining in office and com-
plying with all illegalities 'to prevent Russians entering the administration', had decided the previous day to send two Russian
military doctors to call-up areas in Turku and Vaasa provinces,
where no Finnish doctors were available. This brought the long-
suppressed bitterness against the Senators to a head. At 3 p.m.,
when the session of the Senate was to end, people began to col-
lect outside the Senate building. The crowd quickly grew, as is
usually the case. People were preparing to demonstrate against
the 'traitors', a word heard here and there in the crowd, who
were about to leave the Senate building. Only three Senators
came out . . . They were hailed with whistles and shouts. According to sources, two of them fled into a doorway. Soon after this,
the Procurator Johnsson was seen running away home . . . The
police showed themselves to be utterly incompetent to deal with
the situation. In general they did nothing to get people moving
on the pavements and at street corners, or to close off the streets
leading to the square, or to prevent more people thus joining the
crowd.

Suddenly, at around four o'clock, a troop of Cossacks came
galloping down Alexander Street. After a short 'council of war'
with General Kaigorodov, who had called out the Cossacks . . .
a number of them careered into the square. Others rode up on to
the pavements and began to use their whips in a most brutal manner on the crowds of spectators who were quietly standing there.

A grey-haired man who was passing by was attacked by two Cossacks and received a bloody mouth. A young Polytechnic student tried to save himself via an entry into the university building from Alexander Street, but as he went up the steps, he noticed the door was locked. A couple of Cossacks jumped off their horses and attacked him on the steps in a most violent manner. The great steps of the Nicholas church were full of people, some of them street urchins. The Cossacks mounted an assault on these steps, but were met by a hail of stones and turned back . . .

There is as yet no precise information on the number of wounded and injured. Thirty people were treated for cuts at the infirmary yesterday. Many more received whip-cuts and even flesh wounds, but did not go to the infirmary for treatment. The information supplied by the press on these events has been reduced to completely rudimentary intimations by the censor . . .

('Bref från Helsingfors, Den 19 april 1902. Kosackdåd.', *Fria Ord*, 22 April 1902.)

57 'THE RUSSIAN OPPOSITION AND THE FUTURE OF FINLAND' (1902)

The question has frequently been raised of late as to what we might expect, if anything, of the revolutionary movement in Russia. Opinions in this matter have been and are still very divided, almost as much as views on whether or not we should enter into relations with this movement, whether or not we should support it and how this should be done. Such are the prevailing conditions and the prospects for the future that these questions have acquired such great and topical importance as to merit an answer from each and everyone who has not yet given up hope of a brighter future for our country.

Up to now we have comforted ourselves with the hope that a shift at the top will take place, that through our efforts we will succeed in compelling the monarch to see the dubious nature and damage of the policy he has permitted with regard to Finland. We now know that such hopes have been in vain, that there is no longer any justification for them, and that even if a change in policy towards Finland were brought about in this way, even if this should occur in the face of all likelihood, this would not be sufficient for us to build our future on. We know that the word of the Emperor which for almost a century has protected us is no longer regarded as binding against the political vagaries of the times. This is why we know that only the replacement of the Russian autocracy by a governance bound and limited by law can provide guarantees for the undisturbed advancement of our country and our nation. And finally we know that we ourselves are powerless to regain that which has already been taken from us, powerless even to defend the social order built up bit by bit over a thousand years, and which is now being torn down bit by bit in an orgy of destruction.

We must seek help of a different kind from hitherto, to give our defence greater strength, to press our resistance more effectively against the encroaching power of the autocracy . . .

The time must now be ripe to approach our brothers in misfortune, to get to know their aims and their methods of achieving them. Now is the time for us and everyone else in the same situation to join together in common struggle for the common cause, uniting forces and thereby securing a far better prospect of success than if the fight is carried on by isolated nationalities, groups and individuals . . .

The different nationalities, parties and groups should easily be able to agree on a common aim, which is the most immediate and important, viz. the winning of political freedom through the abolition of the autocracy. What form the new, free constitution will assume will be a matter for a future popular parliament to decide; what will be the relationship of the nationalities of Russia to a constitutionally free Russia must be left to them alone to decide as they think fit.

The time must be ripe for a union of the oppositional elements. A common programme must be drawn up, the opposition as a whole drawn together in a common, purposeful organisation, which will be able to direct the forces of the whole to achieve the aims of the whole, and will use the methods available to the best possible advantage to achieve these aims. It is in this sphere that the way to co-operation with the Russian opposition is clearly laid out for us Finns.

('Den ryska oppositionen och Finlands framtid', (Z[illiacus]), *Fria Ord*, 12 September 1902.)

58 'THE RUSSIAN OPPOSITION AND THE FUTURE OF FINLAND' – A DISSIDENT VIEWPOINT (1902)

. . . This point of view overlooks the fact that our opposition and the opposition in Russia have distinctly different motives. Whilst our task is to try and preserve the existing constitution from a revolution from above, the Russian opposition seeks to overthrow the constitution which legitimately exists in Russia. On the one hand, therefore, there exists a conservative standpoint in the best sense, on the other an openly revolutionary one. How it is possible in practice to bring together these antithetical tendencies, one of which entails a firm adherence to that which is legally valid, whilst the other calls for the abolition of all existing forms, is difficult to understand.

It may be that the idea is for a common aim to be found for the present in the effort to introduce a constitutional form of government into Russia, such as is legally valid in Finland. This however ignores the fact that a form of government which has proved itself to be suitable for one people cannot easily be introduced to another people having a different history and living under different circumstances and conditions . . . Whether the Russian opposition can achieve its ends for the duration by revolution is on the whole doubtful, for in revolutions it is usually the most radical elements which come out on top, and Russia would probably be given an extremely liberal constitution as a result, which would soon prove impossible and lead to new revolutions. For a people so long deprived of freedom as the Russians, liberal institutions, if they are to be permanent, can only be introduced gradually and with careful regard for the particular natural abilities and historical circumstances of the people.

If, therefore, it is doubtful whether we could be of use to the Russian opposition in its efforts, it is certain that any attempt to interfere in the affairs of Russia would be fateful for our country. Such a policy is directly opposed to the juridicial status Finland has been guaranteed in the union with Russia, and which we must try to maintain with all our strength. This position implies that Finland is free within itself, i.e. independent of Russia in its internal affairs. From this it necessarily follows that the Finnish people are duty bound to avoid meticulously any interference in

Russia's internal affairs. And this we must do, even when our own right to freedom from interference is not respected. Otherwise we may find ourselves sharing the fate of the Russian people. If we were to make common cause with the Russian opposition, the inevitable consequence would be that we would share the fate of that opposition, whether it succumbed or emerged victorious. Even in the latter event, we could not successfully demand to be allowed to keep our special position. If we were to take part in the common work of introducing free institutions into the Russian Empire, we would also become ourselves participants in these institutions and lose our own . . .

We can therefore gain nothing, but lose a great deal by linking up with the Russian opposition. One thing which we should certainly lose by so doing has not yet been considered so far. In the event of links really being forged between the revolutionary party in Russia and a section of the opposition in Finland, a very large percentage of those who now support the policy of the passive resistance would simply reject this line and stand aside from all resistance rather than have anything to do with such opposition people. In other words, it would be tantamount to a kiss of death for a broad-based Finnish policy of resistance.

('Den ryska oppositionen och Finlands framtid' (probably written by R. A. Wrede, a member of the passive resistance), *Fria Ord*, 25 September 1902.)

59 'THE PASSIVE RESISTANCE AND THE RIGHT OF SELF-DEFENCE' (1903)

When our misfortunes began nearly five years ago, it seemed as if our people would stand united on the foundations of the law. One need only remember the first mass address and the grand deputation.

But quite soon one or two appeasers began to appear. During the course of the year, a major compliance party with Yrjö-Koskinen as its leader and *Uusi Suometar* as its mouthpiece gathered around the Senate. The friends of the resistance had to give up the idea of a united resistance and prepare themselves to fight against internal as well as external enemies.

A separate 'resistance party' was formed, and our resistance took the name from the start of the 'passive resistance'. For almost five years we have held out. We have stood fast by the law and refused to act against it. Not even our bitterest enemies could say that we have used unlawful methods. Our enemies, not us, have used violence in this country. Against their violence we have resisted only by refusing to obey.

But ever since Bobrikov was given dictatorial powers in Finland this spring the incidences of violence have daily risen in number. The government heaps crime upon crime; banishments, imprisonment, disturbances of domestic peace, violence against women, assaults, are the order of the day. The flower of our nation is deprived of its liberty in its own country. The worst elements, the grasping, the incompetent, the pusillanimous, the mendacious, win salaries, titles, positions of honour.

Every thinking man in Finland is now asking himself the question: What is the use of passive resistance in such circumstances? . . .

It cannot be helped if despondency sets in at the thought that many of our protests are words in the wind, and that our passive resistance, *which would surely have led to victory if we had all been united*, may in the long run be unable to stop the advance of our enemies. The passive resistance is not without significance. A fairly general tax strike, if fines are levied by taxation, can still be effective. The resistance of local government areas can also be successfully continued. A military service strike, even if it is less successful than that of this year, makes the full application of the Russian military service law impossible. Wherever the passive resistance shows itself, it proves that there are still men and women in Finland who can distinguish between right and wrong and dare to do what is right . . .

It would be a mistake to put all one's confidence in the passive resistance in the future because defeat after defeat will finally maim the powers of resistance, and it is an insult to our human dignity to allow ourselves to be treated by Bobrikov and his men as we are now. We must put up a resistance which is seen and heard and felt, a resistance which puts fear into the heart of the enemy. Otherwise his insolence will grow out of all proportion, whilst our own spirits sink beyond view . . .

What is there that we can do immediately?

We can in certain instances take up self-defence!

. . . We do not urge anyone to avail himself of the right to self-defence, for such a matter rests with each individual to decide, and he must consult the only counsel there is in such cases; his own conscience. What we have sought to maintain is that in certain cases we may find in self-defence a way out of the situation in which we now find ourselves. We can go over from passive to active resistance and still remain within the bounds of the law . . .

The idea of self-defence is also an idea of the future, which more than any other can raise up despondent and embittered minds. From this idea a new, active resistance will emanate.

We must not forget that what we do must in the end be directed towards a future when the Finnish people will be masters in their own country and take their fate in their own hands. The road to this future passes through suffering and strife. It is like all other peoples' road to freedom – it passes through blood. Now our fate seems dark. But there will come a day when the watchword 'a free Finland' is no longer suppressed or secretly whispered but is shouted out loud over the whole country. There will come a day when 'a people degraded to the depths of despair shall stand up in defence of their fathers' land'.

Let us prepare the way for that day!

('Det passiva motståndet och rätten till nödvärn' (Arvid Mörne), *Veckans Nyheter*, 15 October 1903.)

60 THE GRANTING OF DICTATORIAL POWERS TO GOVERNOR-GENERAL BOBRIKOV, 9 APRIL 1903

To Our Governor-General of Finland:

In Our desire to secure a closer national unity within Our Empire We have sanctioned measures to bring the Grand Duchy of Finland into conformity with the main body of the Empire, but the execution of these measures has met with open opposition from a section of the Finnish population. Malevolent persons, seeking to turn against the government a peaceable people reluctant to follow their incitements, have not shrunk from committing acts which have disrupted the peace of the community, and have even dared to perpetrate open acts of violence against persons faithfully carrying out their duties. In normal circumstances such breaches of the peace would be dealt with by bringing the guilty to trial and by other prescribed legal methods. At the present moment these methods cannot be used since certain officials, and in particular, the judicial system, are not only failing to co-operate in the maintenance of public order, but do themselves frequently set a pernicious example by flouting the law. As We wish to restore order in Finland and protect law-abiding people from the influence of rebels, We have seen fit to grant certain powers to the top administrative officials in the Grand Duchy of Finland for the preservation of national order and public peace, for an interim period of three years . . .

(*Suomen Suuriruhtinaanmaan Asetuskokoelma*, no. 35. (Helsinki 1903))

61 THE PROGRAMME OF THE FINNISH ACTIVE RESISTANCE PARTY, ADOPTED AT THE FOUNDING MEETING IN HELSINKI, 17 NOVEMBER 1904

1. The party seeks to draw the attention of the people of this country to the lack of legal protection which now exists in the country, and the connection this has with the powers of the Russian autocracy; to the necessity of and justification for an energetic, active and ruthless resistance to tyranny and its instruments; to the freedom movement in other parts of Russia and to the benefits of co-operation with the opposition parties in these countries. The party seeks to undermine the traditional feelings of loyalty towards the monarch of the people, and to strengthen their feelings of freedom :

(a) by the publication and circulation of different kinds of literature on these matters.

(b) by working for the distribution of weapons amongst the population.

(c) by financially supporting a combat group formed within the party, which shall have the right to call itself 'the combat group of the Finnish Active Resistance Party'.
N.B. The combat group will pursue its activities independently, but shall seek the consent of the 'inner circle' in every instance when it might wish to issue proclamations signed 'the combat group of the Finnish Active Resistance Party'.

(d) in other ways determined by circumstances.

2. The party will support the work which has for a long time been performed by private individuals for the assistance of the Russian revolutionaries.

(Printed in H. Gummerus, *Aktiva kampår 1899–1910*, (Helsingfors 1925) pp. 115–16.)

62 THE GENEVA PROGRAMME OF THE RUSSIAN OPPOSITION (1905)[4]

1. The complete transformation of the present Russian Empire in accordance with democratic, republican principles on the basis of a universal, direct, equal suffrage with secret ballot.

As a means to this end :

2. The convention, with provisions guaranteeing absolutely free expression of the will of the people (freedom of expression, press, assembly and association, guarantees of the inviolability of the individual, release of all imprisoned for political or religious convictions), of a constituent assembly of representatives of all the countries of the Russian Empire, with the exception of Poland and Finland, on the basis of universal and equal suffrage through direct elections and a secret ballot.

3. With regard to Finland, which retains its position as an autonomous constitutional state and therefore will not participate in the election of the central constituent assembly, the parties severally represented at this conference concur with the desire of the Finnish people, especially the proletariat, for the convention of a constituent assembly, elected in accordance with universal and equal suffrage, direct election and secret ballot.

4. The convention, parallel with the constituent assembly in Petersburg, of a constituent diet in Warsaw.

5. The dissolution of the old relations and the establishment of new between the above-mentioned parts of the Empire through free agreement between the above-mentioned constituent bodies as sovereign representatives of the nationalities.

6. The convention for the Caucasus, as an autonomous part of Russia and united to it by federation, of a constituent assembly with the task of transforming the entire internal organisation of the country on a democratic, federative basis and of taking part

[4] The Geneva conference took place between 2–9 April 1905.

in the working out of guarantees for the autonomy of the Caucasus on the lines hitherto mentioned.

The Central Committees of :

The Socialist-Revolutionary Party (Russian)
The Polish Socialist Party
The Armenian Revolutionary Federation
The Finnish Active Resistance Party
The Georgian Federalist-Revolutionary Socialist Party
The Latvian Social Democratic Party
The White Russian Socialist Gromada

(Printed in H. Gummerus, *Aktiva kampår 1899–1910*, (Helsingfors 1925) pp. 126–9.)

63 THE ACTIVISTS' PLANS FOR INSURRECTION (1905)

. . . The Finnish Active Resistance Party will seek to bring about an insurrection in Finland at the same time as a revolution breaks out in Russia, and as soon as the heads of the administration are removed, will convene a constituent assembly in Helsinki on the basis of a universal, equal and direct suffrage conducted by secret ballot.

The question of drawing up a detailed plan for the insurrection decided upon was then discussed. The meeting was told that the final *coup* in Petersburg would be prepared for by riots in the towns and in the countryside. Extensive peasant uprisings are at present eagerly being prepared in all the provinces of the Empire. The moment of revolution is at hand.

In Finland, the idea has been that the revolt should begin at the same time as the final decisive act takes place in Petersburg. The most immediate objective of the revolutionaries is to disorganise and overthrow the home government and administration and to prevent all troop movements to Petersburg.

After a lengthy discussion, during which a number of speakers thought that things would be best arranged if a start were made in Helsinki, whilst others felt that a *coup* in Helsinki should be preceded by riots taking place simultaneously in all county towns,[5] and differing opinions were expressed as to whether the

[5] This means the seats of the provincial governors.

attack should be aimed in the first place against the troops or against the higher administration, it was decided :

to authorise the central committee to work out a detailed plan for the creation of a national insurrection.

(Minutes of the meeting of the Finnish Active Resistance Party, 14 May 1905, in *Suomen aktiivisen vastustuspuolueen arkisto*, (the party archives) Finnish States archives.)

64 'SCANDINAVIA AND FINLAND. A SOLUTION OF THE SWEDISH–NORWEGIAN QUESTION' (1905)

. . . The union between Sweden and Norway while it existed constituted a guarantee of peace in northern Europe. The break-up of the union has made the situation in the Scandinavian peninsula rather different, in that a threat to the European balance in relation to Russia's intentions vis-à-vis the Scandinavian countries, principally Norway, has arisen. Even if these intentions cannot be realised in the immediate future, they will certainly re-emerge at the first opportune moment. No-one who follows Russia's world policy can doubt this. It has been said that the political separation between Norway and Sweden will bring the two peoples closer together. The breakup of the union will thus strengthen the situation in the peninsula, especially as it is hoped that Denmark will now be more willing to associate itself with the two brother nations. But there are no real grounds to support the fulfilment of this hope. It would be to misjudge the susceptibilities of human nature if one were to believe that the separation between Sweden and Norway will only serve to strengthen the ties of friendship between them. Norway has broken with the union in a way which for a generation hence will keep alive a feeling of bitterness amongst the Swedes. If we are to face reality, we cannot close our eyes to the fact that the dissolution of the union has substantially weakened the feelings of kinship in the Scandinavian peninsula, and with this its defensive strength as well, for a long time to come.

The civilised states of Europe, from the point of view of their own evident interests, cannot view this situation with indifference. The Scandianavian north is a significant cultural factor in our part of the world, in that a threat against it is a threat to the culture of the western countries as a whole . . .

An attack on the Scandinavian peninsula is only to be feared from the east, from Russia. A land attack must take place across Finland. A seaborne attack will never succeed, since the risk for the attacking party is too great. Turn the Scandinavian peninsula figuratively into an island, and the balance in the north is guaranteed. This will take place through the interested powers *declaring Finland a neutral buffer state, guaranteed by them, between Russia and Scandinavia.* The time for such a step will be when peace is concluded between Japan and Russia. Even if the two belligerent states should make up their differences without interference, Britain, America, Germany and France have such important interests to protect at the conclusion of peace that a *congress of the powers* will be an absolute necessity. However much the economic and political interests of the powers may conflict, they all have a common interest in the preservation of the European balance in the north. The continued existence and integrity of the Scandinavian countries, threatened by the breakup of the union, must unite them all, both from the political as well as the cultural point of view. All that is needed from the powers mentioned is a joint declaration of intent and Scandinavia will be assured from attack from the east in future by the neutralisation of Finland. Russia, laid low by the war, will be unable to raise any material obstacles to this. But what is more, every clear-sighted person in Russia will be forced to admit that the neutralisation and separation of Finland from Russia, far from damaging any of Russia's vital interests, will be of benefit. Finland was conquered to become a protective wall for the new capital Petersburg. An enemy wishing to attack Petersburg would find his best prospects in an attack via Finland. If Finland is neutralised under the guarantee of the powers, this will create the most effective protection for the Russian capital, which will then become unassailable from the north coast of the Gulf of Finland. The neutralisation of Finland, seen from a purely self-interested angle, should benefit all parties, not least Russia . . .

('Skandinavien och Finland. En lösning af svenska-norska frågan', (Axel Lille – mimeographed pamphlet) *Kagaalin arkistoa – Ur Kagalens arkiv*, ed. E. Estlander (Helsinki 1939) pp. 19–20.)

The 1905 Revolution and its Aftermath

The revolutionary strike movement which broke out in the Russian Empire at the end of October 1905 was slow to spread to Finland, partly as a result of the initial hesitations of the railwaymen on the vital Valkeasaari-Petersburg section of the main line to Russia (65). As was the case elsewhere in the Empire, the railways played an important part in the development of a nationwide strike movement in Finland.

At first the strike was genuinely 'national' in character, with widespread co-operation between political groupings and social classes. As the objectives of the political groupings began to diverge and the labour movement came to realise the strength it had acquired during the strike, this co-operation soon began to founder (71). The constitutionalists sought a return to the status quo ante Bobrikov, with the added institution of a democratic parliamentary system; but like the Finnish party, they preferred to work through the established institutions of the country to achieve this end (66, 69). The socialist strike committee in Tampere urged the election of a provisional government in Helsinki which would then convoke a national assembly, a demand somewhat belatedly supported by the activists (68, 70). The election of the provisional government took place in Helsinki on 4 November, but the termination of the strike in Russia and the Tsar's manifesto rescinding most of the acts imposed on Finland during the previous five years robbed the election of any significance (72). The socialists on the central strike committee accepted the inevitability of ending the strike, but in a mood of bitterness which was widely reflected in the press and in the new militancy of the labour movement (73).

The general strike strengthened the confidence and swelled the ranks of the hitherto politically insignificant Social Democratic

Party. It also made it more aware of the potential of the Russian revolutionary movement. However, the party continued to maintain a careful distance from the revolutionary commitments of its Russian counterparts. The party council refused to sanction a general strike during an uprising of Russian troops on the Sveaborg fortress in 1906, and the party conference resolution on co-operation with the Russian revolutionary movement in August of that year was careful to emphasise the special nature of Finland's relationship with Russia, which afforded Finland the opportunity for democratic activities (74, 75).

The revolutionary events of the strike week helped stimulate discussion of Finland's future, but of the political groupings in the country, only the tiny activist 'party' came out openly in favour of sovereign independence – and even then, after considerable debate (76).

65   THE OUTBREAK OF THE STRIKE ON THE RAILWAYS, 28–9 OCTOBER 1905

TELEGRAM OF 26 OCTOBER FROM THE STATIONMASTER OF THE FINLAND STATION, PETERSBURG, TO THE TRAFFIC CONTROLLER, HELSINKI (ARR. 3 P.M., 26 OCTOBER)

Everything still quiet here, traffic running as usual. Station guarded since yesterday afternoon by 88 infantrymen, ordered here by the gendarmerie. No guard on the line anticipated. Traffic on all Russian lines totally suspended. Meat prices rose steeply today; prime cuts 34 kopeks a pound. Major factories also on strike today.

TELGRAM OF 28 OCTOBER FROM PETERSBURG (SENT 5 P.M.) TO A NEWSPAPER IN HELSINKI

5 p.m. quiet on Finland Station. Station guarded by one company Moscow guards, three battalions and two squadrons plus Cossacks in surrounding area. These troops have orders to shoot at first attack by strikers.

Petersburgers departing en masse for Finland. Lack of trains. Mood of Finnish railway personnel calm.

Today telegram from Helsinki from 'a group of workers' with demand to join strike. No pickets have visited station personnel or railway workers urging them to strike. On the contrary strikers seem to have decided to ignore Finnish and Tsarskoe Selo lines.

[A meeting of railway workers in Viipuri decided that evening to stop traffic to Petersburg at 6.00 a.m. the following day.]

TELEGRAM OF 29 OCTOBER FROM HELSINKI STATION TO ALL STATIONS IN DISTRICT NO. 2 (EVENING)

Since 6 a.m. both passenger and goods traffic stopped on section Valkeasaari-Petersburg. Post being carried by automobile between these places. Private telegrams to be sent by state telegraph not to be accepted.

TELEGRAM MESSAGE OF 30 OCTOBER FROM TERIJOKI TO RAILWAY HEADQUARTERS, HELSINKI, (12.10 A.M.)

Impossible to reach Valkeasaari station. Despatched this morning our train crew and small number of private individuals to and from Valkeasaari. Highly doubtful if traffic can be maintained east of Viipuri and on Karelian line. Petersburg completely cut off.

(Printed in S. Roos, *Nationalstrejken i Finland*, vol. 1 (Helsingfors 1906) pp. 24–38.)

66   THE DEMANDS OF THE CONSTITUTIONALISTS, 31 OCTOBER 1905

1. The prevailing coercive regime, together with the dictatorship and all illegal decrees must immediately be abolished, and the unlawfully appointed Russian civil servants and other Russian functionaries whose governance has simply been directed towards depriving the Finnish people of their nationhood must be dismissed without delay.

2. The country must have a Minister State-Secretary who, unlike the present holder of this office, must enjoy the full confidence of the people; the present members of both departments of the Senate must also be replaced by competent Finnish citizens, faithful to the law, who enjoy the confidence of the broad mass of our people.

3. All the creatures of the illegal regime must be dismissed and

those civil servants unlawfully deprived of office by that regime reinstated and given necessary compensation.

4. The Finnish members of the so-called committee on the codification of state laws must immediately request to be relieved of membership of that committee.

5. Measures are to be promptly taken so that the students Westlin and Eriksson may return to their native country and the worker K. Procopé, who was taken to Russia and condemned there by court-martial, may be returned to Finland to stand trial in a Finnish court.[1]

6. In view of the fact that the present Governor-General has continued to uphold the illegal regime in the country and has furthermore shown himself to lack the qualifications necessary for a holder of the office of Governor-General, Prince Obolensky should be asked to leave his post immediately.

7. The ordering of the country's affairs on a lasting basis must be left to a people's parliament, based on the principle of universal, equal and direct suffrage; to this end an extraordinary diet must be summoned forthwith.

A proposition ought to be presented to the representatives for a new, modern form of government for the country, containing amongst other things regulations on the responsibility of the government to parliament, on the freedom of the press, assembly and association and the inviolability of the individual.

(Printed in S. Roos, *Nationalstrejken i Finland*, vol. 1 (Helsingfors 1906) pp. 166–7.)

67 RESOLUTIONS PASSED BY A MEETING OF THE CITIZENS OF PORI, 31 OCTOBER 1905

1. Citizens of Pori! We fully accept the demands of our Russian brothers and sisters for the abolition of a tyrannical autocracy, the overthrowal of the throne of our perjured Emperor Nicholas II and the democratisation of the system of government.

2. Since we have not the confidence and respect for the Minister State-Secretary of Finland, the Procurator and Senate which are essential for the peaceful advancement of our country, and

[1] The two students made an unsuccessful attempt on the life of a police chief in Vaasa in 1904, Procopé killed a colonel in the gendarmerie in 1905.

since the Governor-General as well as all the Governors have revealed themselves to a greater or lesser extent to be agents of tyranny, this meeting of thousands of citizens of Pori demands that they publicly and irrevocably surrender their posts within twenty-four hours of receiving this demand, if they wish to save the Finnish people and themselves from untold consequences.

3. Representatives of the people are to be immediately convened, and they are to draft a new, democratic form of government and constitution for the country; if this is not possible, a national assembly, elected by universal, equal and direct suffrage is to be convened to draft a democratic form of government and constitution which will guarantee both the spiritual and material living conditions of the inhabitants of this country.

4. (a) We demand that our unlawfully appointed burgomaster resign his office forthwith, and that he be replaced by a popularly elected person enjoying the confidence of the people;

(b) that the unlawful district office be abolished for good;

(c) that the gendarmerie be abolished forthwith, never to be publicly permitted to exist in future . . .

Some 10,000 people were present at the meeting.

(Handwritten resolutions in the Finnish Labour Archives, file no. 323 (471) '1905'.)

68   THE 'RED' MANIFESTO, 1 NOVEMBER 1905

The committee, elected to watch over the interests and rights of the people, presents for the approval of the meeting the following proposals:

1.(a) Those detestable toadies, who have succeeded in securing office in the Senate by creeping to the Russian bureaucracy, and who have shamelessly trodden underfoot not only the law but also the people's deepest sense of justice, should immediately resign their offices.

(b) To replace the departing government, the inhabitants of Helsinki shall elect a provisional government of men who conscientiously respect law and justice, who hold the affairs of our fatherland dear and who enjoy, as far as possible, the confidence of the whole nation.

The election shall be by secret ballot, and all inhabitants of the capital over the age of twenty-one shall be entitled to vote, irrespective of sex. Each voter shall only have one vote. The city magistrates shall immediately proceed to the organisation of the election.

(c) The first task of a government so elected shall be the calling of a national assembly. Before this takes place, the provisional government shall not undertake any reforms which might take up national rsources: the government shall however be entitled to use these resources to strengthen the internal independence of the country. All governmental actions must be public, and the government shall be responsible for its action to the national assembly.

2. As the privileged classes in different parts of the country seem to be eagerly agitating for the calling of the Diet, the proletariat declares that it can under no circumstances accept the convention of a diet which is based on the prevailing four-estates principle of representation. If, in spite of this warning, a class Diet is convened, the workers of this country give the privileged classes fair notice that the events of recent days will be repeated with renewed vigour as soon as the Estates assemble.

A national assembly, armed with full powers of legislation, shall be immediately called instead. For the election of the national assembly, every Finnish subject of good reputation, irrespective of sex, who has reached the age of twenty-one, shall have equal and direct voting rights.

The town magistrates and communal councils in the country shall in due course of time see to it that no practical hindrances are allowed to prevent or delay the convention of the national assembly.

3. We honour and love the noble people of Russia, although we hate from the bottom of our hearts the detestable bureaucracy which of recent years has represented the Russian element in this country. We have no particular wish to separate from mighty Russia, if only we receive assurances that the best elements in Russia will take over the reins of government there and if the course of events does not otherwise make such a separation inevitable. In any event we demand that Finland, although remain-

ing an inseparable part of Russia, be recognised as a special state with complete rights of self-government and legislation.

4. With regard to the practical application of the principles of civil rights, we demand :

(a) Citizens may hereafter have absolute freedom to meet and discuss matters of common interest. No kind of official supervision, even of a formal nature, shall be tolerated.

(b) Citizens shall have the right to form societies and associations of a political, economic or idealistic nature. They shall only be obliged to give notice of the formation of such societies.

(c) The spoken and written word shall immediately be recognised as free of control. No regulations or impositions which in the slightest way curb these most natural rights of the individual and the free citizen shall hereafter be tolerated.

With this manifesto we turn to the Finnish people with the request that all who have suffered from political or social oppression may unite around the great ideals for which this manifesto is the spiritual standard-bearer. It expresses all that, consciously or unconsciously, is nearest to the heart of all freedom and justice-loving citizens. Therefore let all the more or less unsuccessful resolutions which have in recent days been drawn up in different parts of the country be withdrawn and let each and every one prepare himself if necessary to seal with his heart's blood that which is written above.

[Tampere, November 1 1905]

The sub-committee set up by the aforementioned (strike) committee :

YRJÖ MÄKELIN   EETU SALIN
VIHTORI KOSONEN   HEIKKI LINDROOS
SIIRI LEMBERG

(Printed in : *Suomen historian dokumentteja*, vol. 2, (Helsinki 1970) pp. 266–8)

69 'A LAWFUL NATIONAL ASSEMBLY' – THE PROPOSAL OF THE FINNISH PARTY, 2 NOVEMBER 1905

The demand has been made for the immediate summoning of a national assembly to legislate new fundamental laws for our country.

Such a line of action is tantamount to embarking upon the course of revolution, which cannot but lead to the gravest difficulties. We feel ourselves obliged to raise the demand that the people themselves must take part in the making of the new constitution. This end can be achieved completely legally if the convened Estates, in agreement with the monarch, cause a change to be made in our fundamental laws so that the question of a new constitution can be considered and decided upon by a general national assembly.

For this reason we have decided that the monarch be requested to issue a manifesto as follows :

The monarch shall authorise the new provisional Senate, after consultations with individuals from different social classes, especially the working class, to draw up a proposal for parliamentary reform, based on a unicameral system, with members elected by universal and equal suffrage;

The Estates, to be summoned immediately, shall be presented with a proposition which entrusts the right to consider and decide upon the above-mentioned proposal on the reorganisation of the representational system to a national assembly, elected on the basis of universal, equal and direct suffrage for every Finnish citizen over 21 years of age, by means of a provisional adjustment of the constitution.

(Printed in S. Roos. *Nationalstrejken i Finland*, vol. 2 (Helsingfors 1906) p. 398.)

70 THE DEMAND OF THE FINNISH ACTIVE RESISTANCE PARTY FOR A NATIONAL ASSEMBLY, 3 NOVEMBER 1905

A Diet or a national assembly – this is the question now occupying the thoughts of many, constituting the main point of discussion at meetings where citizens seek to thresh out the demands of the hour.

The Finnish Active Resistance Party has long held a view in this matter. It has considered it at a joint meeting with all the revolutionary parties in the Russian Empire, and the decision of that meeting was that the transformation of the conditions vital to the different peoples bound together within this Empire must take place through the people themselves, that is, through representative assemblies, where one social class does not work separately from another, nor any one citizen possess more votes than any other, but where all the members work together, are equally important and are elected by their fellow-citizens on the basis of universal and equal suffrage.

The course of events has proved that we were not mistaken as to the correct solution of a situation which we anticipated and which has now taken place. We can now maintain that no other satisfactory outcome of the events of the past few days exists.

Some demand a Diet. Some say that we should not depart from our ancient laws, our constitution. Well, let us examine this demand to see what it entails and how it can be achieved.

A constitutional Diet can only be summoned by the ruler, and he alone can raise the question of an amendment of the constitution at such a Diet. A 'legal' Diet therefore means that, having rendered the ruler powerless, we would once more surrender ourselves for better or for worse to his pleasure, to a ruler whom we have learnt through many years of bitter experience to mistrust deeply.

Some have also advanced the idea that a Diet convoked in the customary manner should first convene and then issue a call for a national assembly. Such a step does not however lie within the competence of the Diet, but would entail a transgression of the constitution : the whole thing would become a comedy, lacking any sort of justification and would only be a waste of time.

Finally the view has been put forward that the participants at the last Diet should convene and summon a national assembly in the name of the Diet. The members of the Diet have ceased to be members with its dissolution, and are at present nothing more than ordinary private citizens. Some say that they more than any others have the confidence of the people, since they were elected by the people. This is not true. None of them has been elected by the real people, many of them have not even been elected, and the majority of the Diet has forfeited the confidence of the people through its willingness to yield on the question of the ten millions.[2]

Why stick so obstinately to the past? New times demand new men, new circumstances demand new methods. Let us be united by the great idea: the good of the people through the people themselves. Let us set the initiative here in the capital, and the whole country will gratefully follow. Let us choose a few men who possess the confidence of the country, who will take over the task of running a paralysed government and who will without hesitation summon the representatives of the people to a national assembly. Only thus will a firm foundation be laid down upon which the Finnish people can build a future in freedom and hope.

(Printed in S. Roos, *Nationalstrejken i Finland*, vol. 2 (Helsingfors 1906) pp. 491–2.)

71 THE LAST DAYS OF THE STRIKE – EXTRACTS FROM THE MINUTES OF THE NATIONAL STRIKE CENTRAL COMMITTEE, 2–5 NOVEMBER 1905

[2 November]

The deputation sent to agree upon co-operation with the constitutionalists arrived and reported that the constitutionalists still hold by the old legal methods . . . when asked what guarantees they could give that a one-chamber assembly would be accepted by the Diet, J. Castrén and Prof. Bonsdorff promised to supply these without saying what they would be. Sakari Castrén had suggested that an unofficial national assembly be convened, elected on the basis of universal, equal and direct suffrage. This would function side by side with the Diet and would use its authority to prevail upon the Diet to accept the resolutions of the national assembly. Comrade A. Rissanen said that the motives of the constitutionalists were that if attempts were made to obtain from the Tsar a manifesto in accordance with our demands, this would be breaking the law, and therefore an arbitrary act, which the Tsar could cancel at a favourable moment.

[2] This was the sum (10 million marks) agreed upon by the Diet of 1904–5 as compensation for the repeal of the 1901 military service law: the law was in fact suspended.

It was resolved not to give up the demand under any circumstances that the Governor-General should provide the country with a provisional government of which half the members shall be social democrats, and that this government should summon a legislative national assembly as its first duty.

It was resolved upon the suggestion of comrade E. Perttilä that all discussions with other parties be terminated since they do not serve any further purpose . . .

A six-man delegation of constitutionalists came and spoke of their visit to Petersburg, where they arrived at 11 a.m. [the previous day]. They reported that from their observations, people in Petersburg were generally, for example in the port, back at work, and the shops were open. Even the railwaymen's strike was not complete . . . Finally the delegation made the following proposal for a settlement : eight permanent and four deputy members from each party would be elected to a committee which would propose an unofficial national assembly, which in turn would propose the reform of the parliamentary system and under threat of a strike compel the Diet to approve this. Since it had been finally decided to break off discussions, the matter was allowed to rest.

[3 November]

It was proposed that a provisional government be elected on the fifth of this month, and that this be announced at today's meeting, and that representatives of other parties be invited to propose candidates.

[4 November]

A request was received from the town council to put up posters in the streets announcing the termination of the strike. It was resolved not to agree to this request, since the contents of the [Tsar's] manifesto were not known.

[5 November]

The delegation which had visited the Governor-General gave a report. They had tried to outline the views of the Finnish proletariat. The Governor-General argued that the manifesto would satisfy everyone, and pledged his possessions that the ruler would accept no other reform decision but one based on the principles of one chamber and universal suffrage. He also proposed that the provisional government could be elected as a committee to consider parliamentary reform . . .

Vallin proposed that the strike be immediately terminated. Continuation of the strike would be rebellion against the manifesto, and this would lead to bloodshed.

Sirola proposed that the strike be immediately suspended and recommenced before the decisive decision of the Diet.

. . . It was decided to end the strike on Monday [6 November] by eleven votes to three.

(Minutes of the strike central committee, Labour Archives)

72 THE NOVEMBER MANIFESTO GRANTED BY THE TSAR, 1905

We Nicholas the Second, by God's grace Emperor and Autocrat of all the Russias, Tsar of Poland, Grand Duke of Finland, etc.

Whereas we have received for Our final consideration the humble petition of the Finnish Estates of 31 December 1904 concerning measures for the return to the rule of law in Finland, We have found this worthy of Our attention and this shall be carried out. Furthermore We have graciously ordained for the further advancement of the privileges of the Finnish people as defined in the laws of the constitution that proposals for important constitutional reforms shall be drafted for presentation to the representatives of the people.

In consequence whereof We do order that the basic regulations appertaining to Our manifesto of 15 February 1899 shall be suspended until the matters therein mentioned shall be dealt with by the legislative process, and We desire the repeal of the following :

The law of 2 February 1903, concerning measures for the preservation of political order and the general peace . . . and the decrees of 10 November 1903 whereby the department of the gendarmerie was granted official status in the Grand Duchy.

The twelfth paragraph of the law of 10 July 1902, concerning the amendment of the formula and arrangements for proclamation of statutes and government decrees in the Grand Duchy of Finland.

The law of 8 September 1902 on the amendment of certain sections of the regulations governing the Imperial Finnish Senate, the law of the same date on the extension of the powers of the

Governor-General of Finland, the law of 26 March 1903 concerning the confirmation of the instructions for the Governor-General of Finland and his assistant, and the law of the same date on the amendment of instructions to the governors, and the military service law of 12 July 1901 :

The law of 31 July 1902 concerning the amendment of regulations governing employment in the civil service in Finland, the law of 14 August 1902 concerning the procedure whereby administrative civil servants are to be discharged from office, the law of the same date concerning the procedure for prosecuting civil servants for offences against their office, and the law of 2 July 1900 concerning public assemblies.

Furthermore We do instruct the Senate to consider without delay other laws mentioned in the petition which are in need of alteration.

We have also seen fit to authorise the Senate :

1. To prepare a proposal for a new Parliament Act embodying reform of the Finnish people's assembly fitting for the times, by the adoption of the principles of universal and equal suffrage to the election of people's representatives.

2. To prepare a proposal for a constitutional decree which shall recognise the right of the people's assembly to supervise the lawfulness of the actions of the members of the government and secure the rights of speech, assembly and association for the citizens of the country, and

3. To prepare a proposal for the freedom of the press and to issue immediately a proclamation suspending the activities of the censor.

And We expect the Senate to prepare these proposals . . . in time for them to be presented to the Estates which are to meet in an extraordinary Diet which We have this day resolved to summon.

We sincerely hope that these measures granted by Us, which spring from Our care for Finland's wellbeing, will strengthen the bonds which unite the Finnish people to their ruler.

(S. Roos, *Nationalstrejken i Finland*, vol. 2 (Helsingfors 1906) pp. 747–8.)

73 A SOCIALIST SUMMARY OF THE NATIONAL GENERAL STRIKE OF 1905

Economic life in our country has once more resumed its former course. The general strike is ended – *but only temporarily.* Will that titanic struggle be resumed once more, and if so, why? Certainly it will be resumed, because the working people have not yet got what they demand, that which they have a right to have . . .

The struggle begun by the workers of these past few grand days was at first completely national and patriotic, but now it is changing, through force of circumstance, into a class struggle. The Red Manifesto was originally a national proclamation, the expression of a mighty national ideal, but the gentry[3] made it into a class proclamation. *Let it therefore be so from now on.*

The ideals expressed in the workers' proclamation, and the demands, were completely objective, speaking for all true freedom-loving citizens who hold human rights dear, but the upper classes could not fit into this pattern, since power is more dear to them than the interests and happiness of all the people.

The upper classes got what they demanded; they got power, the calling of a Diet. The upper classes are preparing for the election campaign and the working class is preparing for a general strike, a class strike, for the struggle has become a class struggle.

That fight will be principally concentrated on the constitutionalist group, against the Vikings and their agents, as they have shown themselves to be contenders for power, a sort of clique wishing to speak and act in the name of all the people . . .

(' "Punanen julistus", työwäki ja perustuslailliset', *Kansan Lehti*, 11 November 1905.)

74 THE FINNISH SOCIAL DEMOCRATIC PARTY AND THE RUSSIAN REVOLUTIONARY MOVEMENT: EXTRACTS FROM THE MINUTES OF THE PARTY CONFERENCE (1906)

Yrjö Sirola: I have already expressed the view that the class struggle should not spread across the frontiers of one's own

[3] The epithet 'herrat' cannot be adequately translated into English; I have therefore made a simple straight translation.

country. I meant that a reciprocal sort of class conflict could endanger the independent status of Finland. It could provide the Russian autocracy with a weapon against our special privileges . . .

Let us draft a line of procedure . . . which will best help us to promote the Russian liberation movement. The struggle for liberation in Russia has already benefited from our incomplete independence, and in a number of respects. Russian liberals can show that peace and order prevail in Finland, for example . . .

Thus . . . generous aid, personal support and sanctuary to be offered to the Russian revolutionary movement, insofar as we are able to give it, but no participation in the Russian liberation movement which endangers our national rights of self-determination or the legal existence of our party unless such would be of considerable advantage to the Russian liberation movement . . . *Severi Alanne's motion to the conference*: The Finnish Social Democratic Party clearly sees that neither the political position won by this country through revolutionary struggle in the recent general strike nor even the political concessions which have likewise been gained from a reluctant upper class can be permanently secure as long as unlimited or even ostensibly limited tsarist power in Russia retains absolute powers of disposal over the fates of the Russian people and the nations, including Finland, associated with them. It therefore regards it as essential henceforth to bring all its efforts to bear principally upon the weakening and overthrowal of this power and thereby openly to proclaim its willingness to support the struggle now being waged by the proletariat and fighters for freedom in Russia, to the best of its ability. In this struggle the party approves of no other methods than those based on and aimed at liberty, fraternity, humanity and equality.

The proposal of the committee on tactics : . . .
(c) Because the party fully understands that as long as the present system of government in Russia continues, there can be no shadow of security for the internal rights of self-determination for Finland, nor full guarantees for the regular continuation of peaceful legislation, the party regards it as its solemn duty to stand solid with the liberation movement of the Russian people, taking note however of the possibilities which the special situation of

Finland affords for the realisation of complete political democracy in our country, and leaving the final decision to the party council in each instance.

(*Suomen sosiaalidemokraattisen puolueen viidennen edustajakokouksen pöytäkirja*, (Oulu 1906) pp. 220–4, 244–5, 393.)

75 POLICE AND REVOLUTIONARY ACCOUNTS OF THE SVEABORG REVOLT (1906)

MEMORANDUM OF THE POLICE DEPARTMENT (PETERSBURG), 6 AUGUST 1906

. . . For a number of days before 17 July [old style], a considerable number of Russian revolutionaries kept turning up in Helsinki, engaged in disseminating propaganda amongst the troops stationed there and entering into close correspondence with the leaders of the so-called red guards. This aformentioned agitation was apparently intended to be in preparation of a military revolt in connection with the plans of the revolutionary organisations to stir up the troops to revolt simultaneously in several major centres of the Empire.

On the evening of 17 July [old style] there arose a misunderstanding between the lower ranks of a minelaying company on Santahamina and the commanding officers, whereupon the other ranks seized weapons and took recourse to violence. The disturbance quickly spread to the gunners' camp on the other side of the island and from there to the battalion of the fortress infantry regiment . . .

According to information received from our agents, the Helsinki red guard had made the following dispositions at the outbreak of the revolt at the fortress : one battalion under the leadership of a former sergeant in the Finnish army called Lahtinen was to attend to the destruction of a section of the railway line between Helsinki and Petersburg and was to blow up the bridge at Simola : a second battalion was to take up position near the railway line in the Eläintarha park and a third was to group on the Töölö road between the sugar factory and Eläintarha, whilst all other members of the red guard were at the same time to transport weapons out of the town to the Töölö road . . .

TRILISSER'S SPEECH TO THE TAMPERE CONFERENCE OF THE
MILITARY AND FIGHTING ORGANISATIONS OF THE RUSSIAN SOCIAL
DEMOCRATIC LABOUR PARTY, NOVEMBER 1906[4]

I must begin by dispelling the false notion that the Sveaborg
uprising was a pre-planned and organised operation. The Sveaborg uprising began quite spontaneously . . . The Sveaborg uprising . . . took our organisation completely by surprise.

[Trilisser goes on to say that preparations for the revolt had
begun a fortnight before 17/30 July, but that the mutiny
of the minelayers was a spontaneous reaction to the refusal
of the command to pay grog-money outstanding to the
men.]

The town at this time presented an unusual sight. Few Finnish
citizens stayed indoors. Everyone flocked on to the streets. The
workers were gripped by a special animation. They were calling
for a general strike. Proclamations urging strike action appeared
on walls and lamp-posts. These proclamations were signed by . . .
Captain Kock.[5] This last circumstance considerably affected the
further activities of the Finnish proletariat at the time. However
popular the invocation of the name of Captain Kock amongst the
working masses, it was unable in all instances to match the authority commanded by the party council of the Finnish [socialist]
party. Had the latter called for a strike, the strike would undoubtedly have been a general one. However, one must do justice to
the Finnish proletariat. About 250 workers, members of the red
guard, together with a number of sailors, went to the aid of the
gunners on Kuninkaansaari who were in need of marksmen.
Elsewhere, for example in the vicinity of Turku, Lappeenranta
and Riihimäki, (in the first two instances under pressure from the
military organisation) the workers destroyed sections of the permanent way and blew up a bridge. But it must be noted that
there was a lack of planning, and, I would say, of a proletariat

[4] M. A. Trilisser, codename 'Mursky', was a leading figure in the Bolshevik military organisation in Finland, set up in the spring of 1906 to prepare an uprising amongst the troops stationed in the country. The police
did not begin to make inroads into the organisation until 1907.

[5] Kock was actively involved in plans for the revolt, but his own status
within the Finnish labour movement as well as the Russian revolutionary
movement is a matter of some debate.

combat organisation in the activities of the Finnish workers. The red guard showed itself to be an organisation more suited for workers' parades than for spontaneous combat.

It is interesting to note that the Finnish bourgeoisie was not indifferent to the course of events either. If the Finnish workers heroically went to die together with the soldiers in revolt, the Finnish bourgeoisie sought to counteract the workers with all the means at their disposal. Armed units of the Finnish capitalists, the white guard, occupied the tramway system and compelled the employees to operate it under threat of shooting if they did not comply. The white guards (no worse than our Cossacks) fired on the workers attempting to halt the tramway system . . .

(Printed in *Voennye vosstaniya v Baltike v 1905–1906 gg.*, ed. A. Drezen (Moscow 1933), pp. 197–8, 239, 243–4.)

76 THE PROGRAMME OF THE FINNISH ACTIVE RESISTANCE PARTY, ADOPTED AT THE EXTRAORDINARY PARTY CONFERENCE, 5 JANUARY 1907

1. The goal of the Finnish Active Resistance Party in the political independence of Finland, with a republican and fully democratic constitution.

2. The first task of the party is to contribute to the creation of the moral and material preconditions for the sovereignty of the Finnish nation, exercised by the Finnish parliament as a constituent assembly.

For the fulfilment of this task the party will pursue its activities :

(a) by written and oral propaganda :

(b) by working for the formation of a voluntary people's militia and the provision of weapons for this militia :

(c) by supporting the Russian revolution in a manner consonant with the autonomous position of Finland : and

(d) by financially supporting a combat group formed within the party, in the event of political reaction or the reintroduction into the country of a lawless regime of violence necessitating terrorist activity.

DISCUSSION OF PARAGRAPH 1 AT THE PARTY CONFERENCE

Paragraph 1 of the programme, dealing with 'Finland's political independence', provoked a lively discussion, in which a large number of speakers supported the resolution as it stood, whilst others, although agreeing with the party council that this should be the goal of the party, wished to propose a different formula which would aim for federation with the Russian republic rather than so evidently appear to be directed towards independence or internal autonomy. Those representatives who opposed the party council resolution argued that such a programme would be to risk not only forfeiting all support here in Finland but also the sympathies of the opposition parties in Russia, and they maintained that such a programme could create bad blood in Europe.

Against this view it was argued that the idea of independence was far more certain of a sympathetic reception in Finland than that of federation with Russia, that we would not lose anything if the Russian revolutionary parties broke off their relations with us, since we had never had any direct benefit from them, and that the joint resolution made by the Activist Party with the Socialist Revolutionary Party was not contrary to the programme outlined by the party council.

[After a vote, paragraph 1 was approved unchanged.]

(Minutes and programme in *Suomen aktiivisen vastustuspuolueen arkisto*, Finnish National archives.)

The Second Period of Oppression (1907–17)

Finland now had a democratically elected Diet – in which the socialists succeeded in obtaining over one-third of the seats in every election from 1907 – but the autocracy remained. It was even strengthened by a resurgent, crude Russian nationalism, hinted at by Stolypin and typified by representatives such as Purishkevich in the Duma debates on Finland in 1908 (78). The Finns' continued insistence that their special position within the Empire had been sanctioned for all time by the autocrat and was protected by the constitution and institutions of the country ran contrary to the Russian concept of the Empire, in which Russian state interests allied to a growing national consciousness overrode any such particularist niceties. The different viewpoints of the two sides are neatly summarised in the conclusions of the 1909 Kharitonov committee (79).

The subjugation of Finland to Russian state interests was ruthlessly pursued by Stolypin. In 1908 he succeeded in channelling matters which Finnish institutions wished to present to the Tsar through the Ministerial Council, which was to determine whether or not the matter was of general state interest before referring it to the Tsar or the relevant ministry. Two years later the Duma passed Stolypin's bill on matters of state interest, an act which left Finland with the right to initiate legislation on purely internal matters alone. All legislation concerning matters of state interest was to be provided for by the Russian state apparatus. The Finnish Diet was only entitled to voice its opinion and to elect members to the Council of State and the Duma. The opposition to these measures voiced by the Speaker of the Diet in 1908, 1909 and 1910 merely led to the dissolution of the session by the Tsar (82). The Senate gradually became a government of Russian nonentities. Imperial legislation placed the Finnish

*pilot system under Russian control, encroached upon the admin-
istration of the Finnish railway system and in 1912, decreed that
Russian subjects should enjoy the same rights as Finnish citizens
in Finland. This law fulfilled a long-felt desire of the Russian
nationalists to break down the exclusiveness of Finland's situation, but it created much bad blood and resulted in the dismissal
and exile of many Finnish officials, including Svinhufvud, for
failing to observe the letter of the law. The publication of a programme of russification in November 1914 was a final clear indication to the Finns that, unlike the Poles, they had nothing to
expect from tsarist Russia (83).*

*Opposition to these measures was more united than hitherto
but lacked organisation or direction. The major political parties,
now organised for action within a parliamentary system, exhausted much of their energy in fruitless attempts to pass social
reforms and in increasingly bitter internecine feuding. On the
fringes of political life, revolutionaries such as Lenin urged the
Finnish worker to throw in his lot with the revolutionary struggle within the Empire, and the irrepressible Konni Zilliacus pro-
phetically postulated the fate of Finland in the event of future
revolution (80, 81). The activist spirit also revived with the outbreak of war, though now hopes for Finland's future were pin-
ned on Germany, where nearly two thousand young Finns were
to receive military training (84).*

77 V. K. VON PLEHVE ON THE RUSSO–FINNISH CONFLICT (1903)

*. . . The Finnish question should not be considered in isolation
from the full process of development of the Russian state.* Its
origin and its present stage should rather be seen within the context of the awakening of the Russian national consciousness and
the attempts to establish Russian principles of state . . .

From the Russian point of view, the reason for the conflict with
Finland is to be found in the efforts of the Russian government,
by the passing of several legislative measures, to make the Finns
more conscious of the principles which on the admission of the
Grand Duchy into the Empire furnished the basis for the Russo-
Finnish relationship. The fact that the government and public
administration of Finland had quickly fallen into the hands of

native officials, to whom the Russian state idea was completely alien and who regarded all matters pertaining to public life from their own particularist viewpoint, made it essential to reaffirm these principles. The Finnish jurists also resorted to the selfsame particularist viewpoint in their interpretation of all constitutional and judicial acts concerning the Grand Duchy. Because these jurists based their view on a definition of the law which admitted of a separate status for the internal government of Finland, and because they did not consider this view in the light of documents defining the position of the Grand Duchy as a part of the state of Russia, it was natural that they perforce concluded that Finland was a state in itself, having the right to a separate political status. Quite different conclusions are obtained if the documents in question are considered in context . . .

At the provincial Diet[1] of Porvoo in 1809, the assembly of representatives of the people possessed no constituent character; it was not concerned with the relationship between the monarch and the people; and it did not rule on the relationships of the institutions of state to each other. *The provincial Diet only had the right to express opinions, not to make regulations,* as the spiritual father of the provincial Diet, Speransky, put it.

(*Russland und Finnland vom russischen Standpunkte aus betrachtet. Von Sarmatus,* (Berlin 1903) p. 3, 7–8. Sarmatus was von Plehve's pseudonym.)

78 THE FINNISH QUESTION IN THE THIRD DUMA (1908)

PRIME MINISTER STOLYPIN'S SPEECH

. . . It is quite natural that, if Finland and Russia do form a common political entity, then not only must there be a common foreign policy, but also uniformity in a number of other national affairs.

Of course it would be difficult to lay before you a comprehensive list of everything that needs doing, but it is clear to everyone that such a list would include for example, the protection of all

[1] The author makes the point elsewhere that the Porvoo Diet was a provincial, and not a state assembly ('als Landtag, nicht als Reichstag'), a common assertion of the Russian opponents of the Finnish case.

the subjects of the fatherland, the Russian Empire, the defence and supervision of fortifications and coastal waters, the administration of the telegraphic service and of a number of branches of the railway and customs administrations, and finally the regulation of the rights of Russian-born citizens in Finland. These matters are all so close to the interests of Russia that they cannot be resolved by the Finns alone, at least not by the processes of the Finnish legislature. Russia cannot hope to break the legal autonomous rights of Finland nor its internal legislative, special governmental and judicial arrangements. But in questions of general legislation, in certain common issues of government, there must be a common accord with Finland, with regard, of course, for the determining rights of Russia. The Finns view things differently. In their opinion not one single law common to the whole Empire is valid unless confirmed by the Diet. If we adopt this point of view, we find ourselves in an absurd situation. The same question would have to be dealt with and decided by our legislative institutions and the Finnish Diet. Let us suppose that the matter is settled differently by each party so that no joint decision is arrived at; there is then no sovereign power in the whole Empire that could resolve the deadlock. The question would then remain either unresolved or would lead to bitter conflict. This is of course intolerable and I repeat once more that the evil is not to be found in the inactivity or illegal measures of the authorities but in the fact that the whole area of legislation, the whole area of relations between ourselves and Finland is completely unorganised . . .

Voices have been heard to say in Finland, amongst our intellectuals and in the press that the Finnish question has been raised in Russia by the dark forces of reaction. Support is sought from intellectual and supposedly liberal circles for the defence of Finland's rights against the approaching threat of the bureaucracy. Voices are heard in Finland which do not and cannot understand that the firm power which crushes revolution and which as a creative force seeks to reform conditions in the Empire has only one purpose, that is, the establishment of the peaceful rule of law throughout Russia. (Applause from the centre and right.) I cannot understand how a government which seeks to fulfil the will of the ruler and strives in accordance with the representative institutions to provide peace and firm order, based solely on the laws, for Russia, how such a government can be suspected of seeking to destroy an identical order amongst our Finnish citizens. One thing is forgotten in this context, namely that in the creation of a new order in Russia, a new counter-force has arisen, that of Russian patriotism, Russian nationalism, the counter-force of nationalist sentiment. The roots of this movement are to be found in the very layers of society. Formerly the safeguarding of Russia's historical and national rights was solely the concern and duty of the government. This is no longer the case. Now the ruler seeks to rebuild the ruined edifice of Russian national feeling. It is you who are the representatives of this feeling, and you cannot absolve yourselves of the responsibility to preserve these national Russian rights. Russian blood has not been shed in vain, nor did Peter the Great unknowingly confirm Russia's sovereign rights on the shores of the Gulf of Finland. The surrender of these rights would cause irreparable damage to the Russian Empire . . .

P. MILYUKOV'S SPEECH

. . . You showed a certain degree of sympathy, gentlemen, when I spoke of the oppression of the Slavic peoples. (Voices from the right: 'We recognised the argument!') and you acknowledged that I knew something of the matter. Believe me when I tell you, that there is no better cement for binding together men in society than the awareness of national affinity. You understood this. There is no greater fury of desperation than that aroused when the existence of this mutual affinity of peoples is threatened by grave danger. Gentlemen! I must tell you that you have heard this and will continue to hear it together with the voices of reason of those people who, salvaging that which can be salvaged, are trying their utmost to negotiate with the representatives of the Russian government, you will have already heard it said there that if the viewpoint of the extreme right cannot be rebuffed, then it will be the duty of every Finn to resort to self-defence. (Noise from the right. The chairman calls the meeting to order.) You have heard the first cries of despair. This is the first warning . . .

I shall not repeat the facts to you, only please study sometime the consequences of our attempts to smash the Finnish constitution in 1899.

Do you really want to begin this all over again? I appreciate that Finland can of course be crushed. It is after all only a matter of a few army units. But I ask you – can you hold on to the fruits of victory? Will you not bring about the same sort of situation that representative Dmowski so graphically described with regard to Poland? Will you not create new problems for Russian policy at a time when there are already too many old problems to be resolved? Gentlemen! I shall finish, but I cannot but urge you to carefully consider the matter. I appeal to your better feelings, and ask you, can the Russian representative assembly take upon itself the task which General Bobrikov was unable to accomplish? . . .

V. M. PURISHKEVICH'S SPEECH

We right-wingers were pleased to hear the speech of the Prime Minister . . . Finland has been conquered with the blood of Russian soldiers and united to Russia for eternity. Every offence against the rights of Russia, every attempt at some sort of autonomy, is a revolutionary step, but revolutionary deeds must be forcibly crushed sooner or later. Separatist agitation is being carried on before a slumbering Russian eagle . . . The position of Russians in Finland is little better than that of Jews or gipsies. It is quite intolerable to read of the belittling of the rights of Russians in Finland, especially when one remembers the extensive rights enjoyed in Russia by any Finn coming here. The distinguishing feature of our policy in Finland so far has been the utter lack of any sort of logical political programme . . . It is not reaction which is toothless, but the opposition, which wishes to bite the Russian government at a time when it has acknowledged its patriotic duty, and to bite those of us who support it. If we, forgetting our national feelings and duties, start to pay heed to what the civilised west says, and shift our national sentiments to a cosmopolitan course, which cannot but poison us spiritually, then we will find ourselves faced with new and unforeseen surprises . . .

(Extracts from *Suomea koskevat välikysymykset Venäjän valtakunnanduumassa*, (Helsinki 1908) pp. 26–8, 54–5, 65–6.)

79 RÉSUMÉ OF THE VIEWPOINTS OF THE FINNISH AND RUSSIAN MEMBERS OF THE KHARITONOV COMMITTEE ON RUSSO–FINNISH RELATIONS (1909)[2]

THE VIEWPOINT OF THE FINNISH COMMITTEE MEMBERS

1. Finland occupies within the Russian Empire the position of a country which has its own fundamental laws and its own special constitution, which cannot be altered other than with the consent of the Finnish Diet.

2. Legislation on the succession to the throne, the coming-of-age of the successor to the throne, on the regency . . . and on the Imperial Family falls exclusively within the domain of fundamental Imperial laws.

In accordance with the same laws, questions of war, peace and alliance, as well as the concluding of agreements with foreign powers are dealt with.

3. In contrast to foreign affairs, questions concerning legislation, justice and administration in Finland are dealt with in accordance with the fundamental laws of the country, in conformity with which laws for the Finnish people and the Finnish authorities . . . should also be issued.

THE VIEWPOINT OF THE RUSSIAN COMMITTEE MEMBERS

1. Insomuch as Finland is an indivisible part of the Russian Empire, it merely exercises territorial self-government in its internal affairs : this is determined through general Imperial legislation.

2. The fundamental laws of the Empire have the same validity in Finland as in other parts of the Empire.

Fundamental laws provided for Finland are valid only for its internal affairs.

3. Finland's internal affairs comprise those local matters which in no way concern the other parts of the Empire, since, in accordance with paragraph 2 of the fundamental laws of the Empire, Finland is governed by special institutions on the grounds of a special law, but only in these affairs.

[2] A joint committee, established in 1909 to work out details on the juridicial and legal relations of Finland and Russia.

Therefore laws cannot be made for Finland with the aid of the State Council and the State Duma without alteration to the fundamental laws valid in Finland.

. . .

All other affairs concerning Finland shall henceforth, as hitherto, be dealt with in the order prescribed by general Imperial legislation.

The opinion of the Finnish Diet on the matters in the last-named category on which an opinion is demanded shall be accorded only advisory status.

4. In order to satisfy Finland's interests and needs more adequately representatives of the populace of the country shall be summoned to the State Council and State Duma . . .

5. . . . The introduction of representatives of Finland into the State Council and State Duma will not safeguard Finland's position to any appreciable degree . . .

(Swedish version printed in A. Langhoff, *Sju år såsom Finlands representant inför tronen. Minnen och anteckningar åren 1906–1913*, (Helsingfors 1922) pp. 368–70.)

80 V. I. LENIN, 'THE TSAR AGAINST THE FINNISH PEOPLE' (1909)

The Black Hundred highwaymen of the Winter Palace and the Octobrist scoundrels of the Third Duma[3] have commenced a new assault on Finland. The destruction of the constitution which protects Finnish rights from arbitrary Russian autocracy, the bringing of Finland into line with the rest of Russia by special decrees illegally enacted – this is the purpose of this assault, the origins of which can be seen in the Tsar's decree determining

[3] The Black Hundreds were a force of reactionaries, used to deal with revolutionaries and Jews. The Octobrist party, founded after the October revolution of 1905, was composed mainly of right-wing businessmen and landowners.

the question of military service without reference to the Diet and in the naming of new senators from amongst the ranks of the Russian bureaucracy . . . By destroying democratic, free Finland, the tsarist government and its agents seek to destroy the very last traces of the victories won by the *people* in 1905. This is why, as the Cossack regiments and artillery batteries speedily occupy the town centres of Finland, this is a matter which concerns all the Russian people.

The Russian revolution, which the Finns supported, forced the Tsar to relax his grip, which for a number of years had held the Finnish people by the throat. The Tsar sought to extend his autocracy to Finland, whose constitution the Tsar's forebears and he himself had sworn to honour, but he was then forced to agree not only to the expulsion of the Bobrikovist hangmen from Finland and the repeal of all his illegal decrees, but also to the introduction of universal and equal suffrage into Finland. Having now stifled the Russian revolution, the Tsar has returned to his old tricks, but with this difference : he now feels that he can obtain support not only from the old guard, paid spies and the like, but also from the clique of propertied men, which under the leadership of t he Krupenskys and Guchkovs feature in the Third Duma in the name of the Russian people . . .

The Finnish proletariat knows that it must fight in the most difficult circumstances. It knows that the western European bourgeoisie, flirting with the autocracy, will not involve itself in the affair, that the property-owning social circles in Russia, partly bought off by the policies of Stolypin, and partly corrupted by the lies of the Kadets,[4] will not give Finland the moral support which it received before 1905, and that the arrogance of the Russian government has grown enormously since it succeeded in striking down the revolutionary army in Russia.

But the Finnish proletariat also knows that the political struggle is not resolved at one go, that it demands sometimes many years of tenacious effort and that the victory goes in the end to the one who has the power of historical progress on his side. Finnish liberty will win, because without it the freedom of Russia is unthinkable and without the victory of liberty in Russia, economic progress in Russia is unthinkable . . .

[4] The Constitutional Democratic Party; liberal, sympathetically disposed to Finland.

In Finland the fight for the freedom of all Russia is being waged. However many bitter moments this new fight may bring to the heroic Finnish proletariat, it will create new bonds of solidarity between the Finnish and Russian working classes, and will prepare the working class for that moment when it will be able to carry out to its final conclusion the work set in train during the October days in 1905, and continued through the memorable days of Kronstadt and Sveaborg.

(V. I. Lenin, *Polnoe sobranie sochinenii*, vol. 19 (Moscow 1961) pp. 127–30.)

81 KONNI ZILLIACUS ON THE FUTURE OF FINLAND (1906)

... Every Finn knows that the allegations of separatist plans for Finland have been and are sheer fantasies. It is quite natural that, during a period such as the Bobrikov era, thoughts should turn to the security our country could enjoy if it were independent of a power which is being used to crush its rights. But there is as little evidence of the sort of plans Novoye Vremya so often talks about as there was earlier ...

It is only now, when the Russian revolution has revealed the daylight to us, when absolutism has had to give way to a quite different system of government, that the following questions have arisen, of their own accord: what have we a right to, what can and what should we do under such circumstances?

The agreement which was entered into by the Estates of Finland in 1809 and which still determines the relation of our country to the Russian state, was made with the Emperor and Autocrat Alexander I and his successors, whose power in Finland was given certain limits within the agreement. The agreement binds us to the Russian *Empire*, is entered into under prescribed prerequisites concerning the organisation of the Russian state and the authority of government, concentrated in the hands of the monarch. Does this agreement bind us also to a Russia where these necessary conditions have completely, or for the most part ceased to operate? Indeed not. Even the transformation of the Empire into a truly constitutional monarchy, where the people themselves, through their delegates, exercise determining authority, should clearly necessitate a new agreement with the new Russian state. A province shares the fate and fortune of the rest of the commonwealth without more ado, a state which is not so closely united to the commonwealth does not.

Circumstances could therefore arise which would give us the right to decide whether we still wished or did not wish to remain united to the state of Russia.

Would Russia be resigned to our taking advantage of this right? That is far from certain; but it is not inconceivable that in a new Russia, the point of view that alien nationalities should be granted full freedom to join or leave the Russian state could make itself felt. At least one Russian party already openly proclaims this principle, as is well known. Neither is it inconceivable that one or more European states could find it in accordance with their own interests, for the security of world peace, to separate Russia from the rest of Europe by a row of neutral 'buffer states' of which Finland could be one. Other possibilities, such as, for example, that of Russia falling victim to anarchy, can be passed over here.

It can be seen from the above that there are conceivable occasions when we might be able to make a decision to become politically independent of Russia . . .

In terms of external politics, such a separation would clearly result in a number of difficulties of an international nature. The example of Norway shows just how easy it is for a small nation to be led astray by such difficulties and the intrigues which are associated with them. Under similar circumstances, we too would certainly be unable to avoid pressure from diverse directions aimed at forcing us to elect one or another available prince as king, which would be of little advantage to our internal unity and even less to the certainty of our future as a state . . .

Without going further into the question, it should be clear from the above observations that it cannot and must not be answered without attention being given to all its many different and important aspects. It is also evident that, on the whole, it cannot yet even be given a decisive answer; the reply to the question must remain subject to developments in Russia. Until there is a definitive point reached in these developments, we ought to resolve, without allowing ourselves to be frightened by the Russian chauvinists' accusations of separatism, that at the decisive moment we shall be free to determine the political position of our country.

('Finsk separatism?' (K. Z[illiacus]), *Framtid*, 5 January 1906.)

82 THE PROTEST OF THE SPEAKER OF THE DIET, AND THE REACTION OF TSAR NICHOLAS II, 1909

THE OPENING ADDRESS OF THE SPEAKER, P. E. SVINHUFVUD

[18 February]

Your Excellency, [the Governor-General]

The Diet of Finland is embarking upon its duties at a time when the Finnish people are deeply perturbed to learn that the presentation of Finnish affairs to our supreme sovereign ruler is still made in accordance with procedure unacceptable in Finnish law and disastrous in practice.

Confident that the humble petitions of the Diet and the Imperial Finnish Senate on this procedure will not be ignored the Diet of Finland, through me, asks Your Excellency to convey the Diet's sentiments of humble loyalty and respect to His Imperial Majesty the Grand Duke.

THE DISSOLUTION OF THE DIET

[22 February]

We Nicholas the Second . . .

Make known unto Our faithful subjects of the Grand Duchy of Finland:

In opening this session of the Diet, the Speaker took it upon himself, in contradiction of paragraph 24 of the Parliament Act of the Grand Duchy of Finland and despite the fact that his attention had been drawn to Our statutes, to express on behalf of the Diet improper criticisms of the resolution of the State Council of Ministers, duly confirmed by Us, concerning the procedure for dealing with Finnish affairs which have a bearing upon the interests of the Empire. This criticism shows that the Diet fails to comprehend properly the true significance of this piece of legislation, which is intended only to protect those interests of state which have always had to be secured.

Since We observe, by virtue of the fact that such improper criticisms have been voiced, that the Diet has not been guided by an awareness of the real interests of Finland, which are inextricably bound up with those of the Empire as a whole, We cannot under present circumstances expect any profitable outcome of the labours of the Diet in its present composition. Having therefore ordained the holding of a new election, We have seen fit to dissolve the present session of the Diet as from 9/22 February of this year, and, in accordance with paragraph 18 of the Parliament Act ... to summon a new Diet in the city of Helsinki on 1 June (new style) 1909 ...

NICHOLAS

Tsarskoe Selo, 8/21 February 1909

(*Valtiopäivät 1909. Pöytäkirjat,* p. 28, 50.)

83   THE RUSSIFICATION PROGRAMME OF 1914

A programme for Finland concerning legislative and other measures, drafted by the preparatory committee set up together with the special committee for Finnish affairs, has been confirmed at the highest level.[5] According to the programme, two main groups of measures are to be implemented. The first group relates to *the consolidation of state authority in Finland, the safeguarding of the observance of laws and the maintenance of essential order in the country,* and the second *to the bringing about of a closer economic and political relationship between Finland and the Empire.*

The following measures belong to the first group :

The handing over of cases against Finnish civil servants who abuse their offices to the deliberations of courts in the Empire.

The revision of the regulations relating to disciplinary responsibility of civil servants and the rules governing service, in particular the questions of the limitations of irremovability of civil servants.

The amendment of their form of oath and their right to belong to political parties.

The education of civil servants for administrative office in the Grand Duchy of Finland and particularly the establishment of professorial posts in Finnish law in the higher institutes of learning in the Empire.

[5] This programme was the work of the Korevo committee, set up by Stolypin to deliberate upon Finnish affairs.

The introduction of the Finnish and Swedish languages as subjects in educational establishments in the Empire and the introduction of Russian to the prescribed subjects of the student examination for entry into the [Helsinki] Alexander University.

The preparation of a law designed to apply to Finland the regulations concerning the state of emergency.

The revision of existing regulations concerning the Governor-General of Finland, his aide, and the governors and in connection with this, the revision of the rules for the Senate.

The transformation of national administrative boards from the collegial system to boards of which the heads have the final right of decision.

The reorganisation of the attorney system in Finland.

The revision of the legal regulations governing the police and members of the gendarmerie in Finland.

The preparation of joint laws for the Empire and Finland concerning the press, unions, associations and general assemblies.

The safeguarding of the interests of the Russian crown, in particular the revision of the regulations governing deliveries to establishments in the Empire.

The fulfilment of the demand of the authorities in the Empire for the enforcement of matters not in dispute in Finland, and the fulfilment of the demands of Finnish officials in other parts of the Empire.

The establishment of a separate legal advisory department within the Chancery of the Governor-General of Finland and the appointment of people entrusted to defend the accused in local courts.

The creation of a procedure for dealing with matters concerning the outstanding demands of the Russian crown in Finland, and vice versa.

The placing of educational establishments in Finland and the Alexander University under the control of the Ministry of Education.

The bringing of the Finnish postal and telegraphic system into a common postal-telegraphic district, which will control the transport of mail by rail as well as the railway telegraphic system, as far as the regulations for its supervision is concerned.

The extension of the general regulations governing the telephone system to Finland.

Finnish participation in the expenses of defending the state.

The preparation of a law common to the Empire and Finland concerning aviation.

The implementation of measures to prevent the import of weapons and firearms into Finland.

The placing of the Finnish railways on an equal footing with the Imperial railways in regard to technical matters, and the extension of the general regulations of the Russian railways to the Finnish system with regard to the direct traffic connections between the latter and the Imperial railway system.

To the second group belong the following measures :

The settlement of questions relating to the Greek-Catholic religion and church in Finland.

The placing of Orthodox schools in Finland under the direction of an Orthodox institution.

The unification of the Finnish customs system with that of the rest of the Empire, and in particular the question of the position of Russian goods, sugar and meat etc., which enjoy privileges in the Finnish market.

The opening of state savings banks in Finland.

The granting of the right to private banks and similar credit institutions established within the Empire to open branches and promote their banking activities in Finland.

The protection of the activities in Finland of trade, industrial transport and other such companies, established in other parts of the Empire.

The revision of legislation governing the Finnish railway tariff, and the transfer of such particular tariff questions to the tariff section of the Ministry of Finance where they also touch upon the interests of the Russian railway network.

The settlement of the Finnish monetary system with the intention of uniting it with the monetary system of the Empire.

The division of land to the landless in the best way possible, and a general settlement of their circumstances by the extension of the activities of the Peasant Bank to Finland.[6]

[6] The Finnish Diet had failed to settle the vital question of the landless peasant in Finland, and it had been a favourite ploy of the Russian authorities to hint at some sort of favourable land division to win support; this paragraph contains an echo of the Stolypin land legislation in Russia.

The participation of the Finnish state in the costs of the state over and above the expenses of defence, especially with regard to the costs of the Foreign Ministry.

The revision of the maritime law in Finland and other regulations governing navigation, in particular the question of the right of Finnish vessels to cabotage and the return of canal dues after passage through the Suez Canal.

The preparation of new regulations concerning the Finnish mercantile fleet.

The preparation of a law common to the Empire and Finland concerning acceptance of or liberation from subject status.

The settlement of the question of the right of native-born Russians to Finnish citizenship.

The bringing in line of material for statistical research, the scope of research, the time it covers and the form of statistical tables, and:

The extension to Finland of the laws of copyright valid within the Empire.

('Ett afgörande på högsta ort', *Hufvudstadsbladet*, 17 November 1914.)

84   THE MEETING AT THE WAR MINISTRY IN BERLIN, 26 JANUARY 1915, CONCERNING THE TRAINING OF FINNISH RECRUITS

Present: three representatives of the Ministry of War, one from the General Staff (von Zimmerman), one from the Admiralty Staff and one from the Foreign Ministry.

The proposal had originally envisaged the training of a Finnish auxiliary corps which would support the Germans during a landing in Finland, but according to statements from the General Staff and Admiralty Staff 'a landing is not possible at present'. Nevertheless, the offer to send two hundred young Finns to Germany specifically for military training was accepted at the meeting. The aim of this training was 'to show the sympathy of Germany for Finland, to make known the cultural achievements and the military spirit of Germany, but mainly to enable them to carry out military tasks in the events of an active advance into Finland or a Finnish uprising'. Participants in the course are to travel in smallish groups to Berlin in the first instance, where they will be lodged through the auspices of the General Staff in association with the Finnish Committee.[7] Those selected for the course are to be young, educated men of good family, recommended by trusted representatives . . .

It is not desirable for the Finns to remain in Germany for any period of time after the course. It is nevertheless not required that they return to Finland. Participants in the course will be advised to return to Sweden, where they are after all more conveniently situated and where they can familiarise themselves with the weapons to be found there. Their stay there can be explained to the Finnish authorities on pretext of study, visits to institutes of higher learning, or to relatives, etc. To permit them to stay in Germany until an invasion of Finland takes place is out of the question.

The course is to begin in the middle of February at the instruction camp of Lockstädt, near Altona . . . The purpose of the instruction is 'the acquisition of a military spirit, infantry reconnaissance and covering, trench construction, destruction of railway lines and sabotage of all kinds, including harbour mouths and ships, guerrilla warfare; drilling instruction will be at a minimum'.

The course is estimated to last 'provisionally for four weeks, possibly longer' . . .

. . . Clothing will be in conformity with the uniform of the *Jugendwehr*,[8] so that it will be easier to maintain the secrecy of the enterprise . . .

(Notes of the meeting, made by Herman Gummerus, in Swedish and German, in *Suomen vapauttamisen ulkomaanvaltuuskunnan Tukholman kanslian arkisto*, Finnish National Archives, Helsinki.)

[7] The Finnish committee was founded in November 1914 in Berlin on the initiative of a number of Finnish expatriates.
[8] i.e. the scouts.

Part III

REVOLUTION, CIVIL WAR AND INDEPENDENCE

From March to October 1917

The collapse of the autocracy in March 1917 produced an immediate crisis of authority. The Provisional Government, anxious to win over the Finnish people to the Russian war effort, was prepared in its manifesto of 20 March to abrogate the Stolypin legislation and to convene the Diet, with a promise of a new constitutional settlement by legislative procedure. It soon showed itself unwilling however to concede to Finland the degree of internal independence which the socialists and a growing number of 'independence line' politicians now sought (86, 87, 91). In the view of the Provisional Government, the rights of the ruler had not disappeared with his demise, but had passed to his successor in authority (90). To this argument was added the embellishment of Russian nationalism – the Provisional Government, as trustee for the Russian people whose will was to find ultimate expression in the National Constituent Assembly, could not grant away any part of the territory of the former Empire (94).

During the spring and summer of 1917, the political initiative in Finland lay with the Social Democratic Party, represented in the coalition government and with an absolute majority of seats in the Diet. The party's stated aim was complete and internationally guaranteed internal independence within the framework of indissoluble union with Russia, but encouraged by Bolshevik support for self-determination even to the point of separation, and exasperated by the failure of the Senate's interim proposals on the transfer of certain powers of the former ruler to the competence of the Senate, the party began to shift to a more full-blooded demand for national sovereign independence (86, 87, 92, 98, 99). The socialists were not alone in seeking separation from Russia. The activists in Stockholm and Germany were working to this end, and sought to enlist German support (88). In the Diet, a number of non-socialist 'independence' men gave their support to the Soviet-inspired law on supreme power, which sought to

*break the deadlock in negotiations between the Senate and Pro-
visional Government by proposing the simple transference of
powers to the Diet. Only foreign and military affairs would remain within the competence of the Russian government
(101).*

*It should be noted that this law did not settle the question of
national sovereignty, which the Soviet congress had been very
careful to place within the terms of reference of the National Constituent Assembly – a point somewhat neglected by the Finnish
socialists (100). It was enough however to anger the Provisional
Government and its supporters (102). Strengthened by the collapse of anti-government elements in the July days, the Provisional Government dissolved the Diet in a manifesto which
clearly outlined the government's whole attitude on the Finnish
question (103). Kerensky's willingness to agree to an interim
agreement worked out by the non-socialist members of the Finnish Senate in September did not mark any significant shift of
opinion from this position (105).*

*By the time of the October elections, the necessity of independ-
ence had become an accepted political assumption, even if there
remained differences of opinion on how independence could best
be achieved. The main issue of the election was who was to control the future destiny of Finland – a bourgeois bloc, openly acting in collusion with Russian bourgeois imperialism to deny the
Finnish people their national and social rights (as the socialists
maintained) or a red terror, backed by indisciplined Russian
troops and bent on exploiting economic distress and social tension to foment class warfare (as the non-socialist parties claimed)
(106). With the final collapse of the Provisional Government,
whose real powers in Finland had ebbed away during the autumn,
the question of the exercise of authority was thrown squarely into
the lap of the representatives of the Finnish people.*

85 THE ORIGINS OF THE MANIFESTO OF 20 MARCH 1917

[After news of the February revolution reached Helsinki, the
bourgeois and socialist parties formed separate delegations to
consider the situation. The following accounts illustrate the
nature and course of their discussions.]

1.

The discussions held within the parliamentary delegation on what our demands should be were markedly cautious, owing to the fact that the situation was still uncertain, and we for our part lacked any sort of means of forcefully pushing through far-reaching demands or of defending what might possibly be obtained. One of the most important points of discussion was the question of international guarantees which was raised by me on Wednesday . . .

Another vital question was whether or not we should now consider a more precise regulation of the relationship between Finland and Russia, in the form of a treaty, than that provided for in the fundamental laws and by the act of Porvoo . . .

[Sunday 18 March]
[Discussions with Admiral Maksimov and Rodichev, the provisional commissar for Finland.]

Admiral Maksimov said (in Swedish) that Finland at the present moment could obtain even more than it had had before. He said that he was now reiterating what he had suggested by telegraph to Petersburg, namely, that we should have our own Finnish troops. The relationship between Russia and Finland ought to be built on trust and this had to be complete . . .

Mr Tokoi greeted Mr Rodichev in the name of the Finnish working class. What had happened in Russia had also opened the way to political influence and material advancement for the working class in Finland. He hoped that it would be possible to draw up a programme of the workers' demands immediately and expected that it would be accepted on the Russian side, inclusive of guarantees for political and economic advancement. He thereupon gave a brief indication of the main points of the programme which the social democrats wished to have accepted (without however demanding that they should be included in the manifesto; something of which he said nothing). Mr Tokoi demanded the confirmation of legislation approved by the Diet, which he enumerated, as well as the safeguarding of the right of the people in respect of the freedom to associate and congregate and the freedom of the press. Those imprisoned should be freed and the state law legislation [of 1910] rescinded. He also demanded a settlement of the foodstuffs problem, and legislation on the tenant-farmer situation and taxation.

Mr Rodichev replied that there were no obstacles to the confirmation of laws passed by the Diet; freedom of association, congregation and the press would also be accorded and a statement to this effect would be made in the manifesto. As far as the freeing of prisoners was concerned, this had already been decided, and a decree would be published on this without delay . . . The abolition of the 1910 state law legislation must rest with the forthcoming constituent assembly. The present government is provisional and therefore cannot do this, but its consent would be promptly given . . .

Other illegal laws would be rescinded, some immediately by the government, others by the constituent assembly when it convened. The Diet would be summoned. The other desired aims put forward on behalf of his party by Mr Tokoi were internal Finnish affairs . . .

Mr Rodichev now took up a matter which, as the statement made by Admiral Maksimov revealed, was clearly much in the minds of the representatives of Russian authority, namely, the military question. He remarked that he knew that Finland had hitherto desired and demanded to have its own army again . . . Admiral Maksimov declared that the Russian troops also fought for the freedom of Finland. Germany was the enemy of liberty and if Russia were to be defeated by the Germans, there would follow a reaction in Russia and in Finland as well . . .

Mr Danielson-Kalmari gave assurances that the cordial words of the Admiral on Finland would evoke a response in wide circles. But on the question of an army people were divided in their opinions, as had already been pointed out. We did not wish to shirk our responsibilities towards the state, but we had been prevented from having our own army and oppression had turned our sympathies from Russia and its cause.

Admiral Maksimov observed that the new Russia was no longer what the old had been. You should fight for social liberty side by side with Russia . . .

(E. Estlander, 'Manifest av 20 mars 1917 och dess uppkomst', *Från brytningstider*. Ny serie, (Helsingfors 1921) pp. 289–99.)

Petrograd, Saturday 17 March 1917
12.00 a.m.

2.

To the Social Democratic Party executive and the Finnish Trade Union executive

The new government has overcome the first difficulties and is more or less generally acknowledge by the whole country as the new government. The workers too support the government and social democratic proclamations point out that this is now a political and not a social revolution. It is generally recognised as essential that all forces should combine to support the new order. It is of course regretted that Guchkov has refused to join the government, but it is hoped that he will eventually agree to serve.

It is quiet in the city. Everywhere one sees the people's militia with their red flags and rosettes. There is no truth in the rumour that troops were to have been sent to Petrograd to crush the revolution.

The Finnish bourgeoisie here have acted swiftly, and Seyn [the Governor-General] has been arrested at their insistence. They believe that a manifesto relating to Finnish affairs should speedily be obtained, since it could be too late within a matter of days. Peräläinen is firmly of the opinion that the position of the government is quite secure, since it enjoys the support of all the revolutionaries, and in view of this the settlement of the Finnish question does not have to be made within a matter of days. Today we have spoken with D. D. Protopopov, the assistant to the Minister for Finnish Affairs, Mr Rodichev. The discussion was of a precursory nature as we learnt that Rodichev himself had travelled the previous night to Helsinki where he would in all probability be having discussions with the politicians there.

Rodichev regards himself merely as a temporary minister, since a new Finnish State-Secretary has to be appointed to look after Finnish affairs here. Both Rodichev and D. D. Protopopov are well known friends of Finland. Rodichev's other assistant is Dr Ramot, an Estonian nationalist and member of the Duma. The Finns here are of the opinion that 'now anything can be pushed through' if only we make haste. The return of the old order is generally regarded as absolutely impossible.

The greatest problem is the shortage of foodstuffs. If it gets

F

worse, the government could find itself in a tight situation. Foodstuffs must be sent from Finland, even if we have to put up with
even more suffering than hitherto. The Finnish workers will surely
understand the importance of this matter.

A strike in Finland would not only be unnecessary, but very
damaging, because it would hinder the export of foodstuffs to
Petrograd. Amongst both Russians and Finns here there is extreme anxiety that there will be no general strike in Finland. Try
as hard as possible to prevent one! Telephone other areas immediately and inform them of this!

Traffic between Viipuri and Petrograd has been restored on
Friday. The Finnish railway workers' committee here has decided to keep traffic running as much as possible.

If you can, let us have some instructions and information.

K. H. Wiik   O. Tokoi   Väinö Tanner

(The original copy of this report is in the Finnish Labour
Archives, Helsinki, file 329(471)5 : 328 '1917'.)

86   FINLAND AND RUSSIA IN THE POST-REVOLU-TIONARY SITUATION

1. THE NON-SOCIALIST VIEW, MARCH 1917

[30 March]

Mr Paasikivi gave an account of the visit of members of the [par-
liamentary non-socialist] delegation on 29 March to see the
Russian Minister of Justice, Kerensky.

. . . Mr Kerensky gave assurances that there was no threat of
danger from the old order, since it no longer had any support. But
there was definitely danger from the foreign enemy. He said that
he had come here to find out if the Provisional Government could
rely on Finland . . . Mr Kerensky then took up the matter of
German plotting here and announced that the Provisional Government had resolved to grant a full amnesty for these actions[1] . . .
In answer to the question directly put to him as to whether this
amnesty also covered those who had been in Germany, Mr Kerensky replied in the affirmative, since the reason for going to Germany was of the same patriotic nature as the Irish rebellion. He

---

[1] A reference to the recruiting of young men for military training in
Germany.

also declared that the Provisional Government hoped for a solidarity which would render German espionage futile in this country, but that it did not demand positive aid and participation in the war. For their part, the Finns replied that since a manifesto had been issued and the amnesty was about to be published, they regarded it as their duty in Finland to do what they could to prevent the occurrence here of acts contrary to the interests of Russia . . .

Mr Ståhlberg observed that the general opinion has been that the authority which the Emperor had possessed as Grand Duke had passed to the power of government in Russia. There was also another point of view which regarded as undesirable the transfer of that authority to the Ministerial Council of Russia and perhaps later to a president. Those affairs which could be decided here ought to be separated from those for which the final decision rests with the sovereign authority in Russia. Mr Estlander declared himself in favour of the latter point of view, admitting that it would require legal consideration and would have to be decided when the decision on the form of government was made. Mr Danielson-Kalmari did not wish to admit that all the rights hitherto possessed by the Sovereign passed to the possessor of the executive authority. If we were to become subject to such a shifting master as a ministry, we would find ourselves in a worse position than before. The only decisions that should rest with Petrograd are those which have a bearing on the whole state. In the new form of government this should be arranged along the lines of, for example, the Canadian constitution. Mr Paasikivi observed that the constitutional committee [of the diet] should prepare a new form of government as soon as possible. If legislative decrees were needed before then, the committee would have to work out special proposals for this. Mr Ståhlberg declared that there was a grave danger of thinking that the past had been entirely swept away. Changes had to be made in the legislative procedures laid down for Finland, otherwise we would soon find ourselves at the mercy of all sorts of meetings and military organisations . . .

('Kertomus porvarillisten eduskuntaryhmien välisen valtuuskunnan toimesta', in the Onni Hallsten collection, Finnish National Archives.)

2. THE SOCIALIST MEMORANDUM PRESENTED TO KERENSKY, 29
MARCH 1917

. . . We beg leave to express our opinion openly on how wide-
ranging we feel Finnish liberties ought to be in order to be completely satisfactory.

The autonomy of our country, founded on the treaty of Porvoo
of 1809, which your government has restored, has shown itself by
bitter experience to be too constricted for Finland, nor has it been
sufficient to prevent the outbreak of endless conflicts between
Finland and Russia. The independent development of our country
on the one hand and a long-endured oppression on the other have
left our people with an ardent desire for internal liberty which
is much more far-reaching than was the case a hundred years
ago. You are aware that during the course of the present war,
this desire has manifested itself in the undesirable form of Finnish
youths joining the German army. This sort of thing has not of
course been widely supported, nor have the efforts for independence linked to this movement aroused much response amongst
the people at large. Nevertheless, the view that there can be no
hope of the sovereign power in Russia granting voluntarily a sufficiently free and adequately guaranteed status for Finland has
perhaps been a relatively commonly held one in our country so
far. To the best of our knowledge this suspicion has not entirely
been dispelled or replaced by confident hopes.

If however Russia were now to grant freely such a status to
Finland, such a great historical action would without doubt have
an incomparably happier influence on the future relations of the
two peoples than any concession which Russia might make to
Finland at a later date.

With this in mind, we beg to draw to your attention certain
*principal features of the sort of constitutional relationship between
Russia and Finland*, which we are convinced would be satisfactory to the Finnish people, in order to seek your opinion as to
whether something along similar lines could not be envisaged as
a possible treaty between Russia and Finland . . .

1. Finland, in all its internal affairs an independent state, is in
an indissoluble union with Russia.

2. Foreign affairs, such as questions of war and peace and
political treaties with foreign powers, are to be handled and re-

solved by Russia on Finland's behalf; but where such treaties presuppose measures relating to Finland or may cause changes in the governance, legislation or administration of the law of Finland, they shall only become valid on the Finnish side on condition that Finnish consent is obtained.

3. Trade and other such economic treaties shall be made independently by Finland with other states.

4. The determining of the constitution of Finland within the framework of this treaty, as well as the governance, legislation and administration of the law of Finland shall be internal Finnish concerns. Hence the questions of the form of government, the head of state and his powers would be left to Finland freely to determine.

5. Decisions on the defence of the country, and how it shall be superintended and directed are to be internal Finnish affairs. Russia shall not maintain troops or defence works in Finland during peacetime. (What sort of regulations the treaty should include on the protection of Petrograd by essential fortifications sited in Finland, we have not for our own part yet considered in greater detail.)

6. The Russian Orthodox church in Finland shall be under its own spiritual administration according to its own laws; only the regulation of its social functions to be a Finnish concern.

7. Russian subjects in Finland shall have in the main the same rights to pursue their livelihoods and the same civic liberties as Finnish nationals.

8. In the arrangement of commercial and other joint relations between Finland and Russia, the procedure of bilateral free agreement and parallel legislation shall be observed.

9. Should any question of future joint state institutions or of changes in this treaty occur, a decision can only be reached by similar bilateral free agreement. For the time being Russia will keep its representatives in Helsinki and Finland will maintain its representative in Petrograd to supervise the observance of this treaty and if necessary promote the making of joint agreements in matters concerning both countries.

Consideration must naturally be given to such things as rules for a suitable body to settle matters of dispute and interpretation which will arise from such a treaty.

It would also be fitting for Russia, in order to strengthen the steadfast confidence of the Finnish people and to provide a firmer guarantee, to offer the treaty to some other states, for example France and Britain, for their guarantee. We believe that you will not regard our mentioning this matter as a sign of no confidence on our part in your government, whose friendship and sincerity we have recently had proof of in the manifesto. But simply because your present government is provisional, and there can be no knowing if a like-minded government will always prevail in Russia, such a guaranteeing of the treaty would be desirable, if its existence is not to be subjected to the shifts of temporary political currents.

It is self-evident that only the Finnish Diet has the authority to decide for Finland upon the contents of this sort of treaty. But we have in this document sought to bring to your notice the general direction of the hopes and aspirations of those whose views we know to some extent.

It is also our belief that an agreement of this sort would not be contrary to the real interests of the Russian people. On the one hand, a liberal, democratic Russia would never wish to see Finland, in our opinion, as a springboard for foreign conquest, but as a faithful protector of her north-western frontier. On the other hand, it is obvious that in the area of economic relations, little Finland does not seek and is indeed unable to do harm to Russia, because our country is of necessity dependent on the products and markets of Russia, and therefore in its own interests must seek to maintain close relations with Russia.

In Russia it might perhaps be said that Finland, with such extensive liberties, virtually approaches the status of an independent country. We do agree that Finland's relations with Russia in many areas would formally be entirely free, even though Finland would naturally be unable in general to act without due attention being paid to Russian interests. We would go so far as to say that in our opinion this sort of state would be better for Finland than an unguaranteed independence. And would not the creation of such a status for Finland by Russia be just the right sort of thing to benefit Russia too?

If such an act of state is thought to be within the bounds of possibility, then do you think the Russian government might now present some sort of counter-proposals? Or on what points might you have something to say against a final arrangement of this sort of the legal relationship between Finland and Russia?

(A copy of this memorandum, prepared by Edvard Gylling, Otto Kuusinen and Karl Wiik, is in the Finnish Labour Archives, Helsinki, file 329(471)5 : 328 '1917'.)

3. THE ACTIVIST 'MAXIMAL PROGRAMME', 24 MARCH 1917

The interregnum which has occurred in Russia as a consequence of the revolution and of which the state of interregnum in Finland is a reflection implies that the constitution of Russia, in regard to its foundations and character, is in a state of utter confusion and vagueness. Something new will arise from the old, but so far everything is undecided and in a state of suspense. The most immediate prospect of some sort of organisation taking shape is to be seen in the Russian Constituent National Assembly which is to convene soon; in the background is the mirage of the republic and a federative state, which even now is seen by many as essential.

One need only mention these words, the Constituent Russian National Assembly, republic, federative state, to discover that this is a matter of concepts and outlines of the state which is of immensely enormous scope with regard to Finland as well. What will be the attitude of the National Assembly on the Finnish question, and what will it take its own authority to be? How will the introduction of a republican constitution into Russia affect the relationship between Russia and Finland, which is at present founded on the principle of both countries having a joint *monarch*? And finally the major problem : if Finland remains united to Russia, how will Finland's extensive internal independence fit in with an all-Russian state system?

It is the last question above all that is bound to arouse fears. It is quite certain that Russia will not create a loose state federation, but, as has already been hinted publicly, a federative state, close to the American or Swiss model. Within such a union however, there is a high degree of centralisation; there are usually very narrow limits to the right of self-determination of the member states in respect of legislation, administration and justice. Were Finland to enter into a state system of this sort, either as an ordinary member or as a separate state, its rights of self-determination would be of a lesser scope than the juridicial limits instituted by the 1809 agreement, and much less than what Finland now can and must lay claim to. Were Finland to obtain, on the other hand, the position of a member state, howbeit with priorities or privileges, this could be the source of complications and jealousies.

. . . Finland cannot consent to enter into a Russian state system as an integrated component, even though it were to retain the nature of a state, but it must lay claim to the position of an *état à part*, a state side by side with Russia with its own strongly international characteristics. With this in mind, it is necessary for an attempt to be made to unite leading political circles in Finland around a *maximal programme*. In support of this, the following reasons may be set forth :

1. Finland must under present circumstances seek to attain as much as possible.

2. The question of Finland's future position must, at least for the time being, be kept open so that it may still be the subject of international settlement.

3. There may be significant tactical advantage to be gained from the presentation of a comprehensive and far-reaching programme, which although highly unlikely to be accepted without demur by the other side, will set out a sort of bargaining position and which will prevent a premature settlement with Russia.

4. Since Estonians, Georgians, Letts and others are now demanding autonomy, Finland, conscious of its ancient inviolable rights, its statehood and its national characteristics, must lay claim to first priority above all others; Finland must assert the principle that its position lies on an altogether different legal and political plane than the ambitions of autonomy held by all the other nationalities of Russia.

The maximal programme should most fittingly embrace the following points.

(a) Unswerving observation of the promise to restore fully and unconditionally the national rights of Finland, to which a whole number of special demands, which were not observed in the manifesto, might particularly be added. Such demands include : the abolition of the use of Russian in all correspondence between Finnish officials; the dissolution of the gendarmerie; the right of the Diet to confirm the regulations governing the Bank of

Finland; a law on the acquisition and surrender of Finnish citizenship, etc.

The most vital demand of all, which must take pride of place, is that the Russian Constituent National Assembly shall not take upon itself any authority *to decide constitutionally the juridicial position of Finland*, but may only acknowledge and confirm the rights which already belong to Finland *in a declaratory fashion*, and may come to some sort of agreement together with the appropriate Finnish organ of state on the necessary alterations to the juridicial relationship between Russia and Finland.

(b) Not only the Minister State-Secretary, but also the Governor-General shall henceforth be Finnish citizens.

(c) Unlimited and reliable amnesty in Finland and the immediate dissolution of the military tribunals and their functions in Finland.

(d) The immediate withdrawal of all Russian troops stationed in Finland (which however will probably depend upon the fulfilment of point (f)) and the handing over of the question of defence to the competence of the Diet.

(e) An unconditional promise that Finland shall not be called upon to bear any part of Russia's war costs and state debts (insofar as the Diet does not voluntarily undertake to meet some of the war costs.)

(f) A notification from the Russian government to foreign powers, that is, directly to Russia's allies and the neutrals, and through the agency of the neutral states to her enemies, that the Russian government, at the request of and in concert with the Finnish government and Diet, considers the territory of Finland as neutral until the end of the war, that is, not part of the theatre of war and expects that it will be regarded as such by extraneous powers, *or* : a direct agreement, through neutral channels, between Russia (and its allies) on the one hand and the Central Powers on the other, whereby the territory of the state of Finland shall be considered and treated in the above-stated manner for the duration of the war.

(g) A preliminary commitment from the Russian side consenting to the Finnish question being taken up at the peace settlement with the object of acquiring international regulation, and for Finland thereby to be additionally guaranteed, beside complete autonomy, the following privileges :

(i) Russian troops shall not be stationed in Finland. The defence of Finland shall be Finland's own responsibility. A neutral zone may be created between Russia and Finland.

(ii) Finland shall have : a national and a trading flag, as well as freedom to conclude with foreign powers customs and trade agreements at the very least, the right to appoint at least commercial agents in foreign states and the right to maintain direct relations with foreign powers, by suitable arrangements, such as a department for international affairs or a similar authoritative body, *in all matters in which Finland, in accordance with the demands hereby made, may be equipped to negotiate on the basis of international law.*

(iii) The terms of the international treaty concerning the position of Finland which may be approved by the respective contracting powers, may not be amended without the consent of Finland; Finland must therefore be guaranteed *an independent claim in international law* to its fulfilment . . .

('Ett finskt maximiprogram', Prof. Rafael Erich's memorandum, is to be found in *Suomen vapauttamisen ulkomaanvaltuuskunnan Tukholman kanslian arkisto*, vol. 2, Finnish National Archives.)

87 THE FIRST CONTACT BETWEEN THE FINNISH SOCIAL DEMOCRATIC PARTY AND THE BOLSHEVIKS AFTER THE FEBRUARY 1917 REVOLUTION

On 19 March,[2] delegates of the Finnish Social Democratic Party – comrade Wiik and others whose names I have forgotten, appeared at a session of the Central Committee of our party. A delegate from the Finnish party hailed the victory over tsarism and expressed his confidence that in the new order, the old links between the RSDLP and the FSDP[3] would be even closer and more fruitful . . .

At the conclusion of these words of greeting, a delegate of the Finnish SDP announced that the party's central committee had

[2] The date of this meeting is given as March 24/April 6 in *Deyatel' nost' Tsentralnogo Komiteta RSDRP(b) v 1917 godu*, Moscow 1969, p.45.

[3] The Russian Social Democratic Labour Party (RSDLP) and the Finnish Social Democratic Party (FSDP)

assigned 10,000 roubles for the support of Russian social democracy, and this had been divided between the Mensheviks, who had been given 3,000 roubles, and the Bolsheviks, who had been given 7,000 roubles. In addition, the central committee of the Finnish SDP promised to hold a special collection throughout Finland in aid of the RSDLP.

After the greetings were over, our comrades put a whole series of questions to the Central Committee concerning mutual relations between Russia and Finland, and asking us to give our opinion in this matter. Their first question concerned the degree of autonomy for Finland which our party was prepared to support. Our reply was that we were prepared to support them in every way in the fight for independence. The Finnish social democrats themselves were thinking of the organisation of their own administrative autonomy in the terms of an 'indissoluble union' with Russia. Questions of 'foreign policy, that is, questions of war or peace, the concluding of political treaties and agreements with other powers, would be decided by Russia, even where these concerned Finland',[4], insofar as these treaties did not affect the internal affairs and administrative structure of Finland itself. At that time they had no thoughts of complete separation from Russia. At the Central Committee our Finnish comrades were promised full support in their political struggle for independence, by which we meant for the full independence of Finland, even to the extent of separation, if the Finnish people themselves desired this.

(A. Shyapnikov, *Semnadtsatyy god*, vol. 3 (Moscow 1927) p. 202.)

88 VON BONSDORFF'S ACCOUNT OF THE MEETING IN BERLIN BETWEEN THE FINNISH ACTIVIST DELEGATION AND STATE-SECRETARY ZIMMERMANN, 24 MARCH 1917

[*von Bonsdorff*] . . . As far as we know, the people in Finland are at present remaining calm and are awaiting developments . . . The fact that all the persecutors of the Finnish people and the

---

[4] This quotation is from the memorandum prepared for the Bolsheviks by the FSDP, based closely on the memorandum presented to Kerensky (q.v.)

hated officials have now been arrested, or are to be replaced, has naturally given rise to much joy. That the party leaders and consequently in all likelihood the Diet are entering into negotiations with the Russian government is no indication that the people will wish to receive their autonomy from the hands of that government.

The day before yesterday however, the Finnish people were given a manifesto, and in this manifesto Finland has been promised everything – everything

The thoroughly pro-German Finnish people will in this manner be presented with a temptation of monstrous proportions. The situation is therefore seemingly grave.

If Finland is to be saved, and through Finland, Sweden is to be brought on to the side of Germany in the future, an intervention from the German side is absolutely necessary. Our organisation is working actively at home, but help from the German government would now be invaluable. The fate of the northern countries is about to be resolved for many years to come. A peaceful Finland by the side of Russia could gradually push Sweden into the hands of the Entente. If Germany desires – as we would like to assume – the participation of Sweden in the war, it must act and proceed energetically in Sweden now.

When I had the honour of being received by your Excellency at the beginning of February, I took the liberty of expressing the devout hope that I might hear some observations from Your Excellency on the interest of Germany in Finland and the Finnish question. At that time, Your Excellency told me of his wish to receive me and to help us if there was real danger. The danger is now upon us. Behind the Russian revolution and behind the Russian promises to France lies Britain.

In order that we might continue our work in Finland and Sweden, it is absolutely essential that we obtain an official statement from Your Excellency at once. With such a statement in our possession we could hopefully prevent the Finnish people, who lack support or aid, from allowing themselves to be seduced into believing the promises of the Russians. In this way our people could, when the time is right, declare their independence and probably actively oppose the Russian government.

The statement which I now humbly request on behalf of my colleagues, would only be submitted to individual party leaders in Finland; I undertake the responsibility of seeing that it is not made public.

May I present Your Excellency with what we feel is more or less necessary? . . .

THE ACTIVISTS PROPOSAL/FINAL DRAFT, APPROVED BY THE KAISER, BUT NOT SIGNED BY HIM.

The German government considers as a German interest the attainment of full independence, where possible, by Finland. As a consequence, the German government is willing to work for the attainment of this end, in accordance with conditions prevailing at the time, at the conclusion of peace. Should there be, however, any sort of political bond still existing between Finland and Russia, Germany is prepared to intercede for the maintenance of Finnish autonomy by treaty [as a guarantor power[5]].

(Minutes of the Stockholm activist committee, 7 April 1917, *Suomen vapauttamisen ulkomaanvaltuuskunnan Tukholman kanslian arkisto*, vol. 1, Finnish National Archives.)

89 A STUDENT MEMORANDUM ON THE FINNISH QUESTION, PRESENTED TO A. F. KERENSKY ON 15 APRIL 1917

. . . We have welcomed with joy the ideas of the Russian revolution,[6] but we can in no way consent to Finland being represented within a constituted Russian federation as an equal member of such a federation. In other words, a sort of union would be formed between the Russian federation and Finland : but in any union thus constituted, we would be so weak that, should any sort of controversy arise, we would find ourselves out on a limb. We have had to defend ourselves against Russian tsarism already; in regard to a Russian federation strengthened by national sentiment, our situation would be precarious.

Under these circumstances we can only envisage the final solution of the Finnish question in the shape of absolute sovereignty. Some sort of *modus vivendi* is of course possible on the basis of other principles; but, as we shall reveal to you today, our goal

[5] Omitted in the final draft.
[6] Added in red ink to the typescript.

will always be the creation of an independent Finland, and to attain this goal we will take advantage of every opportunity which presents itself. If the Russian government remains true, our actions will be open and honest.

For the moment we are particularly anxious to know whether there are grounds for hoping that the Finnish question could be resolved in the future in accordance with our desires. We well understand that a question like this can only be worked out in detail at a later date.

Clearly the Russian National Constituent Assembly would not seek to assume the right of determining the constitutional position of Finland, as did the Third Duma . . .

(The memorandum, in French, is in *Ylioppilasdelegation asia-kirjakokoelma*, Finnish National Archives.)

90 A RUSSIAN VIEW ON THE CONSTITUTIONAL POSITION OF FINLAND – F. F. KOKOSHKIN'S SPEECH TO THE JURIDICIAL COMMISSION, 21 APRIL 1917[7]

. . . The Provisional Government has promised legislation on a new form of government [for Finland] : if the law now being proposed [by the Senate] is carried through, the form of government will then be ratified, not by the Provisional Government, but by the Finnish Senate. This law will fundamentally alter the juridicial relationship of Finland and Russia, however. With the disappearance of the monarchy, its rights did not disappear, they were merely transferred to its successors : French jurists consider that the bulk of Napoleon the Third's privileges were transferred to the President of the republic. We are well aware that the interim position is far from sure, but when a form of government is established for Russia, the laws of Finland will also be changed. The Provisional Government considers changes necessary, having quite rightly made a number of promises. The Finnish constitution will find its own development delayed. Many important

---

[7] This commission was set up to consider the proposal of the Finnish Senate for transferring a number of the rights which had hitherto appertained to the monarch to the competence of the Senate itself: these included the convocation and dissolution of the diet, initiation and confirmation of legislation and the approval of the budget.

rights do not belong to the Diet, since they are implicit in the constitutional government of both states. Russia, having become a free country, cannot go so far as to allow the Diet these rights. This is a matter of the internal constitution of Finland in its entirety. *Who* possesses supreme state power in Finland is not an internal Finnish affair. The joint monarchy was the vital fulcrum in the juridicial relationship between Russia and Finland. The rights of the monarchy were formerly passed on, but in a constitutional state, the monarch cannot arbitrarily delegate his rights. Otherwise we are led to the conclusion that the monarch could have eliminated himself in Finland, which would have fundamentally changed the position of Russia, since Finland would have been separated from Russia. In the fundamental laws of Russia, the rights of Finland are mentioned as they have a bearing on the juridicial relationship. The Provisional Government has an obligation to the Russian people – it cannot predetermine the matter of the governmental state system of Russia. Alterations to the system of government for Finland to any degree will affect the governmental system of Russia and for this reason the Provisional Government has not the right to change the position of the supreme governmental authority in Finland . . .

('Zasedanie yuridicheskago soveshchaniya pri Vremennom Pravitel'stve, 8/21 aprelya 1917', in *Ministerivaltiosihteerin viraston arkisto. 1917 asiakirjat*, no. 36, Finnish National Archives.)

91 SENATOR TOKOI'S SPEECH TO THE DIET, 20 APRIL 1917

. . . We are still living in a state of revolution. As far as I can see, the revolution has not yet fully run its course. The tsarist regime has of course been overthrown, but side by side with this political revolution a profound social revolution is still going on. In my view, it is impossible at this moment even to begin to predict the form or development of our future form of government. But in the main, I think that there should be no differences of opinion in this matter: as I understand it, liberated Russia, the free people of Russia and the road which the Russian people have set out upon, the road to liberation, cannot but presuppose that all peoples capable of assuming the rights of self-determination shall be given these rights. The entire past history and progress of our people is a living witness to the fact that the Finnish people have over the ages matured into an independent nation, capable of determining its own affairs, privileges and courses. Our whole cultural development has followed its own particular course, our whole economic development is also sufficiently independent, and our whole social structure is so different from that of Russia, that there can be no question of any sort of union of these societies which would be detrimental to both. And I am convinced that free Russia, new Russia – and if I may so, an esteemed neighbour, and may I add, a worthy ally – must also be a fully independent nation, because an independent nation will not tolerate an enslaved and oppressed neighbour and ally. I cannot believe that there would be any disagreement with this amongst the Russian people. And I dare to hope that the Russian people and its leaders, the government, will without delay demonstrate not only in words but also in deeds that those promises which the representatives of the Russian people have made to us will be fulfilled to the letter.

I therefore am emboldened to place my confidence in the fact that the right to self-determination of the Finnish people, the beginnings of national independence, are now placed on a firm footing; our duty is to resolutely and consistently promote this, so that Finnish independence is ensured in the very near future.

(*Ensimmäiset valtiopäivät 1917, Pöytäkirja*, vol. 1, pp. 47–9.)

92 'THE FINNISH QUESTION AND THE RUSSIAN SOCIALIST PARTIES'

... In discussions (with the Mensheviks on April 30), our Russian comrades showed themselves on several occasions to be completely ignorant of the Finnish question, and some of the members of the party executive even voiced opinions which did not greatly differ from those of the Kadets ...

The meeting with the Mensheviks left us feeling that there was little hope of Finland's cause being much advanced by them, since their ignorance of that cause and many other things besides left us with the impression that their attention was claimed more by matters closer to their hearts ...

At the meeting (with the Bolsheviks on May 2), after we had finished explaining as we had done to the Mensheviks the reasons why we had turned to them, our Russian comrades expressed their view: they supported the granting of as wide a right of self-determination to the Finnish people as the Finns themselves desired. If the Finnish people demanded independence, they would not oppose this, for in their view the Russian people and their government should not forcibly compel the Finnish people, any more than any other nation, to remain within the same union. The committee also severely criticised the policy of the Provisional Government on the question of increasing the privileges of Finland, pointing out that they themselves had not the slightest bit of confidence in the present government, which was the government of the capitalist class in Russia and was pursuing its imperialist interests. These Russian comrades thought the attitude of the Finns to the measures of the Provisional Government was too cautious and conciliatory: in their view, the Finns should even give up all attempts to influence the government by diplomatic means, and together with the Russians, declare war on it.

(*Työmies*, 10 May 1917. Written by E. Huttunen, one of the delegates sent by the party.)

93 A SOCIALIST ATTEMPT TO AMEND THE RUSSO–FINNISH RELATIONSHIP. MINUTES OF AN AUDIENCE WITH PRINCE L'VOV, 23 MAY 1917

... Senator Tokoi added that in regard to the main objections to the Finnish proposal, an understanding was reached the last time that the Provisional Government would be unable to decide the question of the transfer of certain matters to the competence of the Finnish Senate and the Governor-General before the Constituent Assembly met.[8] For this reason the Social Democratic group, forming the majority in the Diet, had privately discussed this matter and not wishing that the Provisional Government, at any event before the Constituent Assembly, should give up any of the prerogatives of supreme power, had composed a special

---

[8] This probably refers to Tokoi's previous discussions with members of the Provisional Government on 23 April.

proposal relating to this matter, having the character of an agreement between the Provisional Government and the Diet. Here Senator Tokoi handed printed copies of this proposal to Prince L'vov and Prince Shakhovskoy.[9]

The chairman of the constitutional committee [of the Diet], Mäkelin declared that this proposal did not essentially differ from that worked out by the Senate. He thought that the juridicial relationship of Russia and Finland had not ceased with the revolution. He declared that he could not understand why the Provisional Government hesitated in giving its approval to the Senate's proposal. Though not wishing to threaten in any way, he expressed grave misgivings as to what might happen were the proposal to be rejected by the Provisional Government. He announced that the movement for the complete independence of Finland was growing day by day because of the unwillingness of the Provisional Government to accept the proposal. He declared that if things went on like this, neither the Diet nor the Senate could be answerable for the consequences . . .

Mäkelin enquired if there were any answer he might take back to Helsinki?

Prince L'vov, in his résumé, said that hopes of some sort of agreement being reached within a month of the last negotiations were not justified : on the contrary, the differences of principle of 27 March[10] still remain and have even become more pronounced : the Russian governments believes in a oneness of power, whilst the Finnish governments consider that there are two juridicial aspects. It is true that revolutions are not foreseen in constitutions, but the governments of Russia, it seemed to the Minister-President, wished to remain on legal ground whilst the Finns for their part were proposing their own kind of revolution of the legal order : on such a matter, in the opinion of Prince L'vov, on such an important issue, there could only be an answer of 'yes' or 'no'.

[9] This proposal envisaged the transfer to the competence of the Senate of all matters hitherto the prerogative of the Tsar/Grand Duke, with the exception of such things which would alter the politico-juridicial relationship of Russia and Finland or affect the position of Russian citizens and institutions in Finland.

[10] It is not clear what this refers to: in all probability L'vov meant the Senate's proposals of 7 April. (new style).

('Kratkaya zapiska o chastom soveshchanii u Ministra-Predsedatelya Knyazya L'vova 10/23 maya 1917 g.' in *Ministerivaltiosihteerin viraston arkisto, 1917 asiakirjat*, no. 36, Finnish National Archives.)

94 'THE FIRST WARNING'

The words uttered by Kerensky a couple of days ago in Helsinki, which were loudly acclaimed by the soldiers and sailors listening to the Minister's speech, are a sign which the Finnish public would do well to mull over carefully.

... 'How often people seek to take unfair advantage of the kind-heartedness and open-mindedness of the Russian people? And here in Finland (the Minister here raised his voice) we must be particularly careful, for not only the Germans might interpret our generosity and our love as weakness and impotence.'

It is possible that people in Finland are not sufficiently aware of the significant fact that these words were spoken by such a person as Kerensky ... a man to whom the very idea of committing violence and coercion against other nationalities is repugnant ... But when he made his speech, when he spoke the above words, he was speaking with a very understandable resentment. He was not only speaking as the Minister of War and Navy, who is well aware that the Provisional Government under no circumstances may deprive its people of their rights to their national territory, but also as a political fighter, who has all his life served a firm ideal and who sees that there are those who wish to pervert that noble ideal. As a matter of fact, that which only a few weeks ago was a matter of conjecture is now becoming clear; there are sizeable groups in Finland which seek complete separation from Russia, and which imagine that this will be accomplished in the same way as the separation of Norway from Sweden, i.e. painlessly. A. F. Kerensky observes that this view is quite false, that Russia is at the present moment still strong enough to defend the integrity of her territory against anyone.

What kind of giddiness has seized the reserved and peaceful Finns? Can they not see that they have not and will not have the slightest chance of defeating Russia by force, that any attempt to use violence may lead to irreparable damage, for in these restless, frightening times may not the naval guns start firing of their own accord, without orders from Petrograd?

In what respects does the Provisional Government interfere with Finland's activities? Why provoke confusion? An attempt to take advantage of the momentary weakness of revolutionary Russia, which has just liberated Finland, can give birth to years of bitterness and frustration. Kerensky's words, moreover, show the folly of relying on Russia's weakness.

Kerensky, as well as the fleet and army under his authority – the men of which applauded him – are not for the time being the enemies, but the friends of Finland. The inexplicable tone of condescending impatience and arrogant implacability, which particularly in recent weeks has appeared in sections of the Finnish press and public towards Russia, has probably provoked this first warning. For Finland's sake, it is to be hoped that this warning is fully heeded.

(*Den'*, 12/25 May 1917; written by Ye Tarle.)

95   'THE LIBERTY OF FINLAND AND THE ATTITUDE OF THE RUSSIAN GOVERNMENT'

... When Minister Kerensky recently made a second visit to speak at the headquarters of the Helsinki workers' association,[11] this time to the Russian soldiers and sailors, his lips were heard to utter a warning, which has greatly surprised us. After assuring us that Russia is 'powerful, generous and great', he went on to remark 'how we (the Russians) have to be careful, how often people seek to use the open-mindedness of the Russian to unfair advantage, and here in Finland we must be especially careful, because not only the Germans might interpret our generosity and our love as weakness and impotence'. But also the Finns, he meant to add. To drive the point home, he continued, 'let no-one imagine that the Russian revolutionary people are weaker than the old Imperial power and that there is therefore no need to pay any attention to them'. ...

So far in Finland, only the oppressors have held power : Fin-

[11] Kerensky's first visit to Helsinki occurred at the end of March, when he spoke at the Helsinki workers' headquarters, and met leading Finnish socialists, to whom he gave assurances of favourable consideration for Finland's case.

nish and Russian oppressors, one after another. Now, for the first time in the country's history, the working people have a majority in the Diet. Now the worst class oppression in Finland ought to be brought to an end. The Finnish people ought to be freed from the oppressions and controls of Russian exploiters. The Finnish people's Diet ought to decide upon the form of the Finnish political system. But this is opposed by the Russian Provisional Government . . .

The question is simply one of the rights of the Finnish people to self-determination : no more, no less.

It is not therefore simply a question of a proposal made by the Senate. This is only meant as a temporary arrangement. And we are afraid that even a law along these lines might become merely a scrap of paper later on, when the propertied classes in Russia once more wish to oppress Finland. But its acceptance would nevertheless open the way to a conciliatory arrangement at the present moment, and for this reason, the Social Democratic parliamentary group has given it its support.

The former Russian system of government relied in many instances on the indirect or covert support of Finnish reactionaries. Without this support it would hardly have been able so frequently to reject the wishes and decisions of the Diet. Is a similar policy now being resurrected? Does the Russian government intend to follow the opinion of a small reactionary minority, because it does not attach any importance to the views of the majority in the Diet? Does it intend to follow advice which has never even seen the light of day here in Finland? . . .

The Russian government has now to decide which course it wishes to pursue. If it wishes to renew the fight against a small, unarmed nation that was pursued throughout the whole tsarist period, then we know at least that a part of the Russian people will certainly be on our side. We appeal to the class-conscious workers of Russia : and to the class-conscious social democratic workers of all other countries.

(*Työmies*, 27 May, 1917. Written by O. W. Kuusinen.)

96 TWO DIFFERING FINNISH VIEWS ON FINLAND'S POSITION – ARVID MÖRNE AND R. HERMANSON IN *ÅBO UNDERRÄTTELSER*, 3–4 MAY 1917

A. Mörne . . . It is obvious that the very composite Provisional Government, which must steer a great power through war and revolution, cannot in practice exercise the functions which the Senate has sought to take over in Finland. In the event of the Senate's proposal being rejected, the supreme government of Finland will fall into the hands of the private Russian citizens who are the advisers to the Provisional Government on Finnish affairs. Although these people now belong to the circle of friends of Finland and act in the spirit of the [March] manifesto, they could well be different people tomorrow, inspired by completely different points of view. The Provisional Government does not represent a unanimous position in the Finnish question. Not even all its members have signed the manifesto. Leaving aside the fact that we cannot relinquish the legal foundation upon which the Senate's request lies, it is clear to us that, if the Senate does not get the increased powers of authority it has demanded, both as regards the government of the country and the making of laws, a state of uncertainty will develop, in which 'freedom' runs the risk of becoming an empty word . . . The future is thus more than uncertain. If we want the nation to live, we must stop running after guarantees from a quarter where such things are not to be had. We have only one way out : *to try and change Finland's present constitutional position.*

There are two circumstances which could be thought of as providing the possibility for *the creation of an independent Finnish state.* The first lies in the power we ourselves dispose of if we all rally round the idea of independence. A precondition for unity is *a democratic constitution for Finland and the firmness of its social institutions* : a second precondition is *the work of social reform*, which has been given an impetus with the introduction of the eight-hour working day.[12] If the working people recognise that their welfare rests on sure ground within the protection of the Finnish state, their desire to defend the independence of that

[12] The eight-hour day was introduced in a number of industries following strikes and demonstrations in April, but the bill did not have its final reading until 14 July.

state will grow and strengthen. A rallying around the words of Tokoi ought to be possible.[13] Without such a coming together, independence cannot be conceived, even less preserved.

The second favourable circumstance lies in *the international character of the problem of Finnish statehood*. The time is past when the question of Finland's relationship to Russia was seen by the majority of the civilised nations as an internal Russian affair. The knowledge that the right of national self-determination must be one of the foundation stones in the rebuilding of Europe is gaining ground day by day amongst the peoples of both power groupings. This right can only be denied if it is used by certain individual ruling elements of a nation to stifle the efforts for reform of the labouring classes. But this is definitely not the case with Finland. And, leaving this aside, if any unfree nation seems destined for political independence on the grounds of national, historical and cultural distinctness, then it is surely the Finnish people.

R. Hermanson . . . As the relationship between Russia and Finland implies that the Emperor of Russia is the Grand Duke of Finland, and the arrangements for the succession to the throne is not a part of the Finnish constitution, and its alteration therefore does not fall within the competence of the Finnish legislative powers, it should therefore follow – this may well have been taken for granted – that, if the Emperor as a consequence of sickness, being under age, or for any other reason were prevented from directing government himself for any period of time, the provisional government in Russia ought to be recognised as that of Finland as well. The present Russian Provisional Government is certainly not a normal phenomenon, but the same circumstances which are the basis for the above reasoning indicate that the said government is now recognised in Finland as the provisional government of that country as well. As a provisional government it has already been recognised in Russia, and in Finland by the Diet, when it convened on the order of the said government and complied with its provisions concerning the manner of opening the Diet . . .

('Utveckling af Finlands statsrättsliga ställning', *Åbo Underrättelser*, 3, 4 May 1917.)

[13] This refers to Tokoi's speech of 20 April.

97 'THE FINNISH DEMAND FOR INDEPENDENCE': ARTICLE BY K. H. WIIK, FINNISH DELEGATE TO THE STOCKHOLM CONFERENCE,[14] 19 JUNE 1917

... The Russian revolution with its lofty principles convinced the Finnish people that the hour of their final deliverance had come ...

The events of recent days have been such as to confirm the view held in Finland that complete separation from Russia is the only way to avoid continued friction between the two countries. The Russian bourgeoisie and its Provisional Government has shown in no uncertain terms that it has in no way given up its imperialist leanings – in this respect, it shall suffice to mention the last congress of the Kadet party, where the majority under the leadership of Milyukov resolved to keep the old imperialistic programme. And with regard to Finland, this same policy has found expression in an obstinate refusal to concede the immediate extension of the autonomy of Finland, which the Finnish people have demanded as an absolute essential and which should be a direct application of the principles of the Russian revolution.

The Finnish people will not allow their future to be subjected to the interplay of forces in Russia. Imperialism is of course far from occupying an absolute position in Russian society, but it is still a force within that society and it should no longer be allowed to rule over the fate of our people. If the Finnish people now go their own way and arrange their future on an independent basis, they will be acting in accord with the principles of the Russian revolution, the principles of international social democracy, and in common concord with the truly revolutionary elements in Russia and in the rest of the whole world. Only on imperialistic grounds can one justify Finland being kept against its will under Russian dominance. There may be differences of opinion on what form of political position is from the practical point of view the most felicitous for Finland. But from a democratic point of view there can be no denying the people of Fin-

[14] This conference was called by a commission of socialists from neutral countries, and was given added significance by the outbreak of the Russian revolution and the adhesion of some of the Russian revolutionaries to the idea of the conference as a peace-seeking gathering. Wiik and Sirola were sent to present the case for Finnish independence.

land the right to decide for themselves what that position will be . . .

('Det finska sjalvständighetskravet', *Social-Demokraten*, 19 June 1917.)

98 ALEKSANDRA KOLLONTAY'S SPEECH TO THE FINNISH SOCIAL DEMOCRATIC PARTY CONFERENCE, 17 JUNE 1917

Comrades! In the name of the revolutionary wing of Russian social democracy, I greet you, who are fighting the common struggle for liberty, fighting against capitalist oppression. We have before us a common task and common interests link us in our struggle. These common tasks are the fight against imperialism and imperialist policy, against the imperialist policy of the Provisional Government. This Provisional Government, to which several socialists now belong, is pursuing the same policy of its predecessor (good!). Its policy has not changed at all. This policy of the Russian Provisional Government, especially its war policy, we Russian revolutionary social democrats, socialists, Bolsheviks, fiercely oppose.

It is quite clear that it is also in your interest to maintain an unyielding struggle against the war, for an end to the war (good!). At the same time, we also fiercely oppose the internal policy of the government. This policy of the government is clearly revealed in its oppression of small nations. Particularly noticeable is the attitude of the government towards the Finnish question. It is well known that so far no solution to the Finnish question has been found. The Provisional Government assures us that it will be finally settled by the National Assembly. But we do not know in what way it will be settled by the National Assembly. We revolutionary social democrats, on the other hand, demand that the question of Finland's independence ought to be settled whilst the revolutionary situation continues. And we support the granting of independence to Finland even to the extent of Finland's separation from Russia (shouts of approval, applause) . . .

(*Suomen sosialidemokraattisen puolueen yhdeksännen puoluekokouksen pöytäkirja*, (Helsinki 1917) p. 56.)

99 THE FINNISH SOCIAL DEMOCRATIC PARTY CONFERENCE RESOLUTION ON FINNISH INDEPENDENCE, 18 JUNE 1917

The relationship of Finland and Russia has long been one of oppression and conflict. It must now be changed into a free and secure relationship between the two peoples; the Finnish people must now be freed from political subjugation and tutelage.

The Russian revolution freed Finland as well as Russia from the serfdom of tsarist rule. But the throne of capitalism has not yet been overthrown in Russia, because economic development has not yet reached that stage there. Although it is now wavering, the Russian bourgeoisie may still be able to preserve class dominance on the extensive foundations of private property and the capitalist economy. The Russian bourgeoisie does not wish to relax its grip on Finland either. For reasons of class interest, the ruling bourgeoisie in Russia must sooner or later try to crush and oppress Finland if the opportunity offers itself, be that ruling power democratic, progressive or reactionary. This is why it now proclaims the principle of Russian statedom and sovereignty in response to the Finnish people's struggle for freedom. Russian sovereignty for the Finnish people means political subjugation and coercion by the powers-that-be in Russia, which can flourish just as well within the limits of autonomy which the Russian Provisional Government has now seen fit to offer Finland as within the limits of the autonomy enjoyed by Finland hitherto.

The welfare of the working class majority in Finland will not tolerate such a nightmare. The Russian government cannot be granted the right of confirming Finnish laws, because even the most vital reforms of the Diet might then be rejected in Petrograd to the joy and benefit of the bourgeois reactionaries in Finland, as so frequently was the case before. The Russian government cannot be granted the right to dissolve the Finnish Diet, nor to determine the session of the Diet. It is not right that the Russian government should be able to hinder the extension of the rights of the Diet, and the democratisation of the Finnish form of government in general, both of which are in the interests of the work-

ing class. The financial affairs of state and customs matters are
to be freely determined by the Diet, since if they remained under
the control of the Russian government, this could lead to demands
for forced tax contributions from the Finnish people, burdening
them and holding up their progress in the interests of Russian
capitalism. It is not right that the Russian government can influence the appointment of Finnish government members and
officials, for they may then become agents of oppression. The
Russian government has no rights whatsoever to be the supreme
governmental authority for the Finnish people; Finland must
have, as well as its own Diet, its own government, responsible to
the people and the people's Diet. The Finnish people do not need
a standing army, even when independent. It is however unjust
that the powers-that-be in Russia may keep troops and equip-
ment to Finland, even during peacetime, to further their annex-
ationist ambitions. For, although the Russian troops as private
individuals may be friends of the working people of Finland, the
military might of Russia, which is in normal times controlled by
the Russian bourgeoisie, is a danger to the freedom of the people
and is the backbone of all oppressors of the people.

Finnish social democracy therefore sets against the demand of
the Russian bourgeoisie for authority to subjugate the demand of
political independence for the Finnish people : for other than
within the framework of a Finnish state the Finnish working class
cannot carry on the class struggle undisturbed, safely hold on to
its gains or successfully fulfil its role in the international liberation
movement of the working class ...

The Finnish Social Democratic Party appeals for the support
of social democratic parties of all countries, and above all of those
of Russia for the winning and securing of Finnish independence.
Do not let the political future of the working people, the majority
in Finland, be cast adrift, at the mercy of the arbitrary power of
the Russian bourgeoisie. Finland's case is an international affair.
Adequate guarantees cannot be given by the Russian bourgeoisie
for the inviolability of Finnish liberty. This is why international
guarantees are required, in such a form and on such terms as are
acceptable to the principles of international social democracy and
the future of the Finnish people ...

('Suomen valtiollinen asema', *Työmies*, 19 June 1917.)

100   THE RESOLUTION ON FINLAND, APPROVED BY THE FIRST ALL-RUSSIAN CONGRESS OF SOVIETS, 3 JULY 1917.

Russian revolutionary democracy, which has always supported the fight of Finnish democracy against the russifying policies of tsarism and the Imperialist circles of the Russian bourgeoisie, announces in the name of the All-Russian Soviet congress its readiness to protect and defend, in accordance with its general policy with regard to the national question, the rights of the Finnish people to national self-determination, even to the extent of political independence.

Urging the Provisional Government to immediately embark upon the necessary measures for the realisation of full autonomy for Finland, the congress demands :

1. The Finnish Diet is to be granted the right to legislate and confirm all laws concerning Finland, with the exception of matters dealing with foreign policy, military legislation and military administration.

2. The Finnish Diet is to be granted the right to determine matters relating to the summoning and dissolution of Diets.

3. The Finnish people are to be granted the right to determine for themselves the executive power.

At the same time the congress, in accordance with the view of the Finnish Social Democratic party, regards the final solution of the Finnish question in its entirety as lying within the competence of the All-Russian National Constituent Assembly; only the victory of the revolution, which will be crowned by the founding of the Russian democratic republic, can safeguard the freedom of the Finnish people as well. The meeting therefore calls upon Finnish democracy and in particular upon Finnish social democracy to join the efforts of Russian democracy to secure the victory of the Russian revolution.

(*Revolyutsiya i natsionalny vopros*, vol. 3, (Moscow 1930) pp. 115–16.)

101 THE LAW CONCERNING THE EXERCISE OF SUPREME STATE POWER IN FINLAND, PASSED BY THE DIET ON 17–18 JULY 1917.

Let it be enacted : Whereas the rights of the ruler have ceased to exist, the following shall be valid in accordance with the decision of the Finnish Diet :

1. The Finnish Diet alone shall determine, confirm and order the execution of all the laws of Finland, including those concerned with state finances, taxation and customs. The Diet shall also finally determine all other matters concerning Finland which formerly were decided by the Emperor and Grand Duke in accordance with the laws then in force.

This shall not include matters of foreign policy, nor military legislation and administration.

2. The Diet shall convene as prescribed by law without any special summons and shall determine when the session of the Diet is to be concluded. Until the new form of government for Finland has been legislated, the Diet shall exercise the right in accordance with the Parliament Act (article 18) to decree the holding of new elections and the dissolution of the Diet.

3. The Diet shall decree the executive power in Finland. The highest executive authority shall for the time being be exercised by the Economic Department of the Senate, whose member will be placed in office and dismissed by the Diet.

(*Suomen historian dokumentteja*, vol. 2, (Helsinki 1970) p. 325.)

102 OPINION ON THE ORIGINS OF THE LAW ON SUPREME POWER

1. THE YOUNG FINN PARLIAMENTARY GROUP MEETING, 12 JULY 1917

Setälä : This latest turn to the question [was] quite new to members of the Senate, even Tokoi. Chkeidze had told Tanner that it was a surprise to them as well, they had never envisaged this sort of thing. The government (here) is breaking up, the non-socialist Senators [are] critical of the contents of the law. Military matters apparently would remain under Russian control. Not clear what will happen to internal affairs. Is it the intention to set up a government by proportional elections? Would professionals then be brought into government [if] all appointments were to rest with the Diet . . .

He was in favour of voting against the law and immediate promulgation of the law.[15] If the law is accepted, the government will have to resign.

Enckell: who had arrived from Petrograd, had rushed to seek the views of L'vov, Tsereteli and Kokoshkin soon after the decision of the soldiers' congress [i.e. Soviet congress]. Tsareteli did not reply, L'vov and Kokoshkin said that it was impossible to accept the decision.

Arokallio: A product of revolutionary conditions. The socialists too freely admit that the law is shapeless, but they dare not depart from the decision of the workers' and soldiers' congress. It does however clearly express the independence of the Finnish people and this is the wish of the whole nation. The people demand this declaration from the Diet, it must be said straight out to Russia and to Europe. Enckell [is] unsuitable for his post, he is a great friend of the Entente, a friend of L'vov, and a big businessman himself. He is under the influence of the Kadets.

. . . This law is not a vote of no confidence in the government, but is intended to get away as far as possible from Russia. Strongly defended voting in favour of the law . . .

All voted for immediate promulgation, nine spoke for the law, and five against.

(Notes of the meeting in: Tekla Hultin collection, file LI b, Finnish National Archives.)

2. EXTRACTS FROM KARL WIIK'S DIARY, JULY 1917

[11 July]

Home 8 a.m., 2 p.m. to town; Chkeidze there with several others.[16] 4 p.m. dispute [between the Russians and] Kuusinen on the way to deal with the law.

[15] The Parliament Act specified a majority of two-thirds for the passing of a measure of constitutional importance, and five-sixths for the bill to be immediately promulgated.

[16] This was a group of leading non-Bolshevik delegates to the Soviet congress, sent by the L'vov government to persuade the Finns to drop the proposed law on supreme power.

Dan (Dr Fedor Dan, Russian Menshevik): (1) do we recognise the Constituent Assembly (2) do we recognise the military question as all-Russian or do we wish to resolve it now by an interim law (3) all-Russian institutions: the State Bank and Treasury (4) shall the Russian government together with the Diet take action to clear up the all-Russian questions (5) do we accept the summoning of the Diet to extra [ordinary session] (6) shall we carry out [the law] without the Provisional Government or by agreement with [the government], which enjoys the full support of Russian democracy.

Kuusinen answered: (1) regarding the contents of the congress resolution, two parts.[17] *Dan*: our resolution implies sanction from the temporary government. The law is faulty, as it does not say what is to be done with foreign policy and the military question. *Kuusinen*: you must then urge the government to follow the decision of the soldiers' congress. There will be no conflict on the military issue. This is provisional.

[12 July]

7 p.m. [parliamentary] group [meeting] . . . The question of 'the Senate's powers'. Huttunen . . . gave an account of yesterday's discussions with the Russians. As representatives of the Mensheviks and SRs,[18] they have supported the government, and cannot let its authority suffer; the law must be ratified . . . They asked if we regarded the congress decision of the soldiers' soviets as law. They said that we are too optimistic, for the Social Democrats are not masters of the situation. They continued (the meeting) at the hotel Fennia and tried to persuade us to modify the law and then submit it to the Russian government. Then the definitive settlement [could be] left to the Constituent Assembly. Here they learnt that the law had been approved on the second reading, [and] they acknowledged that the [socialist parliamentary] group could not go back. They suggested that we should send a deputation to Petrograd, having postponed the third reading for a couple of days, and then the government would prepare a manifesto. This way the government would save its face. Huttunen said at this: we have tried this one before . . . They replied:

[17] For the resolution, see document 100. The 'two parts' are the three proposals, and the final paragraph, which the Finns did not much care for.

[18] Socialist-Revolutionaries.

now the situation is different: the government must take the decision of the soldiers' soviet congress into account.

(*Karl H. Wiiks Dagboksanteckningar från åren 1917–18*, p. 34, Finnish National Archives.)

103 THE PROVISIONAL GOVERNMENT'S MANIFESTO ORDERING THE DISSOLUTION OF THE DIET, 31 JULY 1917

The Provisional Government has received the address of the Diet, dated 12/25 July, as well as the text of its resolution, independently determined, concerning the exercise of supreme authority in Finland.

On the basis of its constitution, Finland enjoys internal independence only within the prescribed limits of the juridicial relationship between Finland and Russia, an independence which has always been regarded as founded on the principle of supreme authority being in the hands of one power common to both countries. With the abdication of the last Emperor, his full powers, including those rights over the Grand Duchy of Finland, could only pass to the possessor of the sovereignty entrusted by the Russian people, the Provisional Government. Otherwise the rights over the Grand Duchy would have to be considered as belonging to him to this day.

The Provisional Government, which has publicly sworn to maintain the rights appertaining to the people of the Russian state, cannot surrender these rights before the Constituent Assembly has made its decision.

In considering itself still bound to protect and advance the internal independence of Finland in accordance with its manifesto of 7/20 March of this year, the Provisional Government cannot at the same time grant the Finnish Diet the right to encroach arbitrarily upon the will of the Constituent Assembly and to abolish Russian authority in matters concerning the legislation and governance of Finland.

The decisions reached by the Diet do however alter fundamentally the juridicial relationship between Russia and Finland and gravely violate the Finish constitution.

Let the Finnish people weigh up their fate. It can only be decided by agreement with the Russian people.

Having ordered new elections to be held within the shortest space of time possible on 1 and 2 October (new style) of this year, the Provisional Government has seen fit to dissolve the session of the Diet convoked on 22 March/4 April and to order the convention of a new Diet by 1 November of this year; and let all those elected resort to the town of Helsinki at the time to be stipulated more precisely to fulfil their duties in accordance with the Parliamentary Act.

When the session of the Diet opens, the government will present a bill for deliberation concerning the settlement of Finland's internal affairs.

(*Suomen Suuriruhtinaanmaan Asetuskokoelma*, no. 50. (Helsinki 1917))

104 THE FINNISH SOCIALIST CASE, PRESENTED TO INTERNATIONAL SOCIAL DEMOCRACY, AUGUST 1917

[After a brief résumé of developments leading up to the March manifesto, the article deals with the constitutional conflict.]

But even then [March] there arose a constitutional issue : could a Russian government take upon itself the powers which had earlier appertained to the monarch in Finland? The question is by no means a juridicial one, but it is also of extremely important significance for democracy . . . If, the Finns argue, a revolutionary Russian government accords itself the right to interfere in internal Finnish affairs, then this right passes from one government to the next, and the Finns have thereby renounced a basic principle of their autonomy. And the Finnish Social Democrats cannot understand how a revolutionary government, which has proclaimed the rights of national self-determination as a basic principle, can set itself against such demands.

[The socialist party conference resolution on independence is printed in full.]

It has been said that the demand for independence is nationalistic and that such 'small statism'[19] is inappropriate in a time of

[19] 'Kleinstaatlerei', a term used by Kautsky to describe the Finnish socialists' position.

large-scale economic development. There is certainly an element of nationalism concealed in the demand of the Finnish people for independence, but for social democracy it is a matter of democratic gain. Perhaps we would be understood if we spoke of the possibility of bourgeois Russia pursuing a nationalist and therefore imperialist policy against which we are seeking to defend ourselves. Why should a bourgeois Russian government stand over the representatives of the Finnish people? And why should Finland pay contributions to Russian imperialism?

But if Russia becomes a federation of republics, will Finland not find its place there? This is what we are asked, and my reply is: if we obtain guarantees that this is necessary from a democratic and a progressive point of view, then naturally our own interests will compel us to join. But first, the right of self-determination must be acknowledged . . . And it depends on Russia to what extent Finland will voluntarily associate itself with [such a federation].

The demand for international guarantees has also been sharply criticised. I am referring to the resolution [of the party conference] itself. If it is not yet possible to obtain such guarantees, which from the point of view of international social democracy is desirable, then there should be a promise to put forward this demand . . .

[The article quotes the Soviet congress resolution on Finland in full, and goes on to comment on the last paragraph.]

The last paragraph of this resolution embodies the erroneous conception that Finnish social democracy has entrusted the Russian Constituent Assembly with the task of finally resolving the Finnish question. As the resolution of the Finnish Social Democratic party conference shows, the Finnish view is that the position of Finland is not an internal Russian affair any longer, but is of international significance . . .

('Die Erreignisse in Finnland während der Revolutionszeit', (Yrjö Sirola) *ISK Nachrichtendienst*, no. 19, 16 August 1917).

105   AN ATTEMPT TO RESOLVE THE IMPASSE – THE 'OPEN LETTER' OF 12 SEPTEMBER 1917

With the dissolution of the Diet on 31 July, the work of pushing through the extensions to self-government promised in the March Manifesto had suffered a setback, and a certain amount of disquiet began to manifest itself in leading circles in Helsinki. It was feared that, if the rumours of a Russian dictatorship should come true, Finland would not have taken sufficient advantage of the Russian revolution and would not have accrued such advantages that would have to be recognised as established facts by any reactionary regime which might occur in Russia. Therefore it was proposed that some of the powers of the former monarch such as the appointment of civil servants, the drafting of edicts etc., should be transferred to the Senate; this the Provisional Government could decide upon without the Diet being involved, since the monarch had been able to transfer the said powers to another Finnish authority of his own volition, without changes in the constitution. The proposal was drawn up by the bourgeois members of the Senate after the resignation of the socialists, and the temporary vice-chairman, Setälä, asked me to sound out Kerensky's possible attitude to the proposal. Kerensky had no objection to it, he told me that he was even happy that such a step before the elections would arouse sympathy for the Provisional Government in Finland and would be seen as evidence of the willingness of the latter to meet Finland's justifiable desire for increased self-government . . .

[Kerensky eventually signed the 'Open Letter' on 12 September, in the midst of the Kornilov revolt. No other member of the Provisional Government signed the document.]

The reception accorded the open letter 'concerning the transfer of certain matters to the Finnish Senate's competence' by the press in Finland was in many respects influenced by the uncertain atmosphere and the party conflicts before the election. The analysis of the letter was in part vague. The government was criticised for having sought to bring about a compromise after the failure of the law on supreme authority, and in some quarters there was a failure to understand the fact that the open letter was in no way aimed at seeking a solution to the question of the legitimate exercise of supreme authority in Finland . . .

(C. Enckell, *Politiska minnen*, vol. 1 (Helsingfors 1956) p. 114, 117–18.)

106   ELECTORAL PROPAGANDA, AUTUMN 1917

1. 'THE FINNISH PARTIES IN ELECTORAL PACT'

. . . Now, when all serious-minded elements in our society are aware that the immediate and pressing need of the fatherland is the formation of a strong common front against the irresponsibility and class selfishness of our socialist party, which has squandered great opportunities for extending the independence of our country and has pushed our internal state of affairs to the brink of anarchy – now, when we must hold new elections, which must bring an end to socialist rule here, the necessity and logic of a union of the Finnish parties has come out particularly strongly. In different electoral circles, organisations of both parties have decided to join forces in the election as a common bloc, here and there even putting up joint candidates. Last Sunday both the Old and Young Finn party councils approved of the sealing of an electoral pact between the two parties. Grasping the exigencies of the situation, both party councils have also supported the idea of sealing electoral compacts with other non-socialist parties, and cannot but greatly regret what seems to be a lack of understanding of this on the part of the Agrarians, who should be closest in uniting with both Finnish parties . . .

('Suomalaiset puolueet vaaliliitossa', *Uusi Suometar*, 21 August 1917.)

2. 'ELECTORAL MANIFESTO OF THE INDEPENDENCE LINE'

Citizens of Finland!

You are being called to one of the most important elections of our country's history. This election will affect Finland's future, perhaps for centuries to come. In it an answer must be given to the question, do the Finnish people demand full independence for themselves, and do they regard it as their right to take into their hands the dominion of their own country.

In violation of our rights, the Russian government has dissolved the Diet of the Finnish people. It has been prevented from convening by armed force. Let now the perpetrator of violence hear from the mouths of the people that they are united behind the demand for independence.

There is not one party in Finland which in principle is opposed to the demand for independence. But we must not stop at this. The Diet must now proclaim in word and deed this vital necessity of our people. Our right to self-determination must be recognised and our people's absolute desire to be free and politically independent must be expressed. This resolution must be presented to the Constituent National Assembly in Russia and to all civilised peoples. The voice of our people must be heard at the peace conference. The freedom of our country must be internationally recognised.

Only as an independent people, separated from the fate of an alien people, free of undisciplined Russian troops and an untrustworthy alien bureaucracy, can our people organise their own affairs and fulfil their national ideals. Only on this foundation can peace, security and order be returned to our fatherland.

Citizens of Finland, vote for enlightened and fearless supporters of independence in the elections to the Diet.

Helsinki, 6 September 1917
CENTRAL COMMITTEE FOR THE
INDEPENDENCE LINE

('Itsenäisyyssuunnan vaalijulistus', *Uusi Päivä*, 11 September 1917.)

3. 'RISE YE FROM THE NIGHT OF OPPRESSION!'

. . . The security and hope of the oppressed is to be found in the Diet. Even the greatest exploiters must fear the decisions of the Diet. They got a shock after last year's elections when the people chose as guardians of their interests a majority of social democrats. And the upper classes got a second shock in spring, when the Emperor was overthrown and the Diet began its work.

The Diet passed a provisions law, democratic local government laws, and an eight-hour working day in industry and skilled crafts. The Diet also legislated on the responsibility of members of the government to the Diet, on reforms in the Supreme Courts, and extended the law preventing the eviction of tenant-farmers, as well as other useful laws.

For the first time in the history of the Finnish Diet, the main aim of the Diet was the safeguarding of the rights of the oppressed. But the work was interrupted.

Representatives of the capitalist parties fought bitterly against these reforms. When they were unable to prevent them in the Diet, they hoped that the Russian government would reject them. This the majority in the Diet did not tolerate. The Diet on the contrary, passed a constitutional law which would give the final powers of decision in the internal affairs of the Finnish people to the Diet of Finland.

The gentlemen of the parties of exploitation here in Finland rose against this in collusion with bourgeois power in Russia. The Diet was unlawfully ordered to dissolve. The senators of the bourgeois parties, together with the Governor-General, published this unlawful order. And the people's Diet was prevented from convening by force, by armed dragoons.

But the more powerful is the cry which echoes over the whole of Finland, the demand of the majority of the people :

Freedom from the subjugation of the Russian bourgeoisie !

That subjugation is oppressive, greedy and dangerous to the future of the Finnish people. That power would also be a permanent aid and support for the reactionary circles in Finland and a coercive barrier to democratic progress in our country.

The declaration, contrary to the constitutional laws of the country, that supreme authority in Finland has been transferred to ministers in Russia is a gross betrayal of the people by the Old Finn, Swedish and Young Finn party leaders. This Stolypinite lie must be opposed by the proclamation of the inalienability of the rights of Finland by the vast majority of our people.

The right of self-determination and independence for our people must be demanded. Not one inch must be ceded of the law on Finland's internal freedom, passed by the Diet . . .

('Sorron yöstä nouskaa !' *Työmies*, 15 September 1917.)

107 THE DECLINING AUTHORITY OF THE PRO-VISIONAL GOVERNMENT IN FINLAND: RESO-LUTION OF THE REGIONAL COMMITTEE IN FINLAND,[20] 3 OCTOBER 1917

Comrades – soldiers, sailors and workers.

Supreme state power has hitherto been founded upon the co-operation of classes. Two hostile forces, irreconcilable by their very nature, strive for power: democracy and the bourgeoisie (or the coalition).

The whole course of our revolution has shown how bankrupt and corrupt is the power of this coalition. So far, the land remains in the hands of the landowners, no control over production has been decreed, the democratisation of the army has not been carried out, the secret tsarist treaties have not been published and there has not been a single effort by the government to bring an end to the war by open appeal to all the belligerent nations, for peace without annexations or contributions, on the basis of national self-determination. The coalition has already given rise to four crises of power, allowed the Kornilov conspiracy to mature, and finally, the coalition government has decreed the immediate dissolution of Tsentroflot,[21] encroaching upon the rights of the supreme organ of the All-Russian naval fleet.

There is no place for such a government.

Only power which corresponds to the interests of revolutionary democracy, free of the influences of capitalist circles, and leading towards revolutionary democracy can control the course of the revolutionary struggle for peace, bread and liberty.

Until such power comes into being, the Regional Committee in Finland is taking over direct control of all government institutions in Finland and informs all military organisations that not a single order of the coalition government . . . shall be carried out without the consent of the Regional Committee.

Authority in Finland has in fact passed into the hands of democracy, the only force capable of defending the interests of free countries.

[20] The Regional Committee was the overall co-ordinating body for the Soviets in Finland.

[21] Tsentroflot was the overall co-ordinating committee for the fleet committees, and was dissolved in the aftermath of the July Days' uprising.

('Ot oblastnoi komiteta v Finlyandii', *Izvestiya Gel'singforskogo Soveta*, 22 September/5 October 1917.)

108 THE FINAL ATTEMPT TO SEEK ACCOMMODATION WITH THE PROVISIONAL GOVERNMENT, NOVEMBER 1917

1. MEETING OF REPRESENTATIVES OF THE NON-SOCIALIST PARTIES, 3 NOVEMBER

Ståhlberg bitterly criticised the law on supreme authority, which would overturn our whole constitution. All power would be concentrated in the Diet. He described how the Diet could take one decision after another on the powers of government . . .

Setälä announced that Enckell had come from Petrograd with news of his visit to Kerensky. Kerensky was not prepared to sort out the conflict with the Finnish bourgeoisie, which was at odds with itself. He threatened to close the frontier and to stop any foodstuffs entering the country, and to let loose the Russian troops. Kerensky does not intend under any circumstances to accept the law on supreme authority . . .

2. THE DRAFT MANIFESTO OF THE NON-SOCIALIST PARTIES, 6 NOVEMBER

[This vaguely-worded document, which avoided the issue of who should exercise supreme authority, was taken to Petrograd on the eve of the revolution by the Governor-General. It proved to be a dead letter.]

The manifesto of the Provisional Government to the Finnish Diet and the citizens of Finland.

The Imperial authority having been overthrown, it has become necessary to establish the juridicial relationship of Russia and Finland and the exercise of supreme authority in Finland. As the realisation of the constitutional arrangements by which this settlement will finally be made will take time, the Provisional Government has therefore wished to offer the Finnish people the opportunity now to arrange their own internal affairs on the basis of the Finnish constitution, so that the Finnish people may freely develop their material and spiritual culture within the safeguards of their own judicial system and social institutions. The Provisional Government has therefore decided to surrender executive power in Finland, with the proviso that foreign affairs remain as hitherto within the competence of supreme executive authority in Russia and that Finland does not amend military legislation or legislation or legislation concerning Russian institutions and citizens in Finland without the consent of the Russian government. Furthermore, the Governor-General and his assistants, named by the Russian government, shall be freed from their duties as Finnish officials and the Chancery of the Governor-General shall cease to exist as a Finnish administrative office.

(1 : Minutes of the meeting in the Tekla Hultin collection, file LI b, Finnish National Archives. 2 : K. G. Idman, *Maamme itsenäistymisen vuosilta*, (Porvoo 1953) p. 176.)

The November Crisis and the Declaration of Independence

By the end of October, labour leaders in Finland were virtually unanimous in their belief that a crisis point was approaching (109). Stung by their electoral defeat and spurred on by the increasing impatience of the working masses with the parliamentary tactic, the labour movement switched to a policy of bringing pressure to bear on the rump bourgeois Senate through the threat of a general strike if a programme of social and political reforms – 'We demand' – were not immediately implemented. Knowledge of imminent revolution in Russia and a consciousness of the uncompromising mood of the red guards, organised by the workers and officially endorsed by the party from mid-September, added impetus to the new tactic (110). Nevertheless, the Revolutionary Central Council set up to direct the strike shrank from taking a decision to seize power on 12 November, and once again turned away from the brink on 16 November (111). The decision of the moderate majority within the Social Democratic parliamentary group to support the Agrarian motion transferring supreme power to the Diet was a decisive turning-point. The party radicals were unable to retain the support of the trade unionists for a revolutionary seizure of power, and had no alternative but to end the strike. Kuusinen's analysis of the situation on 25 November graphically illustrates the inability of the left wing of the party to choose between revolutionary means and parliamentary action, a confusion reflected in the ambiguously phrased final resolution on tactics of the party conference (112).

On 26 November the non-socialist majority in the Diet voted its approval of the Svinhufvud list of ministers. In his government programme, Svinhufvud had significantly spoken of safeguarding Finnish independence, which the Finnish people had already morally laid claim to since the Russian government had

forfeited its rights (113). It soon became clear that Finnish inde-
pendence was to be safeguarded by a restoration of law and order
and the ejection of Russian troops: the Svinhufvud government
also refused to negotiate with Russia, as the socialists now de-
manded (114). In Germany the activists renewed their efforts
to obtain German military support at a time when the Imperial
German army was advancing into the Baltic provinces (116).
The Svinhufvud government was finally compelled to turn to the
Soviet government at the end of December, after Sweden and
Germany had made it plain that recognition was contingent upon
Russian approval of Finnish independence. The Soviet govern-
ment placed no obstacles in the way, but some of its members
expressed their open disappointment to Finnish socialists that they
seemed more concerned with the granting of independence than
the revolutionary seizure of power by the workers (119, 120).

109   THE GROWING CRISIS – EXTRACTS FROM K. H. WIIK'S DIARY, OCTOBER–NOVEMBER 1917

[27 October]

[Meeting of the Social Democratic Party executive, at which the immediate demands of the party were formulated: these were to be the basis of the 'We demand' programme of the party.]

Kuusinen did not regard all these points worth making a revolution for at the present. But there will be a revolutionary upsurge in Russia in November and this will have an effect on Finland . . .
Manner: We can no longer even discuss whether or not there will be a revolutionary movement at the beginning of November. The trade union council, the attitude of the bourgeoisie, the formation of the red guards are circumstances which will force a popular movement upon us, even if there is not one in Russia. Whether we can restrain the movement is very uncertain . . .
Gylling: Extraordinarily difficult for us to direct affairs here with a dictatorship of the proletariat. We must therefore try to calm things down.
Kuusinen: We cannot put off things for long, maybe till the middle of November, when we can decide in the light of events in Russia. In the event of a Russian revolution, we will no longer be able to calm things down . . .

[8 November]
6 o'clock meeting at the [Governor-General's] palace with Manner, Turkia, Kuusinen, Pietikäinen, Gylling, Torniainen, Wiik, Rahja and eleven Russians.

Sheinman : Revolution in Russia, although the fight still goes on . . . We intend to have dealings only with the Finnish proletariat. What sort of steps do you want us to take on your behalf? We must answer both for the political and the strategic situation. Russian authority in Finland has ceased, and you have to choose commissars. Your upper class surley does not support Germany for Germany's sake, but out of class sympathy (?) What do you want in the way of help from us, and what help can you give us?

Kuusinen : offered congratulations. This is a success for the European revolution. We have set up a revolutionary central committee . . . twenty-seven in number, which will draft proposals for measures and directives for tomorrow. Could you nominate a couple of people to help us arrange matters, amongst other things, the setting up of a joint commissariat.

Sheinman : we bear the responsibility now both for the revolution and the war. We want to know that we shall not meet with any opposition from Finnish social democracy. We mean to declare a state of war in Finland, directed (1) against the bourgeois guards (2) against German spies. Shishko and Rahja chosen as commissars in the Chancery of the Governor-General. The Bank of Finland must not be interfered with, we must be able to pay the troops. We must have your support, perhaps even to the extent of your overthrowing the government by force. We can support you in your fight, but the initiative must be yours. You must fight against the proposed treaty between the Finnish and the Russian bourgeoisie.[1] If you insist upon Finland's high-sounding rights, Finland will become like another Belgium. We shall arrange things in a social democratic fashion, so that no-one shall suffer; take your point of view into consideration. The red guards can arm themselves for free. Our funds exhausted.

A worker asked if we could seize power today or tomorrow.

Kuusinen added that our plan was to seize power this very week.

I [*Wiik*] : We hope to obtain foodstuffs from Russia.

A Russian worker announced they would help us to obtain food-

---

[1] This probably refers to the planned transfer of certain powers to the Senate.

stuffs only in the event of power passing to the workers. Otherwise it would be (seeking co-operation, i.e. with the bourgeoisie)
. . .

Kuusinen : We are well aware that the cause of the proletariat is bound up with that of the revolution . . .

I asked what advantage there was in an edict declaring a state of war. A Russian worker, who might have been called *Debenko*,[2] replied that it would be used against the bourgeois guards. Up to now the state of war had been directed against the workers, after this, against the bourgeoisie . . .

    (Karl H. Wiik, *Dagboksanteckningar från åren 1917–1918*, p. 63, 68, Finnish National Archives.)

110 FINNISH POLITICAL OPINION ON THE QUESTION OF SUPREME AUTHORITY AFTER THE BOLSHEVIK REVOLUTION IN RUSSIA

1. MEETING OF REPRESENTATIVES OF THE NON-SOCIALIST PARTIES, 8 NOVEMBER

Talas spoke of his recent conversation with [the socialists] Huotari and Huttunen, who assured him that their group remained true to the law on supreme authority. Talas observed that this law was now out-of-date in that there should no longer be any need to give up control over foreign and military affairs. Power should therefore simply be transferred to the Diet, in accordance with the principles of the law on supreme authority, and the Diet would then immediately transfer its executive powers to the Economic Department of the Senate. The socialists said that they could not accept the institution of a regency[3] . . .

Alkio : . . . If we approve the manifesto, the final phrasing of which we cannot control, and the socialists oppose it, then the

---

   [2] Probably, Pavel Dybenko, the chairman of the central committee of the Baltic Fleet, who was present at this meeting.

   [3] The idea of a three-man regency had been discussed by the non-socialist parties in the autumn, but was dropped in the face of Agrarian opposition. It was revived on 8 November, when a motion calling for the election of such a regency was put to the Diet by the Speaker. After the Agrarian motion for the immediate promulgation of the law on supreme authority had been defeated by the socialist programme 'We demand', the Agrarians found themselves forced to vote with the other non-socialist parties for the Speaker's motion, which therefore defeated the socialist programme.

bourgeoisie will have to answer for all the anarchy that will be caused. The law on supreme authority is the only possibility of preserving civil peace in the land . . .

2. TRADE UNION CONGRESS RESOLUTION, 12 NOVEMBER

To the organised workers of Finland :

The Trade Union Delegate Congress now in session has decided having considered ways of staving off the hunger and misery threatening the workers, to associate itself with the ultimatum put forward on 20 October by the Trade Union Council to the Finnish Senate, a demand which the workers of this country have made their own. The reply of the Senate to this demand does not satisfy this congress. A few promises are indeed made, but the government has not even properly tried to put its own promises into practice.

The workers have looked for protection from the country's Diet in this deperate hour. But the bourgeois majority has seen to it that the Diet has spent almost two weeks in session doing nothing. Vital and valuable time has thus been wasted . . . For this reason the Trade Union Delegate Congress demands that the Diet must this very day show whether or not it wishes and is able to help the workers in this desperate situation.

To save the working people of this country from starvation and to enable them to develop their own livelihoods, it is essential that the legislature as well as the executive power of our country be immediately organised on democratic principles. The Trade Union Delegate Congress therefore demands, in common accord with the 'We demand' programme of the Social Democratic parliamentary group and the party council, that the Diet in its session beginning at 1.30 p.m. today must order the Senate to promulgate immediately the law on the exercise of supreme authority in Finland, passed by the Diet on 18 July last . . . the law on the eight-hour working day, the local government laws and the law on the right of the Finnish Diet to assess the legitimacy of the government and its actions as well as other laws confirmed by the Diet on the basis of the above-mentioned law on supreme authority.

If the Diet does not now start to carry out the reforms demanded and long awaited by the workers in the way outlined above, this will be seen as an indication that the Finnish bourgeoisie does not intend to set about an effective amelioration of the living standards of the working people, such as the abolition of the misery of food shortages, the curbing of unemployment and the emendation of many other crying injustices, but intends to leave the workers exposed to hunger and misery.

This being so, the congress sees no other way to save the desperate plight of the working people other than the immediate commencement by the organised Finnish workers of a vigorous and forceful fight against the bourgeoisie for their rights and for bread. To this end, the Delegate Congress orders workers organised in the trade union movement to be ready to start a general and nationwide strike on receipt of orders.

The responsibility for these measures shall fall solely upon the bourgeoisie.

(1 : Minutes of the meeting in the Tekla Hultin collection, file LI b, Finnish National Archives. 2 : *Toiset valtiopäivät 1917*, *Pöytäkirjat* vol. 1. pp. 98–9.)

111 THE ABORTIVE SEIZURE OF POWER – THE GENERAL STRIKE, NOVEMBER 1917

1. SIROLA'S ACCOUNT OF THE ACTIVITIES OF THE REVOLUTIONARY CENTRAL COUNCIL

. . . The Bolshevik seizure of power in Petrograd seemed to offer the long-awaited opportunity for the Finnish proletariat to settle accounts with the propertied classes. This was especially evident in the fact that the popular movement in different parts of the country seemed to have exceeded the limits which had been defined in Helsinki . . .

A vital vote took place at the meeting of the Council on 12 November. The proposal 'that for the time being the bourgeoisie is to be pressured to carry out the "We demand" programme' was accepted, by eighteen votes, as against eight votes for a proposal 'to take power immediately into the hands of the workers' . . .

2. THE STRIKE DEMANDS OF THE REVOLUTIONARY CENTRAL COUNCIL, 14 NOVEMBER

1. The government must organise effective means to combat the shortage of foodstuffs and unemployment, bearing in mind

the proposals of the Trade Union Council and the demands of organised labour.

2. The law on supreme authority, passed by the Diet, is to be declared valid and in force.

3. All other laws passed by the Diet during the summer are likewise to be immediately brought into force, especially the eight-hour working day act and the local government laws.

4. Firm guarantees must be given that old age pensions, taxation of high incomes and capitalist war profiteering will be realised and that a start will finally be made on freeing the tenant farmers, as well as the extension of political suffrage to all over twenty years of age. As the best guarantee for the fulfilment of these demands we demand the calling of a Constituent National Assembly.

3. DIFFERENCES IN THE SOCIALIST CAMP: MINUTES OF THE SOCIAL DEMOCRATIC PARLIAMENTARY GROUP'S MEETING, 14 NOVEMBER

[The meeting was asked to consider a proposal made by the Agrarians for a motion to be put in the Diet for the transfer of supreme authority to the Diet, in accordance with the terms of the 18 July law. This provoked the following reaction from the Revolutionary Central Council.]

The Social Democratic parliamentary group ought to know that, since its initiatives and demands in the Diet have not led to any kind of result, the organised workers of Finland have taken it upon themselves to press these demands . . . Furthermore, the Council wishes to inform the group that with the situation at its present stage, they have no authority to decide upon matters which are the concern of the Council, and it urges the group to tell the Agrarians that it is the view of the Council that they should turn to the workers' Revolutionary Central Council if they wish to negotiate on these matters . . .

V. Jokinen: Two organs ought not to be fighting each other at a time of crisis. One must submit to the organ with the determining authority . . .

Jalava: Many members of the group do not approve of the dictatorial power which the Central Council is trying to exercise over the group . . .

[The meeting finally voted 54 to 13 to support the Agrarian initiative, thereby decisively rejecting the view of the Central Council.]

4. THE AGRARIAN MOTION, APPROVED BY 127 TO 68 VOTES IN THE DIET, 15 NOVEMBER

Since it has not yet been possible to elect the regency council, to which the Diet has decided to grant the exercise of supreme executive authority in Finland, the Diet resolves to exercise itself, for the time being, the power which appertained to the Emperor-/Grand Duke according to existing statutes.

5. REVOLUTION DEFERRED – MEETING OF THE REVOLUTIONARY CENTRAL COUNCIL, 16 NOVEMBER

[In the early hours of the morning of the 16th, the Diet voted to accept the immediate promulgation of the eight-hour day and the local government laws.]

After these decisions had been taken by the Diet in the early hours of 16 November, the Council met to consider the situation. On behalf of the Helsinki workers' guard, it was announced that the opinion amongst its members was that what had been done so far was unsatisfactory, and that the workers ought to seize power throughout the country. The convention of labour organisations in Helsinki took the same view.

The position was weighed up in the ensuing discussion. A number of speakers observed that, since some concessions had been obtained from the Diet, a section of the workers might think a continuation of the strike unnecessary ... It was also suggested that now might be the time to try and bring about some sort of coalition government in which the socialists would hold the decisive majority. A motion to this effect, which argued for an even stronger pressure being put upon the bourgeoisie by strike action until the formation of this coalition government, was however rejected by fourteen votes to eleven. The majority thought that the struggle had to be continued further, with an effort to take power into the hands of the workers. Most of those left in the minority announced that they would loyally abide by the decision of the majority ...

[The Council was then reorganised, its twenty-seven members being reduced to sixteen. The trade union members had already showed signs of backing out of the decision to seize power, and this soon became apparent in the decision of the reformed Council.]

The reformed Council met and considered that, since such a large minority was of a different opinion, the Council could not this time promote the seizure of power by the workers, but would work on to increase the pressure on the bourgeoisie.

6. THE DECISION TO END THE STRIKE, 17 NOVEMBER

[At a confused meeting of the Council on 17 November, it was decided to call off the strike; the following proclamation was issued the following day, with dissenting comments added by the trade unionists.]

Class struggle without a general strike.
Working men and women of Finland!
The offensive of our common mighty struggle, which took the form of a general strike, has now been completed.
The bourgeoisie's dark schemes for seizing power have been dashed to the ground. They failed to win the Imperial powers for their Senate or their three kings, as they sought to do. Authority has been acknowledged as resting with the people's Diet. A more democratic basis has been provided for communal politics . . . Likewise the eight-hour working day for industrial and craft workers has been confirmed. Without the workers' general strike the bourgeoisie would probably have emasculated or destroyed these reforms.
Bread has not however been obtained, nor is there any certainty in general of any alleviation of the wretched food shortage or of the prevention of black marketeering. A general strike is of no help here. On the contrary, if the general strike at such a time were to be continued for long, farmers and other profiteers would have an even better chance of persecuting the striking workers through shortages of milk, meat, butter and even bread, and employers could also put the screws on by stopping wages. This is why the fight must be continued in a different guise, in the Diet and outside it, not simply in the form of a general strike.
The form of the struggle may change, but the struggle does not. The weapons of our workers' guards must be kept in safe stores. Prisoners taken by the guards are to be set free, but in

return we demand an absolute assurance from the bourgeoisie that men on the labour side are to be free of all harassment by officials for any deeds committed during the strike . . .

Our Central Council is now terminating its functions and will dissolve, transferring its powers to the Social Democratic Party executive. The task of the Social Democratic parliamentary group will be to try and form a red workers' government, which will protect as best as it can the gains of the general strike and other interests of the workers.

Comrades, our cause must go on! Be ready and arm your ranks. The armistice may be short.

[The union members wanted a red government to be formed independent of the Diet, which was no longer in session, and which would carry through the 'We demand' programme.]

(1;5 : Sirola's account is in *Vapaussodan arkisto*, file 1 A 2 Finnish National Archives. 2 : *Työväen Vallankumouksellisen Keskusneuvoston Tiedonantolehti*, 14 November 1917. 3 : Minutes of the SDP parliamentary group, 14 November, in Finnish Labour Archives. 4 : *Toiset valtiopäivät 1917, Pöytäkirjat* vol. 1, p. 147. 6 : *Työväen Vallankumouksellisen Keskusneuvoston Tiedonantolehti*, 18 November 1917.)

112 THE SOCIAL DEMOCRATIC PARTY CONFER-ENCE, 25–7 NOVEMBER 1917

KUUSINEN'S REPORT TO THE CONFERENCE, 25 NOVEMBER

Since the recent general strike would have broken out in any case, it was therefore natural that steps to direct it were taken by central party organisations. But in planning this sort of massive effort, the question of aims had first to be decided. Some thought that the workers ought to seize power by revolutionary means, others thought that parliamentary action was still feasible. Indeed, efforts had been made to pursue this last-mentioned course of action in order to resolve the issues which the workers wish to see settled, but so far these efforts have met with little success. Therefore the question of what to do is still unresolved. To this question there can only be two answers : either a seizure of power by the workers, or a further attempt to secure the workers' position and guard their interests by parliamentary means. If power is wholly given over to the bourgeoisie, this would mean, in the opinion of the speaker, that the so-called law on supreme authority would not be brought into operation. Neither could there be any question of real reforms. Bourgeois class domination would be stronger than ever. There would also be no hope of, for example, a general amnesty for acts committed during the general strike.

As for the second alternative, i.e. the seizure of power by the workers, it could have any number of consequences. The workers could in any case maintain control of power only until the national assembly met. Even so, the gains which the workers have so far won should nevertheless be protected so that they would not be lost in the event of defeat in the elections.

If the workers were to follow this course of action, they would then need to control power for a least half a year. During this period the power of the workers could be established and strengthened. We must not however forget the difficulties which this course of action would throw up, with the affairs of the country in the chaotic state they are at present. We must bear in mind, amongst other things, that socialist control would in no way cover the whole country. For example, Ostrobothnia would remain outside the area of control. In fact, socialist exercise of power would in general be difficult – at least in the beginning – but it could probably become stabilised in the course of time. But if the bourgeoisie in the end manages to obtain control, then it will be more cruel in its revenge than the most savage working class elements, as the final days of the Paris Commune demonstrated.

The Social Democratic Party executive has prepared no motion on this question, but leaves the party conference with full authority to decide which of the two above-mentioned lines of action it wishes to adopt . . .

J. Raitio declared that it must be one of the greatest misfortunes for the party that membership of labour organisations had grown out of all proportion in recent months, and that irresponsible elements had then been able to acquire an influential position. This being so, it would appear that the erection of a workers' dictatorship was impossible and it must therefore be forgotten. There had to be some sort of way out of the impasse, however, and there appeared to be no other course but compromise with the bourgeoisie to form a government which would carry out the workers' demands . . .

E. Haapalainen thought that the party had made a big mistake in entering into a general strike. There had been no unity whatever at the moment of conflict. For this reason the fight had become disordered. The party leadership should have made it clear when it entered into the fray that it was only to be a carrying out of peaceful strike action, and not a revolution. As there were no clear indications to this effect, the masses went into action with revolution in mind, and this is why it is now difficult to stop this movement. It must be continued. As long as power remains in the hands of the bourgeoisie, the bread question will not be satisfactorily settled . . .

THE RESOLUTION OF THE MODERATES, PRESENTED TO THE CONFERENCE, 25 NOVEMBER

3. On the matter of government, raised at this conference, the assembly declares:

In our economically underdeveloped country there are insufficient grounds for a dictatorship of the proletariat, which at present enjoys some support within the party; during the present time of hunger and unemployment it would even add further to the sufferings of the working class.

A purely social democratic government, lacking socialist majority support in the Diet, would soon show itself to be deleterious to social democracy in our country, especially at this moment, when the affairs of the country have fallen into a state of complete chaos.

Social democratic participation in a coalition government with progressive elements, if such are to be found, might under compelling circumstances be acceptable on condition that the government has a socialist majority and that its programme meets the most immediate demands of the working class.

THE MAJORITY RESOLUTION OF THE TACTICS COMMITTEE, APPROVED BY THE CONFERENCE, 27 NOVEMBER

4. Since in these revolutionary times there can occur situations when the securing of the most pressing demands of the working class . . . can temporarily necessitate the taking over of the powers of government and state by social democracy, or

social democratic participation in a coalition government in
which the bourgeois members are in a minority, then the Social
Democratic parliamentary group and the party council shall
consider at the appropriate time which of the two tactics offers
the social democratic class struggle greater advantage than harm
or danger, and if they reach a mutually agreed decision on the
advantageousness and conditions of one of the tactics, it shall for
the time being be permitted . . .

(The MS. of the party conference from which the speeches and
resolutions are taken is in *Syyttäjistön arkisto*, file Ca 9, Finnish
National Archives.)

113   THE FORMATION OF THE SVINHUFVUD GOV-
ERNMENT, NOVEMBER 1917

[On 24 November, the socialists presented their list for a 'Red
government' to the Diet. The nine-point programme was basic-
ally that outlined in the 'We demand' programme. The non-
socialist majority also presented its candidates for office, and it
was this list which the majority of the Diet accepted two days
later. The new leader of the government, Svinhufvud, clearly
outlined his programme to the Diet on the 24th.]

The most important task which awaits the first Senate appointed
by the Finnish Diet is the safeguarding of Finland's political
independence. The Russian government has forfeited the right
to keep Finland united to the state of Russia. The Russian Imperial government violated the rights of Finland guaranteed by
the rulers of Russia and sought to destroy the judicial system of
Finland; the post-revolutionary government in Russia has for its
part shown itself unable to maintain that permanent authority
which is the basic necessity of all social life.

The Finnish people are therefore both entitled and obliged to
take their fate into their own hands. They must trust that the
people of Russia, in whose name the right of small nations to
an independent political existence has frequently been acknowledged, will not make more difficult the efforts of the Finnish
people to arrange their own affairs on the basis of complete self-
determination.

One of the most important tasks of the government in internal affairs will be to prepare and present to the Diet a bill for a new form of government, based on democratic principles, for our country . . .

All political and social activity at the present moment presupposes a clear understanding of general precepts of justice and a tightening of the rule of order, so that normal life can continue . . .

(*Toiset valtiopäivät 1917, Pöytäkirjat* vol. 1, pp. 182–3.)

114   THE DIET VOTES TO ACCEPT A DECLARATION OF INDEPENDENCE, 6 DECEMBER 1917

[On 4 December, the government presented the Diet with an announcement that it intended to fulfil its first task, the securing of Finnish independence, and would seek recognition abroad: it also hoped that the Russian people and the Constituent Assembly would put no obstacles in the way, but made no mention of seeking agreement with Russia.]

Speaker: The following communication has been given to the Speaker of the Diet:

We request the opportunity to submit for the decision of the Diet during today's plenary session the following: whereas the government has presented a bill to the Diet for a new form of government, on the basis of Finland's existence as an independent republic, the Diet as possessor of supreme authority resolves to accept this principle and also approves of the government embarking upon the measures which it has announced as essential to obtain recognition of Finland's political independence.

Helsinki, 6 December 1917
[signed by five non-socialist members of the Diet.]

K. Manner: I for my part cannot support the motion read out by the Speaker just now, for a number of reasons. I do not wish however to go further into this, at least not yet. In place of the last motion, I propose that the Diet approve the following:

As the possessor of supreme authority in Finland, the Finnish Diet proclaims the principle that Finland is to be an independent republic. An effort must be made to realise this independence by negotiated agreement with Russia. A joint negotiating committee should be set up, composed of an equal number of Finnish and Russian representatives, to make a proposal to this effect. The negotiating committee should also make further proposals for the settlement of relations between Finland and Russia. These proposals should be submitted for the final approval of the sovereign state institutions of both countries. Finland should also seek the recognition of Finland as an independent republic by other states and make treaties with them for the establishment of relations.

To prepare the above-mentioned matters and to draft proposals on them for the approval of the Diet, the Diet resolves to set up a seventeen-man committee . . .

Voting and result : Who approves the Alkio proposal, vote 'aye' : if the 'noes' have it, the Manner proposal is approved.

The voting was 100 'ayes' and 88 'noes'.

Speaker : The Diet has therefore resolved to approve the proposal made by representative Alkio.

(*Toiset valtiopäivät 1917, Pöytäkirjat* vol. 1. p. 306.)

115 THE FIRST OFFICIAL FINNISH APPEAL FOR RECOGNITION, 5 DECEMBER 1917

The Diet of Finland, on the basis of the principles enunciated in article 38 of the Form of Government [of 1772], resolved on 15 November to take possession of the exercise of supreme authority and appointed a government for the country. On behalf of this government and as its leader I have presented a bill to the Diet concerning a new form of government, based on the principle of Finland's existence as an independent republic. I have furthermore solemnly declared before the Diet on behalf of the government – with reference to the frequently expressed assurances of the belligerent states about the granting of full rights of self-determination to small nations – that the Finnish people, in the circumstances in which they now find themselves, are both entitled and obliged to take their fate in their own hands and to seek recognition of Finnish independence from foreign states.

The Speaker of the Diet welcomed this step, which he regarded as in accordance with the rights of the country and the unanimous wish of the people.

There has been no government of late in Russia which has been generally acknowledged either at home or abroad. The representatives of the defeated Provisional Government in Finland, the Governor-General and his assistant have not been at their posts since the beginning of November. More recently, the troops appointed a sailor and a workman as Russian commissars for Finland, but since the constitutional laws of Finland do not recognise guardians of Russian interests appointed in this manner, the Finnish government has been unable to enter into any sort of contact with them.

By their unrestrained behaviour, the Russian troops stationed here have in recent months have caused terror amongst the peaceful population of this country. The intimate relations which in places have been noticeable between the leaders of these troops and hot-headed and unstable elements of society have in a number of instances led to serious breaches of the peace and general order, which must be seen as a direct reflection of conditions prevailing in Russia.

In addition to these grave political tribulations there is a serious food shortage which the Finnish people is now having to combat. The crop failure of last summer and the impossibility of obtaining grain from Russia as well as the difficulty met in realising the projected imports of flour from the United States threaten the nearly three and a half million people of Finland with open famine. This painful situation is made even more difficult by the fact that the disorders in Russia are forcing an ever increasing number of refugees to seek shelter in Finland. These Russian refugees are also consuming the meagre reserves of the country. Moreover, these reserves are also being depleted by the numerous inactive Russian forces stationed here, since they are not certain of regular supplies of foodstuffs from Russia either.

It is therefore of vital import to the Finnish people that the truly isolated position in which the country now finds itself should come to an end. It is vital that the full independence of Finland be realised without delay and that its government manage to establish direct relations with foreign states.

(Svinhufvud's message to the governments of Sweden, Norway, Denmark, France, Britain and the United States. Printed in A. Pakaslahti, *Suomen itsenäisyyden tunnustaminen. Asiakirjakokoelma*, (Helsinki 1937) pp. 5–6.)

116 AN UNOFFICIAL FINNISH CONTACT WITH THE GERMAN GENERAL HEADQUARTERS, 26 NOVEMBER 1917[4]

HJELT'S STATEMENT TO LUDENDORFF

1. Finland is pro-German and during the world war has served the Central Powers, albeit in a modest way.

2. Finland will and must unconditionally break away from Russia and create an independent state in close association with Germany. This can only be achieved by direct or indirect support on the German side.

3. The separation of Finland from Russia and its independence is, in our view, of political, economic and cultural interest to Germany too. It would form the northernmost link of the chain of states which will form a wall in Europe against the east.

4. For Finland to separate from Russia, an invasion by German troops in Finland would be most desirable and would lead directly to this end. An uprising already prepared for would then occur, and the people would make common cause with the German troops.

5. If an invasion on the Finnish coast is not possible in view of the general war situation, a speedy occupation of the Åland Islands would be extremely important for Finland. Finland could then probably do the rest itself. The occupation of the Åland Islands by German troops would be of decisive importance for future relations between Finland and Germany . . .

6. In the event of a prompt ceasefire with Russia a demand by the Germans for the withdrawal of Russian combat units from Finland until its position can be regularised would be of great value. Otherwise Finland's hands are tied and it cannot get out of its present difficult situation.

7. A declaration of full independence by the Finnish Diet will only have the necessary force and significance if it is recognised by Germany.

[4] Hjelt was acting on behalf of the Stockholm-based activists in Germany, but he had been in touch with Svinhufvud before going there, and reported back to him on his return in December.

LUDENDORFF'S REPLY

1. An occupation of the Åland Islands is out of the question this year, though prospects of such an enterprise next year are favourable; this presupposes that the situation in the east is different from that at present. For the time being, we must reckon on the possibility of a ceasefire with Russia.

2. In the event of a ceasefire with Russia Finland must issue a statement that the Finnish people claim the right to self-determination. As a further expression of this right, the demand must be made for the withdrawal of Russian troops from Finland . . .

3. This statement must conclude with the publicly expressed wish for German support for Finland's efforts. General Ludendorff declares that he is prepared to see that the Finnish wish for the freeing of the country of Russian troops is supported at the ceasefire or peace negotiations.

4. Finland must be in a position to add weight to this statement. This is best achieved by strong organisation and preparations for the establishment of a militia.

5. The Supreme Army Command will continue the deliveries of weapons already begun, and will permit the arms despatch already promised be followed by another. Furthermore the Finnish Jäger Battalion will be sent to Finland, partly with arms shipments, partly in small groups via Sweden and Hiiumaa.

6. The question of foodstuffs must be taken up with Berlin. It must not be forgotten that foodstuffs could easily fall into wrong hands, as long as Finland is not free of Russian troops. Support will only be considered after the country is freed of these troops.

(E. Hjelt, *Från händelserika år*, vol. 1 (Helsingfors 1920) pp. 56–9.)

117 AN ACCOUNT OF THE MEETING BETWEEN THE NON-SOCIALIST PARLIAMENTARY DELEGATION FROM FINLAND AND NON-BOLSHEVIK POLITICIANS, 12 DECEMBER 1917

Idman : Explained the purpose of the visit.
Rusanov : Huttunen and Turkia had explained that Finland did not want complete separation last spring. Even now the resolu-

tion of the Diet [of 6 December?] is not liked in Petrograd. He doubted whether the Constituent [Assembly] would meet, the Bolsheviks would prevent it. Probably on 1 January 1918 . . .

Idman : What is your position?

Rusanov : The Finnish example a bad one as regards Estonia, the Ukraine and Armenia. But Finland does have its own reasons, after all. (Idman's view that Rusanov not as favourably disposed as Skobelev.)

Skobelev asked whether an announcement had been made abroad?

We replied, adding in regard to Russia an exception [had been made?] considering the historical reasons.

Alkio : The resolution of the Diet irrevocable, it can only be defeated by force.

Rautapää. No Finn will go into the Senate if attempts are made to restore the old system.

Skobelev : This is your subjective position, what about *Realpolitik*?

Holsti : We are ripe [for independence], large parts of Russia are not, we must break away, because only then will we emerge from the confusion in Russia and at home.

Skobelev promised support, but did not even know of his own election [to the Constituent Assembly]; small group.

Skobelev and Liber : Satisfied that we had no dealings with the Bolsheviks.

Rautapää : The intention of our visit the Diet's address.[5]

Liber : Your purpose is not to submit but to inform.

Reply : Yes!

Liber : In principle they had the same attitude in respect of all nationalities.

Rautapää : Russian troops out of Finland.

Liber : Difficult when they are there for political and not strategical reasons. They do not obey the command. Asked of the possibility of a German invasion of Finland and attack against Petrograd.

Rautapää answered.

Skobelev reiterated the same assurance that the [Menshevik] party

---

[5] There appears to be a discrepancy here, for the Diet only voted to send an address seeking independence to the Constituent Assembly on 22 December.

in principle already well disposed towards us, but what guarantees that the Germans from Riga or the Entente would not come and occupy Finland?

Holsti : Depends entirely on the development of relations between Russia and Germany whether or not Germany will even have any reason to occupy Finland.

Idman : The danger of occupation exceedingly small, Finland is not in the position of Belgium.

Alkio : Finland antimilitaristic; will call no-one to its aid against Russia.

Skobelev : What have the socialists done?

We replied and gave [them] documents.

(Minutes of the meeting in the Holsti collection, file 33, Finnish National Archives.)

118   'RUSSIA AND FINLAND' (DECEMBER 1917)

The bourgeois press in Finland has recently launched a strongly demagogic attack on the government of the Russian republic. The bourgeois papers scream that Russia seems to be the source of all Finland's misfortunes. Things are being made worse by the food-stuffs crisis – and the Russian troops are blamed for eating up all the bread. Financial difficulties are also laid at the troops' door, because they are paid in Finnish currency. The main target for complaints, however, is that Russian troops stationed in Finland side with the proletariat against the bourgeoisie . . .

And now, the final, most terrible sin of helping the Finnish proletariat in their fight with the Finnish bourgeoisie. Yes, we admit to this sin. All our sympathies are with the Finnish proletariat . . . In the end, your bourgeoisie cannot forgive us for this. The net result is this absurd ultimatum on the withdrawal of our troops.

Everyone understands that until peace is concluded, we cannot leave the way open to Petrograd. For this reason we regard the demand of the Senate as simply unworthy of the slightest bit of attention . . .

Proletariat of Finland! Our revolution has lead to the victory of the workers. To you we turn with fraternal regards and an appeal – overthrow the bourgeoisie.

Do not believe the bourgeois press when it says we are against the Finnish people. This it not true. The hard-pressed situation of the Finnish people further strengthens our desire to help you. We have done all we can to ensure that not one gramme of foodstuffs for Finland is delayed en route . . .

Do not believe that we are against independence for Finland. We know our socialist duty as regards the position of the oppressed nationalities.

We are however always and everywhere opposed to the bourgeoisie. We oppose your bourgeoisie as well. We have spoken of this frankly, for the Russian revolutionary scorns concealment of his convictions.

The Chairman of the Finnish Regional Committee
I. SMILGA

(*Izvesiya Gel'singforskogo Soveta*, 7/20 December 1917)

119 EXTRACTS FROM THE DIARY OF KARL WIIK ON THE ATTITUDES OF THE BOLSHEVIKS TO FINNISH INDEPENDENCE

[Friday, 30 November]

6 o'clock, party headquarters.

. . . *Manner* : We told Stalin[6] that no steps should be taken (concerning Finland) before we send negotiators with written proposals. Just recently, at 5 o'clock, Manner had heard from two senators that the bourgeoisie were thinking of proclaiming Finland a republic. Manner had replied to this that the party would not want any action to be taken before we had negotiated with the Russian social democrats. Manner asked if the Finnish government had contacts with the Russian government. Answer : no, the bourgeoisie do not recognise it. *Renvall*[7] : today Enckell is travelling to Petrograd; he is not the Minister State-Secretary but a representative of Finland. Manner advised counselling Petrograd not to make any promises to Enckell.

Smilga[8] : If Finland declares herself a republic, and when the

[6] Stalin had attended the FSDP conference, and had spoken on behalf of the Bolsheviks on 27 November.

[7] Renvall was one of the senators.

[8] I. T. Smilga was the representative of the Soviet government in Finland, and had been chairman of the Area Committee in Finland.

war is over, we shall withdraw the troops, but if this is done by you during the war, you can defend your coasts yourselves. If you want to defeat the bourgeoisie, then do so while the Russian troops are here. Then we can leave with a good conscience. We can leave arms as a souvenir, 20,000 rifles . . .

[Friday, 28 December]

. . . Waited in Smolny[9] . . . *Smilga* told [us] that the Senate had turned to Germany on the question of independence but had received a dusty answer, since Germany wishes to remain on good terms with Russia; then they turned here [to the Soviet government]. (That is why Enckell and Idman are here now to get a proclamation on independence) . . . 3 o'clock with *Trotsky*, who read our proposals and thought the matter could be easily arranged; [he] would support [it] himself. But as a private party man he was puzzled why the Finnish social democrats did not make a revolution. In general, social democratic parties hold back the revolutionary spirit of the people . . .

I [*Wiik*] : on the peasants, their attitude in Finland, and problems of foodstuffs.

Trotsky : For the Bolsheviks, defeat was predicted the day after the revolution (Smilga smiled). The worst thing for a party is to underestimate its own strength . . . Your revolution would stimulate the Swedish workers. If you let the opportunity slip out of your hands, it will be an omission which will not be forgotten (by socialists? posterity?) . . . If independence is the only possibility Finnish social democrats see, then . . . we will prepare a proclamation (on the recognition of Finnish independence) if only a request is made by the Senate.

(*Karl H. Wiiks Dagboksanteckningar från åren 1917–1918*, p. 108, p. 125, Finnish National Archives.)

[9] A socialist delegation, composed of Gylling, Manner and Wiik, had been sent to Petrograd with a request for the Soviet government to recognise complete independence for Finland. It arrived on 27 December, three days before the official delegation headed by Svinhufvud (q.v.).

120   THE RUSSIAN RECOGNITION OF FINNISH INDE-
PENDENCE, 31 DECEMBER 1917

1. K. G. IDMAN'S ACCOUNT OF THE DISCUSSIONS BETWEEN LENIN
AND THE FINNISH DELEGATION, 28 DECEMBER

After we had sat down, Enckell began with a detailed account of
the course of events in Finland since the October revolution,
relating how these events had led up to the declaration of independence. He also explained why the government had not immediately turned to the Soviet government. It had been waiting for
the calling of the Constituent National Assembly. All the Russian
governments so far had always assured the Finns that only the
Constituent National Assembly was entitled to agree to their
wishes. As it now seemed, by all accounts, that there was some
uncertainty whether it would ever by called, and if it did, whether
it would display any vitality, the Senate had decided to turn to the
Soviet of People's Commissars. Lenin's reply to this was that the
National Assembly would indeed soon be convened, 'but the Senate must judge how to proceed, who to turn to'. If it turned to
the Soviet of People's Commissars, the latter would without doubt
immediately recognise Finland's independence. In accordance
with the constitution, the decision of the Soviet would have to be
left for confirmation with the Executive Central Committee of
the soldiers', workers' and peasants' representatives. Lenin believed he could assure us that the matter would meet with no
difficulty there either. After further negotiations on certain other
matters with Lenin we took our leave, saying that we would inform the Finnish government of his reply.

2. CARL ENCKELL'S ACCOUNT OF THE FINAL RECOGNITION, 31
DECEMBER

On Monday 31 December at 3 p.m. the delegation visited the
general secretary once more and handed over the corrected second
copy of the request.[10] According to Bonch-Bruyevich the Soviet
of People's Commissars was to meet later in the evening, and he
asked us to wait for the reply to the government's request in an
anteroom of the hall in which the Soviet held its sessions. At 9

[10] The request had been wrongly addressed to the 'government of Russia'
and not to the Soviet of People's Commissars.

o'clock in the evening, we found ourselves in this anteroom, where there were several typists at work and numerous men, women and children hanging about. In the absence of seating, we stationed ourselves by the window and for more than two hours we witnessed the lively concourse in the room. Through the door which was frequently opened upon the smoke-filled session-chamber of the people's commissars we saw groups of men, eagerly debating . . . A number of times the general secretary came out to the anteroom to give instructions to the typists, and I discreetly endeavoured to ask him whether our business would soon be dealt with. At last – it was already past 11 o'clock and Svinhufvud hoped to be able to return to Helsinki by the midnight train – Bonch-Bruyevich handed me a thin piece of paper, headed No. 101 and dated 18 December (o.s.) 1917, which was signed by seven people's commissars and counter-signed by the general secretary Bonch-Bruyevich and the secretary Gorbunov. It read as follows:

> In reply to the request of the Finnish government concerning the recognition of the independence of the Finnish republic, the Soviet of People's Commissars, in full agreement with the principle of national self-determination, has decided to present the Executive Central Committee with the proposal:
>
> (a) to recognise the political independence of the Finnish republic.
>
> (b) to organise, in agreement with the Finnish government, a special commission of representatives of both parties to deal with the practical measures necessitated by the separation of Finland from Russia.

I thanked the general secretary for the document, and asked him to see if he could arrange for the head of the Finnish government, who had come to Petrograd to receive the recognition, to thank personally V. I. Lenin, the chairman of the Soviet of People's Commissars. Bonch-Bruyevich promised to try and do this, and a little while later Lenin came out of the session-chamber. I introduced Svinhufvud to him and both heads of government cordially shook hands. Lenin asked jocularly: 'Are you satisfied now?', to which Svinhufvud mumbled his thanks, and after a few words were exchanged on the satisfaction which the recognition would create in Finland on Svinhufvud's return with the glad tidings that same New Year's Eve (the train had been ordered to wait), Svinhufvud left for the station. Idman and I remained in Petrograd to await the decision of the Executive Central Committee on the proposal made by the people's commissars. In principle the matter was already settled, but insofar as the central committee had the formal last word, the decision could not be regarded as definite.

(1 : K. G. Idman, *Maame itsenäistymisen vuosilta. Muistelmia*, (Porvoo-Helsinki 1953) pp. 216–7. 2 : Carl Enckell, *Politiska minnen*, (Helsingfors 1956) pp. 201–3.)

Civil War, January–May 1918

The war years placed a great strain on Finnish society. The rampant inflation, food shortages and growing unemployment of 1917 further exacerbated an already tense situation (121, 122, 123). By the end of the year, radical elements in the labour movement were threatening to attempt a seizure of power with or without official party backing (125). On 12 January the Diet granted the Senate the authority it sought to take firm steps to restore law and order (124). This was seen by the labour movement as a whole as an overt declaration of war on the working class, and if anything, it served to weaken the moderates' stand against the revolutionary elements within the Social Democratic Party.

The civil war broke out at the end of January 1918, after the Svinhufvud government had made the white guards the official military force of the state on 25 January, and the Social Democratic Party executive, after lengthy debate, had opted for a revolutionary seizure of power on the same day (128, 129). A red government was set up in Helsinki but despite the socialist programme outlined by Sirola on 24 January and conveyed to the outside world in the appeal to international socialism issued by the party, the Finnish socialists found their justification for seizing power in the defence of democracy against incipient bourgeois counter-revolution rather than in the full-blooded pursuance of the social revolution (127, 130, 131, 132).

For the white forces the war was one of liberation, in which the remaining Russian troops were to be disarmed or driven out of the land along with the misguided Finnish reds with whom they fraternised. The nationalist liberation movement even extended its area beyond Finland's historical frontiers, as Mannerheim's pledge to liberate Russian Karelian shows (133).

The Soviet government, harassed by the necessity of reaching some sort of settlement with Imperial Germany, preferred to main-

tain neutrally amicable official relations with the Finnish government, but the outbreak of civil war – to a large extent prompted by Russian consignments of arms to the red guards – produced expressions of revolutionary solidarity and support (134, 135). In practice however, Russian aid was mostly confined to arms consignments, though a number of Russian troops did fight on the red side (136).

The activists in Berlin succeeded in obtaining German intervention in Finland, although this did not entirely meet with the approval of general Mannerheim (137). The subsequent treaty between the two countries tied Finland closely to German commercial and strategic interests (139). Germany had a particular interest in securing control of the Åland islands, as had Sweden – though the latter had also to wrestle with her neutral conscience in the pursuance of an Åland policy (141).

121   THE ECONOMIC CRISIS OF 1917 : THE STATISTICAL BACKGROUND

(a) POPULATION OF FINLAND 1890–1918

Year	Urban population		Rural population		Total
1890	235,227	(9.9%)	2,144,913	(90.1%)	2,380,140
1900	339,613	(12.5%)	2,372,949	(97.5%)	2,712,562
1910	456,873	(14.7%)	2,658,324	(85.3%)	3,115,197
1917	533,185	(15.9%)	2,812,475	(84.1%)	3,345,660
1918	527,946	(15.8%)	2,801,680	(84.2%)	3,329,626

(Suomen tilastollinen vuosikirja 1943, p.7.)

(b) INDUSTRY IN FINLAND, 1916

	Southern Finland	Central and Northern Finland[1]
No. of industrial plants located in towns	923	310
No. of workers	54,613	11,234
No. of industrial plants located in countryside	1,932	1,529
No. of workers	39,652	12,248

[1] This division corresponds roughly to that of the civil war.

(Suomen tilastollinen vuosikirja 1919, p. 118–19.)

(c) MEMBERSHIP OF MAJOR TRADE UNIONS, 30 JUNE 1917

Union	Branches	Membership	Membership increase since 30 March 1917
Factory and General Workers	358	41,580	35,520
Metalworkers	151	26,174	10,146
Timber Industry Workers	154	15,790	10,474
Transport Workers	76	9,042	5,783
Woodworkers	120	8,844	4,792
Textile Workers	?20	8,700	4,200
Paper Industry Workers	55	7,929	3,617
Total	1,368	150,180	89,571

(*Työmies*, 11 September 1917.)

(d) PRICES OF FOODSTUFFS 1917 (PERCENTAGE INCREASES SINCE 1913 = 100%)

Item	Helsinki	Kotka	Vaasa	Viipuri	Turku
Table butter	184.5	163.5	175.6	96.0	90.9
Potatoes	417.5	341.5	315.2	225.5	424.1
Hard rye bread	225.6	—	270.3	400.0	240.0
Salt herring	302.3	371.2	531.4	—	—
Coffee	441.9	405.3	505.2	546.9	520.1

(*Social Tidskrift* 1918, no. 3, pp. 305–12.)

(e) CONSUMPTION OF FOODSTUFFS 1913–18 (per capita : in kilogrammes)

Item	1913	1914	1915	1916	1917	1918
Wheat flour	63.3	48.9	45.9	74.0	8.6	1.9
Rye flour	187.7	149.9	174.6	157.6	61.0	57.4
Potatoes	115.1	116.5	127.3	116.6	113.0	148.0
Coffee	4.0	3.1	4.0	2.1	1.7	0.2

(*Suomen virallinen tilasto* III : 14 (Helsinki 1920) p. 25.)

(f) STRIKES AND WORK STOPPAGES 1917

Number of strikes and stoppages recorded[2] 478
Of which in 344 wages were given as a reason for striking
          232 working hours as a reason
Number of workers involved   139,550
Of which   46,530 were of diverse occupations
          19,727 were metalworkers
          16,965 were lumberjacks and loggers
          16,167 were agricultural labourers

   [2] This figure is officially admitted to be too low.

(*Statistisk årsbok* for 1918, (Helsingfors 1918) pp. 640–1.)

122   GRASS-ROOTS RADICALISM, 1917

1. TRADE UNION LEADERSHIP AND THE STRIKE MOVEMENT

... The stamp of violence came more and more to the fore in the strikes, not only in regard to the rules and resolutions of the union organisations, but also in attacks on employers and strike breakers (this was particularly the case in farm labourers' strikes). Union officials were threatened, even set upon if their policy was not in line with the views of the workers ... The national union leadership was forced to tag along and the net result was that illegality became recognised as law ...

2. MINUTES OF THE BRANCH OF THE CARPENTERS' UNION (TAMPERE), 1917

[5 October]

... There are a lot of workers with large families who have not had butter for months on end, and they have also had to go without bread for a number of days, not to mention milk, which for many is already a distant memory from the past ...

There was also some surprise at the 'bogey' scares which leaders of our movement have splashed in the columns of Kansan Lehti, amongst other papers, in recent days. This sort of thing was thought cowardly; it was best to get out when the shakes started, because at this moment we need men of drive, and these can always be found ...

[17 October]

... The meeting took up the question of what could be done to prevent our having to eat lichen, which the bourgeoisie are starting to feed us with. It was resolved to make it clear to members that there was no other way but to seize power once and for all and if we have to eat lichen, then the bourgeoisie will have to eat the same helping as the worker ...

3. MINUTES OF THE TRADE UNION DELEGATE CONGRESS, 12 NOVEMBER 1917

Tokoi: ... If the workers in Russia do gain the upper hand and can retain control of political power, then I feel that we too will be compelled to seize power sooner or later ... But we must understand that we cannot carry out an economic revolution, because an economic revolution cannot be made in one country at one time and in another at a different time . . . By seizing political power we can carry out reforms in one or two areas but we cannot carry out a complete social evolution, and we must be clear about this at all events . . .

Haapalainen : . . . I am sure that if we in this country are content merely to engineer a political revolution on behalf of the workers, we are behind the times . . .

Hakkinen : . . . We know that the shortage of foodstuffs has brought matters in this country to the point where we have to decide whether we submit through hunger to bourgeois rule or take up a struggle which will either take us to victory or defeat. In any case, grim death lies before us if we do not fight against it. We will die in any event . . . The workers of our locality are behind any decision that is taken here. They feel that we cannot stand this general starvation any more. Farmers and others there are so overbearing towards the workers who appeal to the provisions boards and individual landowners that it is said of them that they are used to feed corn and meal to their pigs. I can also say with regard to arms that the troops in Tornio have told the workers' guard committee that they can have as many as they like.

Lind: . . . If this congress does not take action, then many in our area have said that the workers there will rise up using their own methods . . . I was explicitly told that if there was no decision taken in this matter then there was no need to come back . . .

> (1 : J. Lumivuokko, *Laillinen ammattiyhdistysliike vaiko vallankumous?* (Stockholm 1919) p. 24. 2 : Minutes in the Labour Archives, Helsinki, file 331.88 674(471) 3 : MS. of the minutes of the congress in the Labour Archives.)

123 SOCIAL UNREST AS A CAUSE OF REVOLUTION – GYLLING'S LETTER TO THE TURKU HIGH COURT, 2 JUNE 1918

. . . The reason why revolutionary elements as it were came together in this way in the party was particularly attributable to the following circumstances :

1. The Russian policy of oppression, which prevented the carrying out of reforms already passed by the Diet, thereby weakening the workers' faith in parliamentary procedure. As is well

known, most of the important reforms passed by the Diet after 1907 remained unconfirmed [by the Tsar].

2. The harsh reactionary nature of the grand bourgeoisie, which caused it to use, even publicily, such tactics as urging the Russian government not to confirm the laws passed by the Diet. Official circles also worked secretly for the same purpose. As the workers were powerless in the face of such tactics, this naturally increased their bitterness and dissatisfaction.

3. Of very great importance to the development of our labour movement was the proclamation of a state of war caused by the outbreak of the world war. Labour legislation, such as it was, even though of very little substance, and the liberty of action of labour organisations were completely throttled. There was also at first a good deal of unemployment, which employers in industry and agriculture used to their own ends. When a period of exceptional profits soon began for industry, this contrast naturally added to the bitterness within the working class.

4 There were certainly plenty of job opportunities in the military work which was then started in the country. Tens of thousands of unorganised peasants flooded to these fortification works. Totally inadequate work direction, work habits, bribery etc. fostered in this work force an undisciplined spirit, which was made worse by the wretched living conditions etc. on the work sites, even if the wages there were reasonable. This work force remained more or less entirely beyond the labour organisations until 1917, and even then the bulk of these workers did not join. The methods of the organised workers did not therefore get the chance to circulate amongst these workers.

5. In addition to the above, there was also the general price inflation and the shortage of foodstuffs, which in 1916 and 1917 began to press more and more upon those with little means. Before the revolution in the spring of 1917 there had been no attempt to deal with this matter, and although in the spring of the same year a provisions law was passed, observance of this law was in practice negligible. When the provisions boards tried to supervise effectively, the effect of their activities on the population, e.g. in Helsinki, was obvious.

It was in these circumstances that the Russian revolution occurred in spring 1917. Needless to say, it found a very favourable soil in Finland. Its influence was felt most immediately amongst the so-called fortifications workers and the workers in factories making war materials for Russia. These working masses were also for the most part outside the Finnish labour movement. The latter with its own independent organisations, forming in a way its own organic self, also viewed the revolutionary influences from the east with an independent eye, and in no way allowed itself to be immediately carried away by these influences. That this finally did happen is the net result of many unfortunate events and their effects . . .

(This handwritten MS. is in the Gylling collection, file 1, Finnish National Archives.)

124   THE SENATE SEEKS POWERS TO RESTORE LAW AND ORDER, 9 JANUARY 1918

. . . The Senate resolved to present to the Diet the following communication :

After lengthy and hard trials and tribulations our country has won national independence. The internal situation in the country however fails to meet even the most basic expectations of this kind of free status. Order in the country is inadequate to protect the lives, property and rights both of our own citizens and of the numerous foreigners resident here. The announcements made every day by the authorities concerned as well as foreign representatives and the press all speak the same language. Only today in the very suburbs of the capital, there have occurred bloody skirmishes provoked by the so-called Helsinki red guards, in which lives have been lost . . . Anarchistic elements from Russia are setting up their bases here, operating quite openly and sowing the seeds of revolution and anarchy amongst the troop units stationed here, who were already in a state of unrest. The situation is growing more serious moment by moment and unless a speedy remedy is found, the country will shortly be brought into a state of complete anarchy . . .

Resolved : that the Diet grant the government the authority to take all measures which it thinks necessary to create a firm rule of law and order in the country.

(Minutes of the Senate meeting, 9 January 1918, in the Finnish National Archives.)

125   THE RED GUARDS DEMAND REVOLUTION –
      MINUTES OF THE MEETING OF THE GENERAL
      STAFF OF THE RED GUARDS, 11 JANUARY 1918

[The failure of the November strike to achieve positive results
caused the growing dissatisfaction with the SDP leadership to
manifest itself amongst the red guards. The party's attempt to
regain control of the guards at a conference called in December proved a failure, and on 11 January, this important meeting, attended by a number of party leaders, tried to resolve
the differences.]

Taimi: As far as I have been able to follow the situation, every
day takes us nearer to a revolution . . . The party press ought to
make clear that everyone should prepare for revolution, and not
rely solely on the red guard . . . I don't expect a Diet revolution.
We must follow the Russian tactic and make a social revolution.
Kiviranta: I am only a witness to that which Taimi has spoken
of. I want to say that the masses and the bourgeoisie are waiting
for the party to split. The party executive has reached the point
where the left will leave. The revolution has not been adequately
pursued, there has been a sort of paralysis. A survey amongst the
guards shows that some 25% are right-wing moderates . . . The
revolutionary elements will go into action if given guarantees of
a convention of a National Assembly, then there will be plenty of
support. The Helsinki guard demands more radical action . . .
Overthrow the Senate, dissolve the Diet. Inactivity will lead to
anarchy.
Manninen: The party conference adopted a parliamentary
policy; this is why the party has been severely criticised . . . The
attitude of the masses is more radical than that of the party executive, council and the parliamentary group. A party conference
should be convened; he believed that a more radical crowd would
attend it. Then a revolution could be carried out . . . The bourgeoisie are rising throughout the land; what will happen in the
countryside where the bourgeoisie have the upper hand – there
will be a bloodbath of the workers . . . Revolutionary control of
power demands a lot of organisation. Must not allow the Russians
to be deprived of their weapons.
Sirola: The party rightists too are beginning to see which way

we are going. It has been a good thing for us that we have been able to keep the party together . . .

Turkia : Things in this country are coming to the point where revolution is inevitable. The bourgeoisie is stronger; our guards are in disarray, splitting the party. From Oulu to Pori will remain outside our control . . .

> (Pencilled notes of the meeting in Vapaussodan arkisto, file IB 29b, Finnish National Archives. The fragmentary nature of the notes has necessitated some interpretation.)

126 SIROLA'S ASSESSMENT OF THE SITUATION, 13 JANUARY 1918

The [Social Democratic parliamentary] group was assigned an important role in the resolution on tactics at the party conference : to consider whether power in some form is to be seized by the workers. Our constituents must be given an account of what is being done . . . In any decision, we should first find out what the true state of affairs is. In this respect, those from different parts of the country should give their accounts.

The bourgeoisie can either begin their attack or carry on concentrating their forces. If the red guards go into action, this can be used by the bourgeoisie as an excuse for attacking. An action could start of its own accord just to relieve the tension. If any groups of workers start to move now, there are three courses open to us : (1) to go along with them in the belief that the majority is behind us, (2) to go along with them out of loyalty, (3) to stand on one side in order to preserve as much of our strength as possible. We must therefore try to estimate relative strengths. This is difficult. The bourgeoisie may have a sizeable army. The Russians here can shift the balance, if they declare for the workers. But since Finland has been declared a republic, this would involve the danger of foreign interference. There is also the important question of whether the workers would retain confidence in the party. The workers should be sure that the party will be with them when the decisive moment comes. We should consider in what circumstances we would go along with them. If the workers get the idea that, for example, the group is not with them, then the group will be pushed aside. Our appraisal will of course depend on what sort of account we get of the situation in the country.

(Minutes of the Social Democratic parliamentary group, 13
January 1918, in the Labour Archives Helsinki.)

127   SIROLA'S ANALYSIS OF THE SITUATION, PRE-SENTED TO THE ENLARGED SOCIAL DEMO-CRATIC PARTY EXECUTIVE, 24 JANUARY 1918

Civil war has begun in the land. If it is not immediately defined,
it will develop into a series of irregular, disorganised and frac-
tious actions . . .

[Sirola proceeds to outline the three facets of the struggle which
must be considered – internal, external and strategic. He then
assesses the chances of remaining on the defensive, the stage
which obtained at that moment, and discounts the chances of
a compromise settlement, which the Diet would not accept
and which would not satisfy the proletariat. The next stage
must then be approached.]

Control of power by the proletariat

As the struggle spreads, there can be no thought of two governments unless the bourgeois government moves to Ostrobothnia
or elsewhere. This would be a threat to the workers' struggle,
since the government and the rump of the Diet accompanying it
could establish links with Germany, Sweden and other foreign
states and obtain help from them in one form or another. We
must therefore take care that the government cannot escape
from Helsinki. The first act of the seizure of power must be the
arrest of members of the government and other bourgeois functionaries regarded as dangerous, the dissolution of the Diet and
the proclamation of a workers' government. At the same time the
state bank should be captured and private banks placed under
the control of commissars. Directives on the control of production and distribution should also be announced (committees for
industry, commerce, agriculture and provisions). The following
should be part of the programme :

(a) The freeing of the tenant farmer and cottagers[3] is not

[3] The unsatisfactory conditions of tenure of the leaseholders in Finland
had long been a bone of contention. The 'cottagers' formed a far larger
group than the tenant-farmers, and their existence was a good deal more
precarious, since their small plot of land was rarely sufficient to provide
them with a living.

enough in the land programme; control over agricultural production should be established, i.e. the land should be nationalised, provisionally in order to stave off famine, and the planning of cultivation should be in the hands of local proletariat committees. It should be directed that the lessees of small farms and crofts (under the control of the committee) and the owners of medium-sized farms (if they agree) supervise cultivation in conjunction with a committee composed of their workers, and large farms should be handed over to the workers' committees. The permanent settlement of land usage would have to wait for future legislation.

(b) To establish workers' democracy, elected administrative organs should be proclaimed in place of [gap in MS] in conformity with the constitution soon to be legislated.

(c) A judicial system based on non-appellant judges and the jury system should be set up.

(d) Universal national insurance on the basis of labour or trade union organisations.

(e) Production should be so ordered that, from being capitalistic it is then gradually changed under the control of the people to co-operative and nationalised production.

(f) The distribution of products should immediately be shifted on to co-operative and communal bodies.

(g) Banks will remain nationalised, and so on.

The details of the programme should be taken under consideration point by point, and it should then be determined whether to try nationalisation in the way outlined above or to declare the control of production and distribution to be an exceptional necessity and to leave further plans to the future. This decision will be influenced by how we regard in principle the question of whether we are to follow a democratic or a proletarian-communist line. Of course, there is no need to fight democracy, indeed we must put our faith in the ability of the working-class majority to adopt before long a programme in which a situation which resembles a minority dictatorship would only be a temporary necessity brought about by a revolutionary state of affairs . . .

(Sirola's analysis, in typewritten MS., is in the Labour Archives, Helsinki, file 323.2 (471) '1918'.)

128 THE REVOLUTIONARY PROCLAMATION OF THE FINNISH WORKERS' EXECUTIVE COMMITTEE, 27 JANUARY 1918

The great revolutionary moment of the Finnish working class has come.

Today the workers of the capital have bravely overthrown the dismal headquarters of the oligarchy, which began the bloody war against its own people.

The members of the criminal Senate were preparing in the very capital of the country the shedding of blood and a treacherous attack upon the organised workers of Finland. They also were guilty of the openly treasonous act of asking the monarchist governments of foreign states to send murder squads to butcher the working people of Finland. The liberty and life of our whole nation was thus in grave danger.

Now all power has been taken away from that butcher-Senate. We have ordered the imprisonment of its criminal members, wherever they are found, for prison should have long since been the appropriate place for such enemies of the people.

It has been resolved to take all powers of state in Finland into the trustworthy hands of the working people of this country . . .

As the supreme body of the Finnish workers' revolution, authorised by the Social Democratic Party executive, we now proclaim that:

all revolutionary power in Finland now belongs to the organised workers and their revolutionary organs.

A social democratic revolutionary government will be immediately formed.[4] Information on its composition will be published at the first opportunity . . .

Peaceable citizens who do not wish to assist the enemies of the workers, need have no fear of the revolution. Owners of small properties in the town and in the country should not believe the lies that the workers want their property. On the contrary, a workers' victory could also improve their social position. The force of labour is the force of justice, which always seeks to avoid unnecessary violence and the suffering of the innocent. But the

[4] The government list was in fact ready by 26 January.

armed helpers of the fallen Senate will be crushed without mercy. Any who have been deluded into joining them should throw away their arms when they see that they have been deceived into fighting against the noble cause of the working people . . .

We believe earnestly that both present and future generations of working people will manifoldly bless this revolution, which will mark a new period of more fortunate circumstances for Finland.

(Published in *Työmies*, 28 January 1918.)

129 THE SENATE'S PROCLAMATION TO THE FINNISH PEOPLE, 28 JANUARY 1918

Incited by a number of power-hungry individuals, a section of the Finnish populace, aided by foreign bayonets and forces, has risen up in rebellion against the Finnish Diet and the legitimate government, forcibly preventing them from functioning and endangering the recently-won independence of the Fatherland. The government of the country has found itself compelled to take all steps at its disposal to put a stop to this treachery. To this end those security forces which have been set up on the authority granted by the Diet for the maintenance of order in the country have been placed under a general command, and General G. Mannerheim has been appointed commander-in-chief.[5] The government commands the law-abiding populace to assist General Mannerheim and his troops in all ways which he considers necessary for the successful completion of his task.

Let those misguided citizens who have risen up in arms to destroy the legal order of society cease at once in this endeavour, and take their weapons to the forces loyal to the government. Should they fail to realise the criminal nature of their actions and submit, then let them remember that their efforts are in any case condemned to failure. The government troops have conquered a large part of the country and are approaching the towns of the south and west, and no opposition will hold them back in their

[5] The government in fact legitimised the white guards which had existed for some months before the January crisis (on 25 January); Mannerheim was appointed to command on 16 January, and left for Vaasa three days later to prepare his troops.

fight for the liberty of the Fatherland against the traitors to this country.

(Printed in *Kansalaissota dokumentteina*, ed. H. Soikkanen, vol. 2 (Helsinki 1969) p. 74.)

130   THE APPEAL OF THE FINNISH RED GOVERNMENT TO INTERNATIONAL SOCIALISM, 18 FEBRUARY 1918

To the Zimmerwald Commission, Stockholm. To the international proletariat! Comrades! We hereby inform you that the Finnish proletariat, suffering from the most grievous privations, faced with the loss of all its revolutionary gains and threatened by the armed guards of the ruling class, has taken up the revolutionary struggle and has overthrown the reactionary bourgeois government. Power has been seized by the working class. With the approval of the Social Democratic party executive, a revolutionary government has been formed – the Finnish People's Commissariat – which has formulated a programme. As well as carrying out radical social reforms, the People's Commissariat has decided to curb the financial power of capitalism by imposing controls on bank capital. The nationalisation of the means of production will be immediately carried out, where the needs of the people demand it. A central council of thirty-five, chosen by the Social Democratic party executive, the trade union movement, and the trades' committees of the workers' red guard and the workers of Helsinki is being set up to check and watch over the activities of the People's Commissariat. Total power is in the hands of the workers. The future reform of the state structure is to be finally determined at a congress, attended by representatives of the national labour organisations. Now, as the workers of Finland, following the Russian example, have begun the social revolution, we send our heartfelt greetings to the International Socialist Commission, and through its medium to the socialist parties of all countries.[6]

[6] The International Socialist Commission was set up in 1916 in Bern to co-ordinate the work of the so-called Zimmerwald International of left-wing socialist groups and parties opposed to the war. The Commission moved to Stockholm in 1917, in preparation for the Stockholm Zimmerwald conference, which failed to get off the ground. The Finnish Social Democratic Party joined Zimmerwald in June 1917.

Class comrades of every country! We proletariats of little Finland know the difficulties we face as a result of our seizure of power and attempts to carry through socialist reforms. Against us is ranged the entire bourgeoisie and their accomplices, who are angrily sharpening the weapons of revenge and who are trying to arouse the peasants against the workers through their nationalist agitation. They are spreading the lying rumour that the socialists are hindering Finland's independence and wish to reunite the country with Russia. Finland's ruling class has nevertheless appealed to the international solidarity of the exploiting classes and is trying to obtain the support of a number of foreign governments. The Finnish proletariat hopes that no class-conscious worker in any country will abet the Finnish bourgeoisie by allowing auxiliary troops to be sent against the Finnish working class. We are also confident that comrades in those countries which have economic links with Finland will do their best to prevent the Finnish workers being starved out. Since the ruling class seek to spread the rumour that, as a consequence of the social revolution, anarchy reigns in Finland, we can tell you that revolutionary order prevails in the country, maintained by the workers' red guard, and that order is only disturbed by the provocation of bourgeois counter-revolution. The revolutionary workers respect the rights of foreigners, and only the bourgeois rebellion against the rights of the workers occasions any disturbance of the peace.

We are aware, dear comrades, that the tactics of the labour movement of each country are determined by the prevalent circumstances of that country, but just as exploitation and oppression are international, so must the struggle against them bear an international character. Finnish and Russian revolutionary blood is being shed at this moment in the common struggle against the oppressors. The necessary conditions for international action has now become a necessity. The revolutionary movement of the working class is spreading from country to country. When will it break out into a general international revolution!

Workers! Men and women! You, who have organised yourselves on the principles of the class struggle to overthrow capitalism, hear the voice of the Russian proletariat, which calls you to the struggle. Rise up against the dominance of the ruling classes, against this disastrous, wretched power which has plunged mankind into misery and the abomination of world war through its system of exploitation and oppression. End the war, over-throw the capitalist governments, participate in the direction of society for the good of the working class and all mankind. In particular we, the workers of a small country, appeal to you, the workers of the great capitalist countries. Save mankind from destruction! This is a question of the wellbeing of future generations! The struggle of the working masses must be spread from country to country. Long live the international socialist revolution! Long live the Zimmerwald international!

Helsinki, February 1918

The party executive of the Social Democratic Party

Y. SIROLA

Commissar for foreign affairs

(*ISK Nachrichtendienst*, 18 February 1918)

131 THE DEBATE ON THE REVOLUTION – 1: DISCUSSIONS WITH THE SWEDISH SOCIAL DEMOCRATIC PARTY DELEGATION, 5 MARCH 1918

Kuusinen: Möller thinks that we are seeking to establish an oligarchy. This is just what we are fighting against. On 23 February the People's Commissariat issued a new constitution for Finland. This is completely democratic. There is nothing to worry about in that respect. When the fighting is over, a general popular referendum will be held. Hitherto the suffrage has not even been universal, but has been denied the workers in many ways, not only through the Parliament Act but also through election falsifications...

Möller: .... Falsifications and the election results certainly cause tempers to rise, but these cannot be seen as real hindrances to social democratic organisation. Other politicians have said that the situation in the Diet would have brought many concessions to the socialists. Your cause would have been undeniably stronger and better if you had not presented a counter-coup against the bourgeois *coup* ...

Eloranta: We have risen up against the bourgeoisie's policy of *coup d'état*. There was no other choice, since the bourgeoisie was already armed.

Sirola: The revolution has not been resolved by the franchise, but by the *coup d'état* and social conditions. The bourgeois reaction occurred in the name of democracy. The bourgeoisie did not wish to support Finnish independence in a democratic manner, they supported German imperialism. They tried to make the white guards the legal security forces and demanded that the workers be disarmed. The revolution therefore occured through force of circumstance . . .

(Minutes of the People's Commissariat, 5 March 1918, ff. 386–7, Finnish National Archives.)

132 THE DEBATE ON THE REVOLUTION – 2 : THE COMMUNIST AND THE SOCIAL DEMOCRATIC VIEWS

1. Above all, we were dazzled by the mirage of parliamentary democracy. If there had been no one-chamber Diet, no proportional representation and no extensive suffrage, and if our party had not won the majority of seats in the Diet in the elections of 1916, then perhaps it would have been a little easier for us to look ahead during the temptation of spring [1917]. But then the path of parliamentary democracy seemed to be unexpectedly smooth and broad in front of our labour movement. The bourgeoisie had no army, not even a reliable police force, nor could they even create one, since that would have needed the consent of the Social Democrats in the Diet. There seemed to be every reason for social democracy to stay on the path of parliamentary legitimacy; by following that path, it seemed that concession after concession could be wrung from the bourgeoisie . . .

In November . . . we decided to back down from the revolutionary struggle, partly to protect our democratic gains from danger, partly in the hope that we could perhaps circle the whirlpool of history by parliamentary means, and partly, no doubt, thinking fatalistically that if the revolution is to come, now or later, it will come in spite of our resistance and that indeed is how it turned out to be . . .

2. The supporters of a dictatorship were accustomed to calling [the decision to seize power, taken by the executive committee set up by the party executive on 24 January] a revolutionary act, but this it was not. It was a *coup* not only against the democratic Diet, but also a minority *coup* within the party, a crime against the resolutions of the party conference, according to which the parliamentary group and the party council should have *jointly*

decided upon the matter one way or another; *neither* of these were heard. Only after the *coup* had been engineered was the party council convened to approve everything that had already happened . . .

If the party had had a longer and more fruitful period of parliamentary activity behind it, things would have been quite different. It might then have been possible to speak of two parliamentary groups, right-wing and left-wing socialists. But only through revolution has the necessity of such a grouping occurred in accordance with circumstances.

(1 : 'Suomen vallankumouksen esihistoriasta. Itsekritiikkiä.' (O. W. Kuusinen) *Kumous*, 5 October 1918, p. 115, 117. 2 : E. Huttunen, *Sosiaalidemokraattinen puoluejohto ja kansalaissota*, (Helsinki 1918) pp. 92–3, 100.)

133   THE WHITE VIEW OF THE CIVIL WAR – GENERAL MANNERHEIM'S ORDER OF THE DAY TO THE ARMY IN KARELIA, 23 FEBRUARY 1918

To all Karelians of Finland and Russia.

On my arrival at the Karelian front I hail those heroic Karelians who have fought so manfully against Lenin's scoundrels and their wretched henchmen, against men who, bearing the mark of Cain on their foreheads, are attacking their own brothers. Lenin's government which promised independence to Finland with one hand has with the other hand dispatched its troops and hooligans, as he himself has declared, to reconquer Finland and with the assistance of our red guards to drown Finland's newfound liberty in blood. Now, when he starts to feel our growing strength, he seeks to deceive our people in a similarly treacherous and dastardly manner, bargaining with the rebels in Finland and promising them Russian Karelia, which his red army is plundering and destroying. We know the value of his promises, and we are strong enough to preserve our freedom and defend our brothers in Russian Karelia. We do not need the charitable concession of a land which by virtue of its blood-ties belongs to us, and I swear in the name of the Finnish peasant army, whose commander-in-chief I have the honour to be, that I will not sheath my sword before law and order reigns in the land, before all fortresses are in our hands, before the last soldier of Lenin is driven not only from Finland, but from Russian Karelia as well. Confident in the rightness and justness of our cause, confident in the heroism of our menfolk and the sacrifices of our womenfolk, we shall create a mighty, great Finland.

('Ylipäällikkö kenraali Mannerheim Karjalan päämajassa', *Karjalan Sanomat*, 26 February 1918.)

134 TROTSKY'S NOTE TO SVINHUFVUD CONCERNING THE INTERVENTION OF RUSSIAN TROOPS IN THE CIVIL CONFLICT IN FINLAND, 29 JANUARY 1918

In reply to your note concerning the intervention of Russian troops in the civil conflict in Finland, I have the honour to inform you of the following : the Russian government, along with your government, considers as intolerable the violent interference in the internal affairs of Finland by Russian military units. To the best of our knowledge, this is also the view taken by the revolutionary Finnish proletariat. But the information which we have received from these units and their commanding officers leads us to believe that counter-revolutionary and chauvinist elements of the Finnish populace are treacherously attacking our soldiers, firing on trains, etc., which has provoked the soldiers into taking the necessary steps to defend themselves.

We agree with you in considering it necessary to clear Finland of Russian troops in the shortest possible time. However, as you yourself have admitted, such an operation can only be put into effect having regard to military and technical conditions and circumstances. We hope that the setting up of the settlements commission will clear up all outstanding questions affecting the interests of the peoples of both countries. For our part, we should like you to inform us as accurately as possible of all cases known to you of violent acts committed by Russian troops against the inhabitants of Finland, so that we can take the appropriate steps in good time.

You may rest assured, Mr President, that the government of the Soviet of People's Commissars is filled with respect and friendship for the independence of the Finnish people.

(*Dokumenty vneshney politiki SSSR*, vol. 1 (Moscow 1957) p. 94.)

135 'THE FINNISH REVOLUTION AND THE RUSSIAN TROOPS'

The victorious revolution in Helsinki has overthrown the bourgeois Senate and transferred power into the hands of the Finnish people. We, as representatives of revolutionary Russia, can only hail the working class of this small, granite country and wish them further success in their struggle. Our slogans of socialist revolution on a world scale are beginning to come true. With her revolution, little Finland links her fate to our own revolution.

The question of our position in regard to Finland has become acute amongst the Russian troops, whom the bourgeois white guards are in fact fighting. For us, Russian revolutionaries, the legal government of Finland is that created by the revolution. The right of revolt against the oppressors is the greatest right of the people. For us all, this goes without saying.

This is however well understood by the Finnish bourgeoisie. The sympathy of the Russian troops for the Finnish proletariat is not a secret to them . . . In the north, in a number of towns, our units have been attacked and disarmed. What has happened to the prisoners, no-one knows. Units of white guards are gathering in the north, organising and preparing for war with Helsinki. What must we do at this present terrible moment?

Should we observe 'neutrality', hand over our weapons to the white guard? It is impossible to imagine anything more disgraceful. Russian revolutionary troops capitulating to white bands?! Nowhere does the doughty Russian soldier lay down his arms to the white guard. Rather death than a betrayal of the revolution.

War without mercy to the white bandits! The bourgeois hirelings will be crushed. Having defeated the bourgeois in Russia, our troops will not tolerate the sneers of the Finnish bourgeoisie. A ruthless settling of accounts with the enemies of the revolution! All our troop units into the fight with the white bands!

They will pay dearly for the violence perpetrated against our comrades. All our troops must be on fighting alert. Our duty towards the Finnish revolution we will carry out to the end.

Chairman of the Finnish Regional Committee

I. SMILGA

(*Izvestiya Gel'singforskogo Soveta*, 19 January/1 February 1918.)

136 THE RUSSIAN CONTRIBUTION TO THE FINNISH CIVIL WAR OF 1918

[13 January 1918]

1. Kallio said that Shottman had informed him that Lenin had officially promised 10,000 rifles and if there are any in store then as many as we can find; we can discuss payment if the workers eventually win – there are machine-guns as well . . .

[23 January 1918]

Arms are on their way [from Petrograd] to the workers' guards. The bourgeoisie are rubbing their hands in anticipation. As it is a matter of 15,000 rifles, machine-guns and rapid-fire guns, the loss for us would be enormous if they were to fall into enemy hands . . .

[The initial euphoria of revolutionary solidarity with the Finnish socialists was almost immediately tempered by practical considerations which faced the new Soviet government. In particular, the necessity of making a harsh peace with the Germans caused bitter debate in the ranks of the Bolsheviks. In a polemical speech to the seventh party conference in March, Lenin sought to find some saving remnant of virtue in this necessity.]

2. We have done all we could. By signing the treaty [of Brest-Litovsk] we have saved Petrograd, even for a few days . . . The treaty orders us to withdraw our troops, who are clearly useless, from Finland, but we have not been forbidden to send arms to Finland. If Petrograd had fallen a few days ago, then the city would have been gripped by panic and we would have been unable to send anything from there, but during these five days we have helped our Finnish comrades – I cannot say how much, they know that themselves.

. . . We have not betrayed Finland any more than the Ukraine. No worker can accuse us of that. We have not withdrawn a single good man of our troops, nor will we do so . . .

. . . It is foolish to try and get me to say how long this breathing-space will last. As the railways have been saved, we shall help both the Ukraine and Finland. We shall take advantage of the breathing-space, we shall manœuvre, we shall retreat.

(1 : Minutes of the General Staff of the red guards, in *Vapaus-sodan arkisto*, file 1B 29b, Finnish National Archives: Letter from the commander of the red guards in Vapaussodan Historian Komitean arkisto, file B III 6, Finnish War Archives. 2 : V. Lenin, *Polnoe sobranie sochinenii*, vol. 36 (Moscow 1962) p. 33.)

137 THE GERMAN INTERVENTION IN FINLAND: MANNERHEIM'S TELEGRAM TO LUDENDORFF, 5 MARCH 1918

In the name of the Finnish peasant army, I beg Your Excellency to convey to His Majesty the Emperor our deep gratitude for the support sent to us, without which we could not now go on to victory in the fight for Finland's liberation. I would personally like to express our most sincere thanks to Your Excellency, and would like to take the liberty of saying that the German expeditionary corps will afford proper and effective aid. We beg to be allowed to suggest the following : (1) that the German troops be placed under Finnish supreme command from the moment that they step on to Finnish territory. (2) That the commander of the expeditionary force proclaim in an announcement to the Finnish people that the German troops have not come to Finland in order to become involved in an internal conflict of the Finnish people, but in order to assist Finland in its struggle against the alien bands of murderers who have made an unauthorised entry into our country. Otherwise the Finns could easily feel themselves to be subjugated, and this could pave the way amongst many groups of people to a bitterness and class hatred which could last for centuries. Under the above-mentioned conditions I consider myself authorised on behalf of the Finnish army to welcome the victorious, valiant German troops and to express the warm thanks of the Finnish people for their support in our fight for freedom.

(E. Hjelt, *Från händelserika år*, vol. 1 (Helsingfors 1920) p. 99, footnote 1.)

138 THE SOVIET–FINNISH TREATY, 1 MARCH 1918

[The treaty, concluded between Russian Federal Soviet Republic and the Finnish Socialist Workers' Republic, was little more than a clearing up of outstanding matters, although it did contain some territorial concessions. The hopes of the Finnish socialists for more are well expressed in the following official announcement of the treaty.]

The other day, on 1 March, a treaty between the Finnish and Russian republics was signed in Petrograd, the result of proposals prepared by a joint settlement committee composed of delegates from both countries. The treaty was signed for Finland by the people's plenipotentiaries Oskari Tokoi and Edvard Gylling.

This treaty is extremely favourable to our country. Russia has willingly surrendered to Finland all the real estate owned or controlled by the Russian state and state institutions in Finland, such as farms and other land and water areas, buildings, factories, the telegraphic system, fortifications, lighthouses etc, as well as state, communal and private property expropriated by the Russian government during and also before the war.

In addition, Russia has surrendered to Finland a valuable harbour site on the Arctic coast, which is larger than Uusimaa province.[7] The harbour there is icefree throughout the year and the coastal waters are rich in fish. When a railway has been constructed to the area, the whole of the north will be offered new sources of income.

The question of whether a part of Russian and Olonets Karelia will be united to Finland is still undecided. This matter was mentioned, but left for a special sub-committee to consider.

(*Suomen Kansanvaltuuskunnan Tiedonantaja*, 4 March 1918.)

139   THE GERMAN–FINNISH TREATY, 7 MARCH 1918

CONFIRMATION OF FRIENDSHIP BETWEEN FINLAND AND GERMANY AND THE SAFEGUARDING OF FINNISH INDEPENDENCE.

Article 1 : The contracting states declare that no state of war exists between Finland and Germany and that they have resolved henceforth to live in peace and amity with each other.

Germany will work for the recognition by all states of Finland's independence. Finland for its part will surrender no part of its territory to a foreign state or grant rights of servitude in re-

[7] Petsamo/Pechenga.

spect of its national territory without prior agreement with Germany...

Article 30 : The contracting states are agreed that the Åland Islands fortifications be demolished as soon as possible, and that the permanent defortification of these islands as well as the settlement of other military and navigational matters relating to the islands be the subject of a special treaty concluded between Germany, Finland, Russia and Sweden : other littoral states in the Baltic may be invited to participate in this treaty at the request of Germany...

Berlin, 7 March 1918

For Finland : Dr E. Hjelt, Dr R. Erich
For Germany : Count von Hertling

(*Toiset Valtiopäivät 1917, Asiakirjat* vol. 3, no. 55.)

140 THE BRITISH REACTION TO THE GERMAN–FINNISH TREATY, MARCH 1918

REPORT NO. 1 TO THE FINNISH SENATE

... As will appear from the accompanying two reports no. 3 and no. 5, the negotiations in the matter of foodstuffs proceeded extremely smoothly until the first of March ... The news of the invitation of the Germans to Finland changed the situation at once. Whilst I was in conversation with the Permanent Under-Secretary at the Foreign Office, Lord Hardinge, on 6 March, he complained of the Senate's telegram to the German Chancellor ... He finally declared that if the Germans had not been invited to Finland, Britain would have granted Finland final recognition. Last Monday I met the Minister for Munitions, Winston Churchill, at the House and he spoke to me along the same lines.

More particularly with regard to the peace treaty between Finland and Germany, I have heard at the Foreign Office that the German promise to guarantee the approval of Finnish independence has caused bad blood. It is said there that as the United States, Britain and Italy of the major states have not yet granted final recognition, it would seem that Finland has somehow sought to threaten these states because they have not yet spoken their last word. And even then, I have been told, not even a totally victorious Germany could expect to be able to force Britain and the United States to grant recognition at the slightest sort of pressure, even if they were to succeed with regard to Italy. It would have been much better, I was frankly informed, if Finland had relied more on the moral duty of the Entente powers to redeem their pledges than on the armed imperialist threat of Germany. To both these points I have tried to reply by way of easing the situation that the present desperate need and the centuries-old slavery that Finland has endured and is enduring know no law, particularly when the opportunity seemed to present itself to become completely free.

Since I have succeeded in making the acquaintance of a civil servant in the joint Intelligence Department of the War Office and the Foreign Ministry [Prof. J. Y. Simpson], who collates and draws up reports on material received concerning Finland, Russia and Scandinavian countries for the War Cabinet, to which only the most important ministers belong, I have argued the case for the necessity of our independence and the need for territorial expansion, i.e. for the union of Russian Karelia and the Kola peninsula, in numerous conversations . . .

(R. Holsti's report, 27 March 1918, in A. Pakaslahti, *Suomen itsenäisyyden tunnustaminen. Asiakirjakokoelma*, (Helsinki 1937) pp. 92–3.)

141 THE ÅLAND ISLANDS QUESTION: THE SWEDISH GOVERNMENT AND FINLAND, NOVEMBER 1917–FEBRUARY 1918

[11 November 1917]

Count Douglas junior . . . has arrived back from a special and very secret mission to von Kühlmann. [The German foreign minister] had asked Douglas, first on 31 October and at a later date, to make an enquiry of the king whether Sweden would be willing to occupy and administer the Åland Islands after an anticipated German conquest of the islands . . .

[12 November 1917]

The government's reply was unanimously negative, pointing out that our sole interest was a neutralised Åland and that it was not in conformity with a genuine neutrality to enter into prior negotiation at the prospect of a possible handing over of a territory conquered by another power during the course of a war . . .

[17 December 1917]

We had a briefing session and soon agreed upon a policy proposed by [foreign minister] Hellner, which asserted the old standpoint : Åland should remain unfortified and neutralised, and in addition Finland's struggle for liberation would be accorded our full sympathy. We would seek to promote this policy at the negotiations now under way at Brest-Litovsk by means of a special emissary . . .

[1 January 1918]

(The *Finnish* question has come to the fore, partly because of the official representation of the deputation which has just arrived for a *de jure* recognition . . .) Hellner, [prime minister] Edén and I took the line that our previously adopted position in the communication relating to the Åland question obliged us to follow the same course. As soon as the existing Russian government recognised Finland, we should announce that we gladly welcomed the ancient frontier land as a free state. Other state councillors were more cautious. The knowledge that Finland is inundated with Russian troops, the uncertain position of the Lenin government, the information that the Germans are disinterested as regards Finland,[3] the uncertainty about what the governments of the western powers and a future Russia might have to say . . . all this caused some hesitation amongst many of my colleagues, and they preferred to consult with Denmark and Norway before we made our decision . . .

[6 January 1918]

This time it seemed that all my colleagues were agreed that recognition should now take place. [Minister of justice] Löfgren and [Minister of finance] Branting were the most hesitant. The former was adamant for a declaration of neutrality as security from the Finnish side so that we did not run the risk of seeing a German base of operations there . . . I myself was of the opinion now as before that Sweden had a strong interest in supporting the liberation of Finland, whereby the Åland question would be brought to a more favourable stage for us . . . Both to lead Fin-

[3] Information supplied to Court Douglas by von Kühlmann, 12 December.

land out of the German camp and to bring it closer to us, a declaration along these lines [i.e. recognition] was desirable. This
was what we decided.

[20 January 1918]

It would be better if we could quietly settle the Åland question, but it does not seem as if this will be so, for we must now
adopt a position without delay, since Ahlström [Sweden's representative in Finland] has sent a courier with the request of 90%
of the population of the Åland Islands to be incorporated into
Sweden. We have had the first discussion about this on Friday.
Edén, Hellner and I were as usual in such matters of the same
opinion. Give Finland assistance, and have Åland neutralised by
agreement with the powers, no hesitation must prevail. [Minister
for church affairs] Rydén and [minister of agriculture] Påboda
[Petersson] adopted an essentially negative position. They argued
that in our possession the islands could become a source of unrest
... and a permanent reason for new demands for defence [ex-
penditure?].

[15 February 1918]

Terrible news from Åland. The Russian soldiers are murder-
ing and looting. We must intervene without delay ... I have
hurriedly ordered an icebreaker and *Runeberg* to sail with *Thor*
to Åland ...

[21 February 1918]

Just as we were ready with our work of pacification ... came
the news that the Germans intend to occupy Åland in order to
invade Finland! The effect is paralysing. The whole of our
Åland operation will be distorted ... In all probability the Finns
are behind this German *démarche*. Their hostile attitude towards
Sweden is pretty obvious ...

(E. Palmstierna, *Orostid 1917–1919*, vol. 2 (Stockholm 1953)
p. 103, 106, 111, 112, 118, 120–1, 124, 134, 138.)

White Finland, Red Russia
1918-20

The Finnish civil war ended in May 1918 but the repercussions
of the war lasted for many more months. The defeated reds fled
to Russia, where in August 1918 the radical elements formed the
Finnish Communist Party, adopting a fiercely leftist programme
which took up the challenge not only of victorious white Finland
but of the struggle for the worker's 'soul' with the reformist socialists in Finland itself (144).

The victorious whites were left with a number of problems, not
least their dependence upon Germany and the threat of an En-
tente-supported white Russia reasserting ancient claims to Finland
(142, 143). The governments of the Entente witheld recognition
as long as Germany remained the protector of Finland; in
November 1918, the British insisted not only on German troop
withdrawals from Finland, but also on the holding of new Diet
elections and the dismissal of leading figures known to be pro-
German. This led to the replacement of Svinhufvud as Regent by
Mannerheim, and the quiet burial of plans for a German prince
to become king of Finland. Finnish independence was recognised
by Britain in the spring of 1919. The white Russians continued to
press for recognition of Russia's historic claims to Finland at the
Paris peace conference, but as Finnish aid for interventionist plans
became crucial towards the end of 1919, cracks appeared in the
ranks of the white generals who claimed to uphold the authority
of mother Russia (146).

Intervention caused a number of problems, especially in Karelia, where a British expeditionary force became involved in local
politics. Karelian nationalism, of which a brief glimpse is given
here, was to a large extent masterminded by Finns (147). The
freeing of east Karelia – which had never been part of Finland –
from the yoke of Russian-Bolshevik tyranny was a favourite theme

of Finnish nationalists. Social democracy did not deny the desirability of a union of brother tribes, but it opposed conquest as a means of achieving this (148). Throughout 1919 friction reigned on the Soviet-Finnish frontier (149). Finnish white volunteers fought in Estonia and mounted a raid into Russia Karelia in the spring of 1919 (145). In Helsinki, white Russian generals intrigued with sympathetic Finnish officers in an effort to bring about a whole-hearted Finnish offensive against Petrograd. In the early days of September the Soviet government put out peace feelers to the Baltic States and Finland. The Soviet peace offer met with a mixed reception in Finland, and with the mounting of general Yudenich's offensive against Petrograd in October 1919 further discussions fell through (150). With the collapse of intervention in the winter of 1919–20 Finland was left with no alternative but to follow the course of the Baltic States and make peace with the Soviet Union. The still unsettled east Karelian question proved a hindrance to peacemaking and in the end the Finnish delegation had to consent to returning two communes occupied by Finnish troops in 1918 to the Soviet government. Finnish attempts to squeeze some sort of guarantee of the right of the Karelians to national self-determination were finally limited to a paragraph in the peace treaty which virtually abandoned the Karelians to their fate (152).

142 SVINHUFVUD'S REVIEW OF FINLAND'S POSITION, 15 MAY 1918

. . . The last four months have been amongst the most decisive in the history of our people. The course of events is fresh in everyone's memory. There occurred a violent rebellion directed against the whole of society, lawful order and civilisation. The origins and causes of this violent rebellion are to be found to the east of Finland's frontiers, but the hatred directed against the social order which was preached and inculcated in the name of the class struggle here at home also played a part in preparing the ground for anarchistic violence. The Fatherland was saved however because the core was sound, because there was a sufficiently powerful element wishing to preserve the social order which fought and overcame this violence . . .

As regards foreign affairs it must be mentioned that since they were last discussed in the Diet, a number of foreign states have recognised Finland as an independent sovereign state. In all, recognition has been obtained from the Scandinavian states, Sweden, Denmark and Norway, and from all the central powers, that is from Germany, Austria-Hungary, Turkey and Bulgaria, in addition to the Russian recognition. Of the Entente powers, France has recognised us, and in addition, recognition has been accorded by Holland, Switzerland, Spain and the Holy See in Rome. We also are informed that many states are ready to recognise our independence as soon as we have settled our affairs and entered into relations with their governments. On the other hand, there are a number of states who have received information of the declaration of independence from the Finnish government and whose recognition has been requested, but who have so far announced their intention of withholding recognition for the time being. This is the position of Britain, the United States, Italy and Belgium . . . In particular mention must be made of our relations with Germany. I take this opportunity to voice our deep gratitude for the invaluable support and aid which mighty Germany and its allies has contributed to the securing and safeguarding of our independence over the past months, especially in the field of diplomacy. Government plenipotentiaries signed two important agreements with Germany this March, agreements of the greatest significance to our existence as an independent state since they are vital ulterior witnesses to the fact that Finland has joined the ranks of civilised states as an equal partner. The agreements will be presented separately to the Diet for the ratification. Relations with Russia have for the time being been broken off, since the Russian government according to our information has elected to support the rebels and recognised the commissariat government set up by them in Finland . . .

(*Toiset valtiopäivät 1917, Pöytäkirjat*, vol. 2, pp. 1073–4.)

143 BRITAIN AND FINLAND – HOLSTI'S REPORT OF A CONVERSATION WITH LORD HARDINGE, 29 AUGUST, 3 SEPTEMBER 1918

. . . Lord Hardinge began by observing that the British government found it impossible to understand how anyone in Finland could doubt for a moment that it was the intention of the Entente

powers to conquer Finland and hand it back to Russia. 'Our programme is firmly nailed to the mast : we will honour the right of
all peoples to self-determination and we consider the securing of
an independent status by Finland as evident. Any talk that we
entertain hostile intentions towards you is merely a German
fabrication.' . . .

To this I remarked that from the point of view of the Entente
powers the Finnish question might well seem very simple, but in
Finnish eyes it was far more complicated. I said that since the
most remote times the Russians had been our arch-enemies, since
we had only fought against the Poles, the Austrians and Denmark-
Norway a few times. Now Germany has militarily defeated Russia
and by so doing has indirectly released Finland from the Russian
yoke. Germany has since directly helped us against the Russian
Bolsheviks and now the enemies of Germany, the troops of the
Entente, are marching southwards along the eastern frontier of
Finland. It is therefore hardly surprising if Finland, with its own
weak armed forces, is again seizing upon German military aid,
especially when it is known that influential Russian circles are
seeking to tempt the Entente powers into agreeing to Finland's
reincorporation into Russia. The situation would be appreciably
different, I remarked, if Britain and the United States had recognised Finland's independence.

To this Lord Hardinge replied as follows :

'The Finnish people should know once and for all that we regard them as quite ready for national independence. It is therefore quite unnecessary for feelings to be agitated and alarmed
against us in Finland to force us to grant recognition when the
Finnish government has even refused to accept this. I can assure
you, he said, that at the right moment Britain will grant recognition and will press Russia to accept the self-determination of
Finland.

I thought this last sentence of His Excellency of such importance that I asked him word for word if I might both cable and
write to the Senate using these very words, and he agreed to
this . . .

(Report no. 73, in A. Pakaslahti, *Suomen itsenäisyyden tunnustaminen. Asiakirjakokoelma*, (Helsinki 1937) pp. 137–8.)

I

144   THE PROGRAMME OF THE FINNISH COMMUNIST PARTY, ADOPTED AT ITS FOUNDING CONFERENCE IN MOSCOW, 29 AUGUST 1918

The Finnish Communist Party is the party of the proletariat and the wage-earning worker and is solely dedicated to the cause of the working class, seeking to raise it to power in order to destroy the bourgeois robber-state and the capitalist economic system.

The Communist Party is founded on the principle of revolutionary Marxist socialism, the principle of communism proclaimed by Marx and Engels which the petty politicians of compromise of a later age have falsely expounded in theoretical sophistries which the old Finnish Social Democratic Party adopted in its programme . . .

The socialist society, for the realisation of which the Communist Party works and fights, is not a new social objective for the worker but a long-standing ideal which has been brought to the stage of fruition by recent economic developments.

Through their own socialist revolution the workers of each country will preserve their own great cause as well as that of the proletariat of other countries and will establish a common international soviet republic for the victory and strengthening of the socialist world order.

The Socialist Soviet Republic of the Russian proletariat is in this context the only true Fatherland of the world's revolutionary proletariat at this present moment, and must be defended by communist of all countries against the imperialist robbers, because the Russian Socialist Soviet Republic is the one common weapon of the proletariat of the world against the bourgeoisie of all countries and their governments of terror.

On these grounds, the Finnish Communist Party proclaims :

1. The workers must vigorously prepare for armed revolution, and must reject any return to the old parliamentary, trade unionist and co-operative fighting tactics of the Finnish labour organisations of pre-revolutionary days.

2. The only acceptable labour movement and activity is that which guarantees the promotion of communism and of the achievement of victory for the coming socialist revolution – any activity of a different sort which makes an appearance amongst the workers is to be sternly condemned, revealed and opposed.

3. By revolution the working class will seize all power into its own hands and set up an iron dictatorship of the workers; – the bourgeois state is to be destroyed, and is not to be replaced by democracy, either before or through revolution.

4. By means of a proletarian dictatorship a communist social order will be created, by the expropriation of all land and capitalist property and by the organisation of all production and the distribution of produce by the organised workers themselves. The capitalist system of exploitation is not therefore to be merely made more tolerable before or even by the revolution.

5. The workers' international revolution and its victory is to be promoted as vigorously as possible and the Socialist Soviet Republic of the Russian proletariat is to be supported with all available resources.

In Finland at the present time, the victory is with the bourgeois butchers. The bourgeoisie has attempted to crush the workers' struggle for liberty with bloody terror. The blood of thousands of our comrades cries out for revenge. Tens of thousands of starving orphans and widows curse their oppressors and wait in agony for the moment of liberation.

The forces of labour are at this moment under the yoke of a terrible class oppression, defeated but not broken.

They will rise again.

Schooled by hard experience they will smash the chains of the butchers' terror.

The bourgeoisie fears this already. It will use all its strength and devilish skills to avoid the approaching day of reckoning.

The Finnish worker must carefully weigh his actions and not allow himself to be enticed into premature and careless deeds which would only weaken the united strength of the workers. The working class must instead gather and organise all its forces for the approaching final and decisive battle.

LET THE CLASSES IN POWER TREMBLE BEFORE THE COMMUNIST REVOLUTION. THE PROLETARIAT HAS NOTHING TO LOSE BUT ITS CHAINS. IT HAS A WORLD TO WIN.

(Printed in O. Borg, *Suomen puolueet ja puolueohjelmat 1880–1964*, (Porvoo-Helsinki 1965) pp. 147–9.)

145 FINLAND – THE PROTECTING WALL OF CIVIL-ISATION': ARTICLE IN *HELSINGIN SANOMAT*, 12 JANUARY 1919

. . . The Finnish people are the only ones who have set about supporting the Estonians' fight in an effective manner. Volunteers from all over the country have rushed and are still rushing to fight in the ranks of the Estonian army for Estonian liberty from the Bolshevik reign of terror. The first international duty which has befallen Finland since its elevation to the ranks of independent nations is great indeed. Only recently freed from the dangerous snare of Bolshevism, it stands on guard for civilisation, assisting its small brother nation against the Bolshevik hordes. But the duty is also an honourable one. The gaze of the entire civilised world is now fixed upon us, and the world at large follows with excited interest the way in which Finland fulfils the duty which has befallen it . . .

This duty is also immensely important from the point of view of our own security and liberty. The preservation of Estonian liberty to a large extent will also protect our own liberty, whilst the collapse of Estonia before the Bolsheviks will mean a further increase in the danger which threatens us still from Bolshevik Russia . . . Those Finnish men who are fighting the Bolsheviks in Estonia are thus fighting at the same time to safeguard the freedom of their own people, and awareness of this has certainly helped bring about the great enthusiasm for aiding Estonia in our country . . .

('Suomi sivistyksen suojamuurina', *Helsingin Sanomat*, 12 January 1919.)

146 A WHITE RUSSIAN MEMORANDUM ON FIN-LAND, MARCH 1919

. . . We have already shown how advantageous the association with Russia was to Finland in the previous century. Finland was assured of a privileged position which it could hardly have enjoyed in association with another state, let alone in a state of complete independence. We therefore believe that, if the degree of autonomy which Finland hitherto possessed could be guaranteed against encroachments upon it, this would be a great advantage for Finland to achieve out of this war. It is difficult to see what reasons would necessitate complete Finnish independence: indeed, independence would constitute a considerable danger for Russia.

. . . In the first instance, it is very easy to see the danger which a foreign policy independent of Russian foreign policy could present. This would imply the possibility of Finland concluding an alliance with Russia's enemies: it only suffices to cast a glance at the map to see that if Finland concluded an alliance with Germany, for example, Russia would be defenceless to the north. Finland forms a geographic unit with Russia, which means that if it were to pursue a hostile international policy towards Russia, this would be as good as surrendering fortified frontier emplacements to the enemy. There are conditions which are sometimes dictated to a defeated country, but to which not one would voluntarily consent.

. . . Of even greater importance than the question of alliances is that of strategic considerations. If Russia in common with other countries has the obligation to defend itself against aggression, it cannot remain indifferent to the prospect of seeing Finland used by its enemies as a base of operations against Russia itself . . .

Russia's forfeiture of the right to control the Finnish coastline with its fleet virtually means that it is impossible for Russia to have a battle fleet capable of repulsing an attack from the sea against Petrograd. Moreover, if Russia cannot prevent a landing on the coast of the Gulf of Finland, if it must guard the land frontier of Finland against the incursions of enemy troops, then Russia will be deprived of land defences too. It is hardly necessary to add that the Murmansk railway would be threatened as well, and Russia would thus be in danger of losing her only icefree port.

It follows that if the legitimate interests of Finland and the desires of the Finnish people lay claim to as much independence in internal affairs as possible, then the truly vital needs of Russia will necessitate that in certain respects, the wishes of Finland must be reconciled to the interests of Russia . . .

(This memorandum, drafted by the former assistant to the Governor-General of Finland (in 1917), Baron Korff, was published in French as: *Quelques considérations sur le problème finlandais*, (Paris 1919) pp. 9–10.)

147   THE EAST KARELIAN QUESTION: MINUTES
      OF A MEETING OF KARELIAN DELEGATES, 16–
      19 FEBRUARY 1919

[General Price was sent to this meeting by General Maynard,
Commander of the Allied Forces in the Murmansk area, who
had learnt of the delegates' intention to press for Karelian
independence; Price read out the following telegram from his
superior officer to the meeting on 18 February.]

The Commander of the Allied Forces does not support proposals
for separation from Russia. Karelian dependence on Russia is of
advantage to both sides. The Commander of the Allied Forces
will safeguard the welfare of Karelia in future if Karelia acknowledges itself to be a part of Russia . . .
    The meeting unanimously resolved :

1. The meeting demands the proclamation of Karelia as an
independent state, whose closer association with either Russia or
Finland will be for the Karelian people to decide. The natural
frontiers of Karelia, taking into account geographical situation
and national ethnic inhabitation, should be : in the south, Ladoga
and the river Svir′, in the east, Lake Onega and the river Onega
to the White Sea, in the north, the Barents Sea and in the west,
the Finnish frontier. The land surface of Karelia would thus be
some 215,000 square versts,[1] in which area there were according
to the 1907 census some 185,000 inhabitants, of which, according
to the statistics, over 60% were Karelian . . .
    2. The meeting elected . . . a five-man 'National Committee
of Karelia' . . .
    3. The National Committee was authorised by the meeting :

    (a) to send at least two delegates to the peace conference, to
obtain recognition of Karelian independence from the states of
the world.
    (b) To take steps to secure recognition from neighbouring
states . . .
    (c) To convoke a 'Karelian National Constituent As-
sembly' . . .
    (d) The National Committee is authorised to draft a con-

───────────────
[1] A square verst is approx. 3,500 square feet.

stitution for Karelia and proposals dealing with the social order, for presentation to the future National Constituent Assembly.

(Minutes of this meeting are to be found in the Ingman collection, file B3 : 1, Finnish National Archives.)

148   EAST KARELIA AND FINNISH PARTICIPATION IN THE INTERVENTION AGAINST RUSSIA : THE DIET DEBATE, 11 APRIL 1919

Alkio : . . . The concept of the Finnish state includes the union of East Karelia and the Olonets region with Finland, and this has been publicly proclaimed many times over the past few years. I proclaim it once again in this assembly. The aim of our endeavours is to free East Karelia from the misery and the thousand-year slavery it has endured under the Russian government. We well know that we cannot carry out this liberation by force and we will not even attempt to do so. But we wish to proclaim to the present world powers that on the basis of national self-determination we Finns demand that the birthplace of the Kalevala must be united with the rest of Finland . . .

Keto : . . . We social democrats have made it clear that we too consider the union of nearby frontier parishes to Finland desirable on the grounds of national affinity . . . But the matter has now assumed an essentially different aspect. The question before us now is, should Russian Karelia be joined to Finland by means of concealed conquest, without our knowing whether or not the people of Russian Karelia themselves have any desire to be united to Finland. We can surely only demand settlement on the principle of national self-determination if the people of a particular area themselves demand the right to be joined to another country . . .

Since I have requested the right to speak, I would like to take the opportunity of expressing my satisfaction that the government appears to have finally given up the planned campaign against Petrograd . . . If such plans are still being considered in Finland, with the intention of attacking the Russian capital, then it must be said once and for all, that plans of this sort could do irreparable harm for our country in the future . . .

In my view, the same is true as regards Russian Karelia. If we try now to unite this area with Finland, even by some concealed form of annexation . . . that is, to unite the whole of Russian Karelia as far as the Kola peninsula to Finland, then we will be excluding Russia from the Arctic Ocean. The exclusion of Russia from the Arctic would unquestionably hinder the future economic development of Russia to a considerable extent and would lead to economic friction between Russia and Finland, which could undoubtedly become a threat to the political independence of our country at some future date, when Russia is more powerful than at present. Finland should therefore be content to pursue more modest objectives in its Russian Karelia policy . . . and as has been said, these objectives ought to be striven for by peaceful means alone.

(*Valtiopäivät 1919, Pöytäkirjat* vol. 1, p. 57, pp. 72–3.)

149 SOVIET–FINNISH RELATIONS, 1919.

The Soviet Russian government protests most strongly against the complete unjustifiable attacks and persistent acts of aggression committed by Finland on the territory of the Soviet Russian Republic, and also against the attempts to cover up these attacks with lying accusations.

The attempts of the Finnish government to ascribe falsely to the Russian Soviet Republic hostile intentions or aggressive deeds . . . can only be regarded as directed towards the creation of an offensive against the Soviet Republic.

The Finnish government cannot fail to know that the Russian Soviet government continues to abstain from any sort of offensive action against Finland and that it is limiting itself at the present to measures of essential self-defence with regard to Finland.

On 17 May, Finnish batteries at Puumala opened fire without any cause on Russian territory on the opposite shore of the Gulf of Finland, with the intention of bombarding the Russian fortress of Krasnaya Gorka. On 18 May, the Finnish forts of Ino and Puumala once more opened fire without any reason against our ships. At the same time, and on succeeding days, there occurred a number of attempts to land troops on the Russian shore of the Gulf of Finland, in which units of Finnish soldiers were involved.

The Russian batteries of Krasnaya Gorka were compelled to open fire in self-defence to silence the Finnish batteries which were firing on them and our ships . . . There is also the matter of the incursion into the Olonets region, in which regular Finnish troops also participated . . . with the approval of the Finnish government . . .

These statements, the lying nature of which is of course well-known to the Finnish government, are undoubtedly a part of the plan of aggression worked out by the Allied powers. These efforts will not however achieve their ends, for the Russian Soviet government will spare no necessary means for the defence of the republic, continuing at the same time to eschew any sort of offensive against Finland. The Russian Soviet government, repeating once more its strong protest, voices its confidence that the Finnish working masses will not allow themselves to be used as tools of the imperialist policy of the Entente, and will help to put an end to the militaristic activities of the present Finnish government.

People's Commissar for Foreign Affairs
CHICHERIN
20 May 1919

[The Finnish government had in its note of 19 May protested against the unjustified Russian bombardment of their coastal batteries]

(Printed in *Dokumenty Vneshney Politiki SSSR*, vol. 2, (Moscow 1958) pp. 169–71.)

150   THE FINNISH PRESS OPINION ON THE SOVIET PEACE OFFER, AUTUMN 1919

1. . . . Mr Chicherin has sent the government of Finland, as well as those of Estonia, Latvia and Lithuania a telegram in which he proposes the commencement of peace negotiations, with the aim of bringing hostilities to an end and of preparing the ground for the establishment of future peaceful relations betweer Finland and Soviet Russia . . .

In our opinion it is obvious that Finland for its part can expect nothing worthwhile from a peace made with Lenin's Russia. During the past months we have seen how Soviet Russia, in spite of the prevalent military situation, has sought to press its doctrines of bloody minority dictatorship upon us in the most ruthless manner . . . We must therefore inform Mr Chicherin that we cannot take up his offer to begin peace negotiations, since this would mean, in our opinion, exposing Finland to Bolshevism and would be a step towards the assimilation of Finland into Soviet Russia.

2. . . . The peace offer of Soviet Russia will surely be welcomed with feelings of satisfaction by the Finnish people, especially the working class. The permanent threat of war and adventures of conquest have been the cause of an unceasing state of nervous tension and an atmosphere of uncertainty in society. This tension has also been increased amongst the workers, who have seen and felt the final objective of these warmongers to be the bloody overthrowal of the Russian workers' commune and the erection of black reaction in its place . . .

3. . . . The method which the right is recommending for a settlement of relations between Finland and Russia, i.e. by an assault on Petrograd, is unacceptable, at least whilst matters are as they are now. But it does not follow from this, that we should accept the position of the social democrats. As we demonstrated earlier when we considered the Bolshevik peace offer, there are a lot of things to be taken into consideration which must be cleared up before there can be any question of starting peace negotiations. Above all, we must act in concert with the western powers in this matter. If they continue their present policy of isolating the Bolsheviks then there is no chance that we could adopt a different policy by making a 'separate peace' with the Bolsheviks, in common with the small states of the Baltic . . . At present, conditions in Russia are still so thoroughly confused . . . Therefore until conditions in Russia have stabilised, our most important duty is to rebuff all hostile dangers and attacks on us from that direction, whether they come via underground routes or any other way . . .

4. . . . If Bolshevik power in Russia is now overthrown, as seems likely, this will take place without Finland having played a direct part in it. Seen from the point of view which we have always held, this is to be greatly regretted. Nothing would have been more natural or more justified than that Finland, whose very foundations Bolshevik power in Russia has zealously sought to destroy, should have done all that it could to overthrow that power. By assisting white Russia in its fight to liberate the country from the Bolshevik reign of terror, Finland would also have been able to promote the favourable settlement of many vital matters and to

bring about good relations between Finland and the future Russia . . .

In general, our country can expect greater social peace with the overthrowal of the Bolsheviks beyond the frontier, and thereby greater expectations for vigorous, confidence-building work . . .

The establishment of good relations with the new Russia will become the major political task for our country after the defeat of the Bolsheviks in Russia. This is a task which is one of the most important that independent Finland has had to face . . .

(1. 'Bolshevikki-Venäjän rauhantarjous', *Uusi Suomi*, 18 September 1919. 2 : 'Neuvosto-Venäjän rauhantarjous', *Sosiaalidemokraatti*, 18 September 1919. 3 : 'Suhteemme Venäjään', *Helsingin Sanomat*, 11 October 1919. 4 : 'Näiden päivien kysymys', *Uusi Suomi*, 17 October 1919.)

151 THE OPENING SPEECHES OF J. A. BĒRZINŠ AND J. K. PAASIKIVI AT THE TARTU PEACE CONFERENCE, 12 JUNE 1920

J. A. Bērziņš : The great Russian proletarian revolution destroyed the previous relationship of [Finland and Russia]. I do not need to delve into the past to give you an idea of the relationship which existed before the revolution. This sad history is familiar to you all. But one thing must be mentioned; the overthrowal of tsarism was not of itself enough for Finland to obtain complete independence. Finland did not receive and could not have received her independence from the hands of the bourgeoisie that came to power in the place of tsarism. The bourgeoisie continued, even if in a more moderate form, the same policy towards Finland that the tsarist Russia of the big landowners had practised for a hundred years before the revolution. Not until the November revolution, with its slogan of peace between peoples and the reconstruction of society along socialist lines and its proclamation of the right of national self-determination as a principle of its international policy, were the old chains which had bound Finland against her will to Russia decisively and immediately broken.

One of the first concrete measures of the Soviet power in the field of international politics was the proclamation of Finland's independence, its recognition of Finland as a sovereign state. This historical political action was intended as the turning of a new leaf in the relations of the Russian and Finnish peoples. It is not the fault of Soviet Russia that this conference, intended to restore peaceful normal relations between Russia and Finland, is meeting some two and a half years after the proclamation of Finland's independence. The Russian Soviet government, resolutely pursuing its policy of peace, has frequently sought to have such a conference convened. Up to now, many hindrances have been placed in the way. The bourgeois circles in Finland have supported the policy of intervention. Moreover, first Germany and then the Entente, in pusuance of their own interests, have sought to prevent the emergence of friendly, neighbourly relations between the Russian and Finnish peoples. We are glad that at last we are able to meet and begin to sort out old misunderstandings and to establish new relations, in a spirit of amicable co-operation. The many peace moves made by Soviet Russia to her enemies have often been interpreted as signs of weakness. By its heroic struggle, proletariat Russia has shown the whole world its strength and forces. In consequence, the attitude of the capitalist countries towards soviet power is also changing. Even the most powerful capitalist states, the victors of the world war, have *nolens volens* been forced to enter into relations with Soviet Russia.

Some warmongering imperialists are indeed still trying to continue the wild policy of intervention against Russia. Whilst opening negotiations with Soviet Russia for the restoration of regular commercial relations, the Entente powers are at the same time still continuing to egg on the frontier states which have emerged from the territory of the former Russian Empire to attack Soviet Russia. All aggressive intentions are alien to the Russian proletariat, but when it is attacked, it will fearlessly repel all blows and there can be no doubt that it will soon emerge victorious from the present struggle.

We believe that this conference, in view of the fact that the Russian and Finnish peoples have clearly expressed the desire for peace, can indeed bring about normal friendly relations between Russia and Finland.

J. K. Paasikivi: In the peace negotiations about to begin we must strive for the creation of a basis for sound political and economic relations between both countries, which will last for a long time to come. We are convinced that this can be achieved, if the ideas of justice and the right of peoples to self-determination, now generally acknowledged as a precondition in the establishment of relations between peoples and firmly recognised by the Russian Soviet government, are regarded as sincerely held guiding principles. The realisation of these principles will without doubt best guarantee the peaceful continuance of relations between peoples.

The matters which will be deliberated upon in our discussions are numerous and many-sided. There are many questions, mainly of an economic nature, dating from the time of the union of Finland and Russian and even from more recent days, which remain to be settled. The past has also bequeathed to us the matter of the territory between the Finnish frontier and the northern White Sea, to which Finland has of old an indisputable right. The final settlement of this question must therefore be one of the aims of our negotiations.

The Finnish people cannot remain indifferent to the fate of their kindred people living on the eastern side of the frontier, whose contribution to Finnish culture has been so great. For this reason, the demand of these people to determine for themselves the necessary guarantees for their political existence must be considered in the negotiations now beginning.

The changed conditions which have emerged from the events of recent years have created problems which must be settled for the future, such as the future economic relations of Finland and Russia, the previously valid regulating features having lost all meaning.

By the equitable solution of such problems, the preconditions for good future relations between Finland and Russia will be created. These relations would be further strengthened to mutual advantage if it were to prove possible to find the means whereby permanent peace in this part of Europe might be secured.

We hope that, despite difficulties that may arise, we are able to obtain satisfactory results in our negotiations. This we may do if only we consistently abide by the above-mentioned principles and if these are calmly and impartially applied to the matters which must be resolved.

(*Suomen ja Venäjän välisten Tartossa pidettyjen rauhanneuvottelujen pöytäkirjat*, (Helsinki 1923) pp. 5–8.)

152 THE RUSSO–FINNISH PEACE TREATY, 14 OCTOBER 1920

1. As soon as this peace treaty comes into force, the state of war existing between the contracting states shall cease and both states shall bind themselves to observe in future peaceful and good neighbourly relations . . .

4. The Petsamo area with its coastal waters . . . shall be immediately surrendered by Russia to Finland, with the coming into force of this peace treaty, to be held in perpetuity and with full sovereign rights . . .

10. Finland shall withdraw, within forty-five days of this peace treaty coming into force, troops stationed in the communes of Repola and Porajärvi, which shall be returned to the state territory of Russia and united with the autonomous region of East Karelia, formed from the Karelian population of the governments of Archangel and Olonets and enjoying the rights of national self-determination . . .

12. The contracting states support in principle the neutralisation of the Gulf of Finland and the whole of the Baltic Sea and bind themselves to work for this end . . .

(*Suomen asetuskokoelma 1921* no. 21 (Helsinki 1921).)

Select Bibliography

M. Julkunen and A. Lehikoinen's compilation, *A select list of books and articles in English, French and German on Finnish politics in the 19th and 20th centuries* (Turku 1967) provides a comprehensive list of works available to the non-Finnish reader. The following general histories and accounts may be recommended:

E. Jutikkala and K. Piirinen, *A history of Finland* (New York/London 1962).

A. Mazour, *Finland between east and west* (Princeton, N.J. 1956).

J. Nousiainen, *The Finnish political system* (Cambridge, Mass. 1971).

L. Puntila, *The political history of Finland 1809–1966* (Helsinki 1974).

Aspects of the period of autonomy are covered by:

M. Borodkin, *Finland: its place in the Russian State* (St Petersburg 1911).

W. Copeland. *The uneasy alliance. Collaboration between the Finnish opposition and the Russian underground 1899–1904* (Helsinki 1973).

J. Danielson, *Finland's union with the Russian Empire. With reference to M. K. Ordin's work 'Finland's subjugation'* (Helsinki 1891).

M. Futrell, *The Northern underground: episodes of Russian revolutionary transport and communications through Scandinavia and Finland 1863–1917* (London 1963).

L. Krusius-Ahrenberg, *Der Durchbruch des Nationalismus und Liberalismus im politischen Leben Finnlands 1856–1863* (Helsinki 1934).

L. Mechelin, *A precis of the public law of Finland* (London 1889).

P. Tommila, *La Finlande dans la politique européenne en 1808–1815* (Lahti 1962).

R. Travers, *Letters from Finland. August 1908–March 1909* (London 1911).

K. Zilliacus, *Revolution und Gegenrevolution in Russland und Finnland* (München 1912).

For the revolution, civil war and early years of independence, see :

M. Graham, *The diplomatic recognition of the border states. 1: Finland* (Berkeley, Calif. 1935).

J. Hannula, *Finland's war of independence* (London 1939).

J. Hodgson, *Communism in Finland. A history and an interpretation* (Princeton, N.J. 1967).

M. Jääskeläinen, *Die ostkarelische Frage. Die Entstehung eines nationalen Expansionsprogramms und die Versuch zu einer Verwirklichung in der Aussenpolitik Finnlands in den Jahren 1918–1920* (Turku 1965).

O. Kuusinen, *The Finnish revolution: a self-criticism* (London 1919).

J. Paasivirta, *The victors in world war one and Finland. Finland's relations with the British, French and United States governments in 1918–1919* (Helsinki 1969).

A. Upton, *Communism in Scandinavia and Finland. Politics of opportunity* (London/New York 1973).

Index of Persons